WITH WELLINGTON'S
OUTPOSTS

WITH WELLINGTON'S OUTPOSTS

The Peninsular and Waterloo Letters of John Vandeleur

Notes and commentary by

Andrew Bamford

Frontline Books

With Wellington's Outposts
This edition published in 2015 by
Frontline Books,
an imprint of Pen & Sword Books Ltd,
47 Church Street, Barnsley, S. Yorkshire, S70 2AS

Edited text and commentary © Andrew Bamford, 2015

ISBN: 978-1-84832-774-0

CIP data records for this title are available from the British Library

For more information on our books, please visit
www.pen-and-sword.co.uk, email info@frontline-books.com
or write to us at the above address.

Printed and bound by CPI Group (UK) Ltd, Croydon, CR0 4YY

Typeset in 12.5/15.6 pt Arno Pro Small Text & 12.7/15.6 pt Arno Pro Display

Contents

~

Plates and Maps

~

Plates

John Vandeleur in later life. *(9th/12th Royal Lancers Regimental Museum)*

'Great Marlow. The Royal Military College', 1817 engraving. *(Anne S. K. Brown Military Collection)*

'Troops bevouack'd near the village of Villa Velha', aquatint by Charles Turner. *(Anne S. K. Brown Military Collection)*

'The village of Pombal in flames', aquatint by Charles Turner. *(Anne S. K. Brown Military Collection)*

'Battle of Fuentes D'Onor', aquatint by Charles Turner. *(Anne S. K. Brown Military Collection)*

'Distant view of Ciudad Rodrigo', aquatint by Charles Turner. *(Anne S. K. Brown Military Collection)*

Lieutenant Colonel (later Major General) Frederick Cavendish Ponsonby, by Thomas Heaphy. *(National Portrait Gallery)*

'12th – the Prince of Wales's – Light Dragoons, c. 1812', watercolour by Reginald Augustus Wymer. *(Anne S. K. Brown Military Collection).*

'City of Coimbra', aquatint by Charles Turner. *(Anne S. K. Brown Military Collection)*

'The Battle of Vittoria, June 21st 1813', aquatint by Thomas Sutherland. *(Anne S. K. Brown Military Collection)*

Sir John Ormsby Vandeleur, oil on canvas by William Salter. *(National Portrait Gallery)*

'Major General Sir Denis Pack', mezzotint by C. Turner.
  (Anne S. K. Brown Military Collection)
'Attack on the Road to Bayonne', watercolour by W. Heath.
  (Anne S. K. Brown Military Collection).
Uniforms of the 12th Royal Lancers, 1814, watercolour by
  Richard Simkin. *(Anne S. K. Brown Military Collection)*
'The Battle of Waterloo', 1815 map after Lieutenant Tyler.
  (Collection of Mick Crumplin)
'View from Mont St. Jean of the Battle of Waterloo', aquatint
  from the 1816 *Campaign of Waterloo*. *(Anne S. K. Brown Military
  Collection)*
'Chasseur de Lord Wellington', engraving by Rulhières.
  (Anne S. K. Brown Military Collection)
'10th (the P. Wales's own) Royal Regiment of Hussars', lithograph
  by C. H. Martin. *(Anne S. K. Brown Military Collection)*

Maps

Preface

~

I first encountered the letters of John Vandeleur during research for a history of the 12th Light Dragoons during the Napoleonic Wars, now published by Frontline Books under the title *Gallantry and Discipline*. The Vandeleur surname was familiar through his more famous near-namesake, John Ormsby Vandeleur, who served as a brigade commander in the Peninsula and at Waterloo, but this young relation was unknown to me. Following up an obscure footnote in an old regimental history of the 12th in which a couple of extracts from these letters were cited, I discovered the existence of the 1894 publication entitled *Letters of Colonel John Vandeleur 1810–1846*, which was listed as having been 'Printed for Private Circulation' by Rivington, Percival & Company of London. Looking at the date range in the title, and bearing in mind the fact that the letters and their author had not cropped up before in the best part of a decade I had spent working on the British Army of the Napoleonic era, I assumed that there would perhaps be a handful of letters dealing with the period in which I was interested, with the remainder being Victorian family papers or accounts of peacetime soldiering. Only when I was finally able to track down a copy of the original text was it revealed to me how wrong I had been, and that in fact what I had in my hands was a positive treasure-trove of letters, almost all of which dealt with the Napoleonic Wars and their immediate aftermath.

The letters quickly established themselves as one of the main eyewitness sources for the latter portion of my history of the 12th, for Vandeleur served continually with that regiment – either as a troop officer or on the staff of his namesake the general, commanding the brigade of which the 12th was a part – from 1812 until the end of the Peninsular War, taking part in the retreat from Burgos, the battles of Vitoria, the Pyrenees, Nivelle, and Nive, and finishing his service with the occupation of Bordeaux. All this was recounted in detailed and lively letters home, as was his subsequent service, again as a troop officer with the 12th, during the Hundred Days. For my immediate purposes this was an excellent resource, but there was more, for the initial batch of letters, covering 1810 and early 1811, were from Vandeleur's earlier active service as an ensign in the 71st Highland Light Infantry during the defence of Lisbon against the invading French under Marshal Massena. The only part of that story missing is an account of the fighting at Fuentes de Oñoro, and that for the very good reason that Vandeleur was badly wounded in that action and left in no fit state to write about it. Lastly, for good measure, a handful of letters from 1819 deal with a family scandal that arose after Vandeleur's younger brother was involved first in a duel and then in the resulting court martial, and the last letter of all gives an account of the participation of a rather older and more senior John Vandeleur – by now a lieutenant colonel commanding the 10th Hussars – in the celebrations subsequent to the coronation of Queen Victoria.

All in all, the letters give an excellent first-hand impression of life as a young officer on campaign and in battle during the Napoleonic Wars, being rendered all the more interesting by their writer having variously served as an infantryman, a cavalryman, and as an aide de camp. That much of this service was spent with the army's outposts – hence the title for this re-issued collection – also adds to their appeal since we have accounts of picquets, patrols, and minor skirmishes, as well as the major battles in which Vandeleur was engaged. All of this therefore renders it all the more remarkable that they have been so little known, despite having been in print for over a century. Neither the listing of memoirs in the back of Oman's *Wellington's Army*, nor the revised and exhaustive version of the same list assembled by Robert Burnham as part of his contribution to the 2006 *Inside Wellington's Peninsular Army*, makes any mention of Vandeleur. Nor, indeed, can one find a citation to the letters in the many histories that have been written of the campaigns in which Vandeleur took part; evidently, the limited print run and restricted circulation of the first and only edition has rendered the text thoroughly obscure, whilst the original letters, if they still survive, remain in private hands. This new printing, then, is intended to give the letters the place they deserve in Napoleonic literature and scholarship.

There is, however, one significant flaw to the original edition, which I have endeavoured to counteract here, and that is the fact that the 1894 text reproduced the letters and nothing but the letters, with no context provided. In the words of the original Preface:

> By desire of his family, and at the request of many old friends, anxious to perpetuate the memory of one who was loved and respected both in his public and private life, the following letters of the late Colonel John Vandeleur have been printed.
>
> Though the letters were private ones, and do not pretend to be a complete history of the exciting surroundings amongst which their author moved, they furnish many interesting side-lights in an epoch so full of glorious memories for his fellow-countrymen.

Interesting side-lights are all very well, and they are certainly there aplenty, but quite a lot of what Vandeleur writes clearly assumes a knowledge that the original recipient possessed but which is lost to the modern reader. Having been working for some time on the 12th Light Dragoons when I first encountered the text, and being aware from work done for an earlier study of the activities of the 71st, many of the more cryptic comments did make sense to me. Even so, others required considerable investigation and enquiry in order to ascertain just what was meant by particular passages. Even with the help of various experts, the precise meanings of some family references, in-jokes, and comments relating to neighbours back in Worcester where the Vandeleur family was then residing, remain hidden. For the most part, however, I have been able to add notes to identify places, military figures, and incidents referred to in the text, whilst at the same time providing a commentary that places the letters in context, discusses any more complex issues arising from Vandeleur's account of his activities, and fills in the occasional narrative gaps in the sequence. What I have not done here is re-tell the story of the Peninsular War, although I have referenced the summary provided to the appropriate sections of Sir Charles Oman's multi-volume history, as well as to other, shorter sources where appropriate. In terms of identification of military figures, two sources have been invaluable; the 'Peninsula Roll Call' compiled by the late Captain Lionel S. Challis, now available in electronic form via the Napoleon Series website, and the published *Waterloo Roll Call* assembled by Charles Dalton. In that they have been used so frequently, I have not provided citations on each occurrence.

For all my additions, however, it must be stressed that those wishing to read only the letters themselves, and to form their own opinions, may do so content in the knowledge that the basic text of 1894 has been reproduced in full, complete with John Vandeleur's occasionally unconventional approach to spelling and punctuation. The only editorial changes, and these stemming from the 1894 publication, are the deletion of a couple of names relating to persons back in England of whom Vandeleur evidently had a low opinion. Otherwise, no editing of content has taken place, and thus the views contained within the letters – sometimes factually erroneous, sometimes clearly showing a lack of faith in the outcome of events – are exactly as expressed 200 years ago. The only concession to ease of reading is that I have added paragraph breaks to those letters that were originally lacking them.

Lastly, in addition to my notes and commentary, I have also included a series of appendices incorporating additional primary-source material relevant to the story. Some of this, relating to the departure of the 10th Hussars for India in 1846, was included with the original 1894 text; the rest is taken primarily from papers held by The National Archives at Kew, and by the Regimental Museum of the 9th/12th Royal Lancers in Derby. I hope these appendices add an additional dimension to the basic narrative provided by the letters, and supply an additional layer of contextual background. The cooperation of the regimental museum and regimental trustees of the 9th/12th Royal Lancers – not least in making available the archival material just mentioned, and also in finding a portrait of Vandeleur himself – has been invaluable in assisting with this project, and I must in particular thank Mike Galer at the museum and Christopher Glynn-Jones of the trustees for their continued support.

Thanks are also due to a number of individuals who have assisted in putting this work together. As always, the members of the Napoleon Series online discussion forum proved able to assist with a number of queries, and on this occasion I must name and give particular thanks to Mick Crumplin, Ron McGuigan, Steven H. Smith, and Dave Worrall. Elsewhere, Ronald Brighouse, Carole Divall and Ian Robertson were of great assistance in using their knowledge of Peninsular geography to help identify the places mentioned in the story, this process in many cases requiring considerable effort to unravel Vandeleur's occasionally novel attempts to provide a spelling for a place name that he had likely never seen written down. Paul L. Dawson shared his knowledge of the cavalry fighting at Waterloo, and David Blackmore and Adrian Philpott theirs of Britain's light dragoon regiments more generally. Dave Brown was again generous in loaning items from his extensive book collection, and Mick Crumplin in providing some of the images for the plates section. Steven Broomfield at HorsePower, the museum of The King's Royal Hussars, was extremely helpful in providing information on Vandeleur's later career with the 10th Hussars. The maps accompanying this book are the combined work of my wife Lucy and of David Beckford, which makes this the third book on which the two of them have successfully collaborated. Michael Leventhal, Stephen Chumbley, Kate Baker, and their colleagues at Frontline Books have been as professional and helpful as always, as has freelance editor Donald Sommerville. As ever, I must close the acknowledgements by thanking Lucy and the rest of my family for their continued support in my endeavours, and in particular my father, Mick Bamford, who has again done a stalwart job as a proof-reader and also assisted with aspects of the genealogical research. Needless to say, responsibility for any errors remains mine.

Introduction

~

Although their surname stood as evidence of a distant Dutch ancestry the Vandeleurs were by the eighteenth century firmly established as an Irish family, having first settled there in 1660. Judging by the marriage matches they made, the family quickly integrated itself into the Anglo-Irish Protestant ascendancy, and by the beginning of the nineteenth century the family tree had begun to sprawl to create a somewhat tangled web of cousins and second cousins, many of them – to the confusion of the historian – sharing the same Christian names. In terms of tracing the descent of the John Vandeleur who wrote these letters, we need to go back a half-century to his earlier namesake, who in 1749 bought what would become the family estate at Kilrush. This John, who died in 1754, was married to Frances Ormsby, with whom he had four children: Crofton, his heir; John Ormsby; Richard; and Mary. The recurrence of Ormsby as a middle name, almost always paired with John as a Christian name, becomes a confusing theme in the family; Frances would have her namesakes down the generations as well.

Beyond the fact that Richard would in due course father a son who would also be christened John Ormsby Vandeleur, who would go on to serve as a brigade commander in the Peninsula and at Waterloo, and to whom we will return in due course, the two youngest children of John and Frances Vandeleur have no further part to play in the story. Returning to the older siblings, Crofton, the heir, married Alice Burton and had a substantial family, beginning with yet another John Ormsby Vandeleur – of note only because his daughter, named Alice for her grandmother, would

John Vandeleur and his Relatives

John Vandeleur
m
Frances Ormsby

Crofton Vandeleur
m
Alice Barton

John Ormsby Vandeleur
m
Lady Frances Pakenham

Richard Vandeleur
m
Elinor Firman

Mary Vandeleur

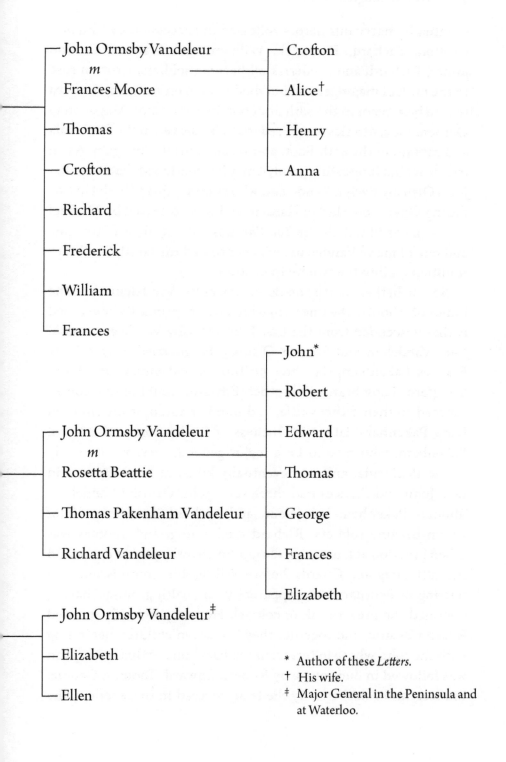

- John Ormsby Vandeleur
  m
  Frances Moore
  - Crofton
  - Alice†
  - Henry
  - Anna
- Thomas
- Crofton
- Richard
- Frederick
- William
- Frances

- John Ormsby Vandeleur
  m
  Rosetta Beattie
  - John*
  - Robert
  - Edward
  - Thomas
  - George
  - Frances
  - Elizabeth
- Thomas Pakenham Vandeleur
- Richard Vandeleur

- John Ormsby Vandeleur‡
- Elizabeth
- Ellen

* Author of these *Letters*.
† His wife.
‡ Major General in the Peninsula and
   at Waterloo.

eventually marry our hero – followed in succession by Thomas, Crofton, Richard, Frederick, William, and Frances. Crofton junior, Richard, and Frederick all became soldiers; Crofton rose to the rank of major general but died in 1806 on Antigua; Richard rose to be a major in the 88th Foot but died at Campo Mayor on 19 October 1809, of a sickness; Frederick also served in the Peninsula as a captain in the 87th Foot, and we shall meet him again. As an irrelevant but interesting point, it may be mentioned that Brigadier John Ormsby Evelyn Vandeleur, who commanded 3/Irish Guards during Operation Market Garden, and was portrayed by Michael Caine in the film *A Bridge Too Far*, was a descendant of this line and one of many Vandeleurs who continued the family's military tradition on into the twentieth century.

So much, then, for the pedigree line of the Vandeleurs, and the junior off-shoots. The line with which we are primarily concerned is that descended from the first John Ormsby Vandeleur, son of John Vandeleur and Frances Ormsby. He married in 1766 Lady Frances Pakenham, daughter of Thomas Pakenham, 1st Baron Longford: Lady Frances's brother, Edward, would in due course succeed to their father's title, and number amongst his children Kitty Pakenham, later the Duchess of Wellington, and Edward Pakenham, who rose to be a major general, served extensively in the Peninsula, and was eventually killed at New Orleans in 1815. John and Frances had three sons, John Ormsby Vandeleur, Thomas Pakenham Vandeleur, and Richard Vandeleur, all of whom became soldiers. Richard died young, and Thomas was killed in action at Laswari in 1803; John Ormsby rose to command the 5th Dragoon Guards before selling his commission and retiring in February 1803, apparently on health grounds, having obtained the brevet rank of colonel. He had previously married Rosetta Beattie, and together they had seven children beginning with the John whose letters form the backbone of this book. John was followed in due course by Robert, Edward, Thomas, George, Frances, and Elizabeth. By the time covered in these letters, the family were living at Barbourne, on the outskirts of the city of Worcester.[1]

John Vandeleur was born in 1793, apparently on 17 May although this seems slightly uncertain since he only says, in a letter bearing that date, that 'This, I believe, is my birthday.' His father was then still a serving officer, and young John was prepared from an early age to follow him into the military profession. In order to give him a suitable grounding, John was sent to the Royal Military College as a gentleman cadet. Established in 1802 under the aegis of the then Colonel John Le Marchant, the Junior Department of the Royal Military College was situated at Marlow and intended to prepare young men for service as officers in regiments either of the British Army of that of the Honourable East India Company. There are no letters from Vandeleur's time at the college, but a brief account of life as a gentleman cadet is contained in the memoirs of William Hay, who would later serve alongside Vandeleur in the 12th Light Dragoons. Hay, a rather light-hearted youth, enjoyed the military aspects but was initially somewhat lazy when it came to the academic work, notwithstanding that, as he recalled, 'no cadet was eligible for a commission until he attained the upper fourth in arithmetic, French, landscape and military drawing, etc.'[2] Young Vandeleur, on the other hand, seems to have applied himself well, and was rewarded with a commission as an ensign in the 71st Highland Light Infantry. With this appointment, his military career began in earnest.

1. Family history primarily from genealogical tables at http://www.stirnet.com/genie/data/british/uv/vandeleur1.php, with details of those who served in the Peninsula from Burnham, 'Lionel S. Challis' "Peninsula Roll Call".
2. Hay, Captain William, *Reminiscences 1808–1815 Under Wellington*, pp. 4–5.

Chapter 1

Defending Lisbon

John Vandeleur received his commission as ensign in the 71st Highland Light Infantry on 9 May 1809, a few days before his sixteenth birthday. At this time, the regiment was enjoying a brief respite after a period of varied and active service and had newly completed the conversion to light infantry that had been ordered the previous year. Originally raised in 1777 as the 73rd, and renumbered as the 71st in 1786, the regiment had always been a Scots one, but had undergone a series of changes that took it away from its original roots as MacLeod's Highlanders. Moves to broaden recruiting away from the highlands saw it given an affiliation to Glasgow in 1808, whilst at the time that young Ensign Vandeleur received his commission it had narrowly avoided losing its highland status altogether. Originally slated to be one of several highland regiments due to be 'de-kilted' in order to increase their recruiting potential, some astute bargaining on the part of Lieutenant Colonel Denis Pack had kept the 71st in tartan trews, until an eventual compromise saw it become the Highland Light Infantry. Trews were in the end replaced with trousers, but instead of a shako the traditional knitted bonnet was to be blocked up into a shako shape, retaining the diced band that distinguished highland units. Pack was also quick to ensure that the regiment kept its pipers.

This neat compromise owed at least something to the distinguished performance of the regiment's 1st Battalion under Pack's command during the South African, South American, and Peninsula campaigns. These had seen the battalion take part in the capture of the Cape of Good Hope and of Buenos Aires, before itself being taken prisoner when the latter city was recaptured by forces loyal to Spain. Pack was eventually able to escape, along with enough soldiers to reconstitute a company's worth of the 1/71st, to take part in the fighting brought about by Britain's return to the Rio de la Plata in 1807. That operation ultimately ended in disaster, but the convention that secured the cessation of hostilities also secured the release of the remaining men of the 1/71st, and the whole battalion sailed for home in September 1807. Reaching Ireland in December, the 1st Battalion was brought up to strength with a detachment of 200 men from the 2nd, and readied for further service. Initially, the expeditionary force being prepared at Cork under the command of Lieutenant General Sir Arthur Wellesley was destined for a return to South America, but Napoleon's invasion of Spain turned the Spanish into allies and the troops were instead earmarked to take part in the liberation of Portugal. Again under Pack's command, the 1/71st fought with distinction at Roliça and Vimeiro, before joining Sir John Moore for his march into Spain. Further distinguished at the Battle of Corunna on 16 January 1809, which enabled the evacuation of Moore's army, the battalion returned home thereafter and was stationed at Brabourne Lees where it began its conversion to light infantry. It was brigaded with the 68th and 85th Regiments, both of which were undergoing a similar conversion from line to light infantry, and was again built up to strength by the arrival of over 300 men from the 2nd Battalion – then stationed in Scotland – as well as direct transfers from the Militia and several new officers.[1]

In theory at least, one of those officers was John Vandeleur. As a new and junior ensign, Vandeleur should have begun his career with the regiment's 2nd Battalion in Scotland, but instead he is returned as being absent without leave, not having joined since appointed. By late 1809, the turnover of officers meant that his

1. Hildyard, Lieutenant Henry J. T., *Historical Record of the 71st Regiment Highland Light Infantry*, pp. 52–71; Reid, Stuart, *Wellington's Highland Warriors*, pp. 159–74.

seniority as ensign now entitled him to a place in the 1st Battalion, but its returns for early 1810 show him as having obtained the Commander-in-Chief's leave to be absent from 30 December 1809 to 24 August 1810, allowing him to complete his military education at Marlow. Thus, it was not for more than a year after his appointment to it that Vandeleur actually joined his regiment, which had in the meantime seen further hard service. In common with the majority of the infantry that had returned from Corunna, the 1/71st had been earmarked for the 'Grand Expedition' against Antwerp, forming part of a light infantry brigade under Brigadier General Francis de Rottenburg along with the 68th and 85th. Taking part in the landing on Walcheren, the battalion remained in the Scheldt until November 1809, incurring substantial losses through the fevers that crippled the expedition. Still on leave, Vandeleur thus avoided exposure to the sickness that could well have ended his military career before it had properly begun. Finally, in the Monthly Return of 25 August 1810, the name of Ensign John Vandeleur appears as amongst the officers present for duty with the 1/71st. The battalion was then stationed at Deal, and already under orders for the Peninsula. Early the following month it sailed, and, with this, the written record of John Vandeleur's military service begins.

In the Downs, 10th September 1810[1]

My Dear Father,

The unexpected tidings which I am going to announce, I hope will not break your spirits. You have met with such changes yourself, to you I may venture to disclose, that by the time you read this, your son, your dear son, has sailed for Portugal. Open it gradually to my Mother, that it may not have too strong effect on her gentle feelings. She is but a woman, and they are not born to suffer such. I will write by the first opportunity, so God Almighty bless you both until my return, which I trust will be soon.

1. In the original text, p. 1.

From your ever dear and affectionate son,
     John Vandeleur

At the time that the 1/71st returned to Portugal, the course of the Peninsular War seemed to be running in favour of the French. Although Portugal had been cleared of the invaders for a second time in 1809, following the allied victory at the Second Battle of Oporto, the subsequent Anglo-Spanish offensive aimed at retaking Madrid had ultimately failed in the face of French numbers, following which the remaining Spanish forces in Andalusia had been smashed and the French advance carried to the gates of Cadiz. Falling back into Portugal, the British troops under the newly created Lord Wellington were now working with the rejuvenated Portuguese Army in order to defend that country. As part of the rebuilding and remodelling of the Portuguese forces, under the direction of Lieutenant General Sir William Beresford, a number of British officers had been seconded to the Portuguese service. For the most part these were regimental officers, but more senior men were also needed as brigade commanders, and one such officer was Denis Pack, who had volunteered for service whilst his battalion was still recovering from Walcheren, and who had been given command of an independent Portuguese brigade.

Pack had envisaged returning to command of the 1/71st once the battalion reached the Peninsula, but he had proved so effective as a brigadier that he was prevailed upon to remain where he was.[1] Accordingly, the 1/71st was taken out to Portugal by Major (brevet Lieutenant Colonel) Nathaniel Peacocke, although he swiftly returned to Britain and command of the battalion went to Lieutenant Colonel Hon. Henry Cadogan who had previously commanded the 2/71st in Scotland. Because so many men were still on the sick list after Walcheren, only six companies initially

1. Pack obituary in Anon., *The Annual Biography and Obituary of 1823*. London, A. R. Spottiswoode, 1823, pp. 345–67.

embarked rather than the full ten: these six contained the fittest soldiers, with the remaining companies coming out to join them once there were sufficient fit men to make up the numbers.[1]

John Vandeleur evidently assumed that his father would have had time to break the news of his departure to the rest of the family, for his next letter – like almost all those that followed it – was directed to his mother. Also in common with many of those that would follow, it was evidently written in several sittings, beginning in this case whilst still aboard ship, but concluding with an impression of Lisbon that can only have been gained after several days ashore.

O.H.M.S. Lisbon, 25th September 1810[2]

My Dear Mother,

We have just dropped our anchor in the Tagus opposite Lisbon. We expect to land this evening or to-morrow morning and march directly forward to Almeida. The City of Almeida has surrendered to the French. A large body of British troops are advancing from Cadiz to join Lord Wellington's army. The Portuguese tell us that they are as strong as ten thousand. The 50th and 92nd are expected every moment to join us, which will make our reinforcement equal to two thousand, so that immediately Lord W. receives the whole twelve thousand it is said he intends to take another brush with the enemy.

We sailed from Deal on Friday the 14th of Septr., and landed on the 25th after a very pleasant voyage. The whole of the men are in good spirits and only wish to engage. Three Hundred of us came in the *Melpomene*, and the remaining three hundred came on board the *St. Fiorenzo*, both frigates.[3]

---

1. Hildyard, *Highland Light Infantry*, pp. 76–7.
2. In the original text, pp. 1–5.
3. HMS *Melpomene*, 38-gun frigate, captured from the French in 1794; HMS *San Fiorenzo*, 36-gun frigate, captured from the French in 1794 and famous for capturing the French frigate *Piedmontaise* in an epic single-ship action off Colombo in March 1808.

They ask as much as 80 dollars for a mule and sixty for a jackass. I think I must put up with a good strong ass to carry my baggage, and occasionally myself. When you write to me, which I hope will be soon, direct to Lord W's army, mentioning my regt., and be sure and direct Light Infantry for perchance we may be detached. We are obliged to carry our own greatcoats and a haversack, to carry provisions, together with a bottle canteen and telescope. We expect Col. Pack to meet us, and we think it probable that 3 companies of the regt. will be on the right of the Portuguese Brigade and three on the left, or else we shall form a reserve to the Portuguese Brigade, so that we will certainly be under the command of Col. Pack.[1]

You have no conception what a beautiful country Portugal is: it abounds with fruit of every description. The finest water-melons sell for 3d. apiece, the finest grapes for almost nothing, and all fruits in proportion. The best port wine for 9d. a bottle, and an inferior kind for 6d. and 4d. a bottle. Remember never wait for answers from me, for sometimes in waiting for answers you may lose the Packets from London. I shall always write to you whenever I hear of a Packet.

We don't expect to remain long in Portugal, for we strongly flatter ourselves that we shall sicken the French in a very superior style, for from the Portuguese we learn that they are very sickly, half starved, and very shy. I trust that you will not fidget yourself the least on my account. Remember old Mrs. Marriot's advice concerning her sons at Seringapatam![2]

You may depend on my sending letters to you at every opportunity, and concealing nothing. I was excessively glad to hear of my father's

1. Lt. Colonel Denis Pack had entered the Army as a cornet in the 14th Light Dragoons in 1791, and served as a cavalry officer until obtaining his lieutenant colonelcy in the 71st in 1800. Commanded 1/71st at the Cape and in South America, then Portuguese service 1810–1813. Promoted major general and commanded Highland Brigade in the Sixth Division 1813–1814, Ninth Brigade in Waterloo Campaign, and Fourth Brigade on occupation duty in France. Knighted 1815, died 1823 aged only forty-seven.
2. A reference to a neighbour in Worcester whose sons had served in India – presumably she had resigned herself to the risks they were undergoing.

great raking. I am afraid he will slip into my shoes among the pretty girls of Worcester. I shall expect next letter to hear of his attending the assemblies. I hope to find him very much recovered against my return to England. Give my sincere love to him.

I have got one thing to ask you as a favour, not to let Thomas join the navy, or go on board ship. I have seen more mischief to a lad done by the midshipmen on board ship than I ever did before in my life. I have only been on board 10 days, and I would rather see my brother a chimney-sweeper than a sailor!

God bless you, my dear mother. Trust in your son's goodness and fear nothing. Remember my love to the family and to the Wakemans and Larkens.[1]

> Adieu! Your ever dear son.
> John Vandeleur.

There is an interesting mixture of fact, supposition, and rumours in Vandeleur's first missive from the Peninsula. The general conception of events is sound enough, with the fall of Almeida on 27 August, allowing the French Armée de Portugal under Marshal André Massena to begin their advance on Lisbon in earnest. With 50,000 Anglo-Portuguese troops against Massena's 65,000, Wellington had based his strategy on trading space for time and falling back towards Lisbon and its surrounding defences. Reinforcements were on their way, both from home and from Cadiz, but insofar as the latter source was concerned, rumour far overestimated the numbers – there were fewer than 10,000 British troops in Cadiz to begin with. Nevertheless, numbers notwithstanding, Wellington had every intention of striking a blow where and when he could, and Vandeleur's prediction of a coming fight accurately prefigures the allied victory at Busaco, won two days

---

1. The Wakemans were a prominent family around Worcester, raised to a baronetcy in 1828; it may be inferred that the Larkens were also neighbours. Judging from later letters, Vandeleur seems to have had a fancy for one of the Wakeman daughters.

after the date of this letter, even if the conception of the French as sickly and unwilling to fight was wishful thinking to say the least.[1]

Similarly wishful was the apparent assumption by the officers of the 1/71st that they would again be serving under their old commanding officer, Denis Pack. With a few exceptions, British and Portuguese troops had not been brigaded together since the Oporto campaign, and on those occasions that this had been done it had seen a single Portuguese unit attached to several British battalions, not the other way around. The misconception is also particularly striking when one considers that Vandeleur names the two battalions – 1/50th and 1/92nd; the West Kents and the Gordon Highlanders – with which the 1/71st would in fact be brigaded. Whilst misunderstanding and rumour must inevitably have played some part in this mistaken belief, fuelled in part by Pack's own stated intention to return to command the battalion, one wonders if there was also an element of wish-fulfilment inherent in it: Pack was a well-known and respected leader, whilst the battalion's temporary commander, Peacocke, was a decidedly unpleasant individual who would – much later in the war – be cashiered for cowardice.[2] With such a contrast, the battalion's officers can hardly be faulted for wishing for a change; thankfully, although they would not get Pack back, the arrival of Lieutenant Colonel Cadogan would give them an officer of equal merit.

Lisbon, Saturday, September 28th, 1810[3]

My Dear Mother,

I take the opportunity of writing, as a Packet sails this evening. By my last letter I informed you we were going to march directly on to join the Grand Army, but much to our disappointment and expectation we were left to garrison Lisbon, along with the Duke of Brunswick-

---

1. Oman, Sir Charles, *A History of the Peninsular War*, Vol. III, pp. 153–281, 341–89.
2. Oman, *Peninsular War*, Vol. VII, pp. 270, 280.
3. In the original text, pp. 5–10.

Oels Corps of Riflemen.[1] I hope we shall not stay long in Lisbon; but our stay is quite uncertain, inasmuch that directly we take off a shirt or a pair of stockings we are obliged to get them washed. We have all bought horses, mules, donkeys, etc. to carry our baggage. I bought a small pony about as big as Neptune, and as rough, a mustache [*sic*], for thirty dollars! As far as I can judge from a horse, I think I am well off: he is strong, never requires any grooming, got a clean back, and above all things is not particular in his feeding, for he eats straw, or sour hay, or grass; in fact he is glad to get anything, and makes no choice. You can seldom find your fine, thorough-bred English horses with so many good points about them. My horse only requires a little antimony and a few good lessons from Capt. Lisdale, to make him look very war-like.[2]

We heard in Lisbon yesterday that the Portuguese troops and some English Dragns. had got in the rear of the French line and had retaken 3 small towns from whence the French derived the most, if not the entire, of their supplies. The Portuguese are said to have behaved very well on the occasion. They took a body of French cavalry about a thousand strong.

I have some good intelligence to communicate to you, which is that there is a compy. vacant, and the senior Lt. expects to be gazetted every day. There is likewise a Lt. who intends making application to Col. Pack for a compy. in the Portuguese service; so there will be two vacant Lieutenancies. There is one ensign who can purchase, so he expects the first; then I am next after him.[3]

---

1. The Brunswick-Oels Light Infantry, twelve companies strong, had arrived at Lisbon on 17 September. See Oman, Sir Charles, *Wellington's Army 1809–1814*, p. 349.

2. Antimony was supposed to improve the appearance of a horse's coat. 'Captain Lisdale' is a mystery: no-one of that name served in the Peninsula. Possibly a Worcester acquaintance or a literary allusion.

3. This reflects normal practice, wherein a vacancy for promotion by purchase was offered first to the most senior candidate within the regiment, and, if he could not put up the money, to the second and so on down the seniority list until a purchaser was found. See Oman, *Wellington's Army*, pp. 198–9.

I hope you received my letter dated the 25th quite safe. I sent it by the *Tonnant* Frigate.[1] This, perhaps, will reach as soon, for it is going by the *Prince of Wales* Packet.

I will try to give you some small account of Lisbon. In the first place I will begin with their religion, which is Roman Catholic, and I am sorry to say that the stoutest and most able men are friars, who, under the veil of the Church, commit the grossest debaucheries and revelries. The commerce of Lisbon and Portugal in General is very extensive, but not beneficial; for I learn from the inhabitants that the countries trading with her engross all the production of her colonies, as well as her own inland commodities; but there is no placing any dependence upon what they say, for they are such a set of lying rascals.

The air of Portugal is not so pure as that of England in my opinion. The soil is very fertile; it produces grapes, figs, melons, pumpkins, nectarines, peaches, pomegranates, apples, pears, etc., all of which are extremely good, but I am told that the Spanish soil is much better, and the fruits also better. They have but little corn; most of the corn is supplied them from England. They have but few horses here; but what they have, although far from being handsome, are very strong, and go through a great deal of fatigue and hardship. All their carts are drawn, or rather pushed forward, by bullocks. They are of a very simple construction; they are nothing but a few boards nailed together to form a kind of flat. The wheels are without spokes; they are like the lid of a barrel; they make the most hideous noise, for the civil power will not suffer the drivers to oil or grease the wheels for fear of smuggling.

You will excuse what I am going to mention. The Portuguese are not the most cleanly people in the world. Like the Scotch they empty the rubbish of the house out of the windows in the night-time after nine o'clock. I was not up to the system the first night I was in Lisbon, and as I was returning from duty to the barracks, which are in a convent, there were the contents of a vessel discharged at me. However, I was

1. HMS *Tonnant*, not in fact a frigate at all but an 80-gun ship of the line, captured from the French at the Battle of the Nile in 1798 and subsequently distinguished at Trafalgar in 1805.

fortunate enough to escape it, but my servant received it full upon his head, and my portmanteau, so it just put him in mind of it, for he had been in Lisbon before, therefore he warned me to keep under the eaves of the houses, for the streets are too narrow to keep in the middle of it. Oh! what a comparison could be drawn between that and Worcester.

They ask most immoderately dear for whatever we want. They asked me 15 dollars for a pair of second-cloth trousers, whereas I have known officers to purchase them in Deal for 12 to 16 shillings. The Portuguese language is a very harsh, but not a difficult one to learn. I have purchased a dictionary and grammar, by which I can contrive to make myself understood with the assistance of a little French, which I find very useful.

The houses in *Lisboa* (as it is called in the Portuguese language) are very high, a family lives on each floor. There is generally an officer billeted on each family. The rooms are in general very well proportioned and very neat and clean, but for all that, they are full of bugs and fleas, which is no small annoyance. The rooms are lined with a kind of tyle [*sic*] resembling the Dutch Pan-Tyle, which is painted in a fancy style; it has a very pretty effect, it reaches up almost breast high. Every room has a balcony – even the *genets* [*sic*]. The doors are immense, just like the *doors of Clains Church*.[1] Then outside there is another door about two inches from the former, with thick bars of wood and iron, just like a prison. I intend to take an airing through Lisbon to-morrow on my charger. The streets of Lisbon are up and down hill, which renders them very unpleasant; when we marched in, several of the officers and men fell or rather slipped down on account of the nails in their shoes. There are some very fine mules in Lisbon, but they are so immensely dear, there is no thought of buying them.

[the rest of this letter lost]

It is rather a shame that the rest of this letter is missing, as the description of Lisbon is a good one. Evidently news of Busaco had

---

1. Presumably the church of St John the Baptist in Claines, a village just north of Worcester.

still not reached the city by the time Vandeleur sent off his letter, unless the reported cavalry action was somehow based on a first garbled report of the battle. Certainly, it is hard to see what else – unless pure rumour – had inspired the story; it is too early by over a week for the recapture of Coimbra by Portuguese irregulars, which was the first occasion when large numbers of prisoners were taken from the French. In all events, however, this would be the last time for a while that Vandeleur would have to rely on second-hand news for the doings of the army, for the 1/71st were soon themselves on the way to the front.

O.H.M. Service, Lisbon, 15th October 1810[1]

My Dear Mother,

I have been much surprised at not hearing from you, but I suppose, nevertheless, that you have written and I have not received your letter. I have been up to *Coimbra* with the Grand Army in Genel. Spencer's Brigade,[2] where we had to build cabins and huts for ourselves. I, thank God, built a very comfortable one with sods and boughs. I was assisted, of course, by the officers of our compy.; we succeeded in making it completely water-proof and air-tight etc. We were then absent 10 days, when Lord Wellington made a good retreat to *Villa-Franca*, to a very strong position there.[3] Lord Wellington wants to draw the French into a snare which he has got at *Marpa*, which is only 30 miles from Lisbon.[4] There is a line of fortifications all across the country, from the sea-side to the Tagus, which can be defended by about 20 thousand, even against almost any number. All the roads about there are undermined and ready to blow up directly we pass, so that no French Artillery or waggons of any description can pass. If we can get them into this snare, not one of them can escape.

1. In the original text, pp. 10–16.
2. Lt. General Sir Brent Spencer, commanding the First Division and Wellington's de facto second-in-command.
3. Vila Franca de Xira, on the Tagus twenty miles northeast of Lisbon.
4. Most likely Mafra, although that town is rather closer to Lisbon.

I came from the army back to Lisbon with 30 sick of our regt. I am sorry I shall have about a month to remain in Lisbon. I have got the Opthalmia in my eyes, but, thank God, I am almost well; for I can see to write almost as well as ever. I took it about a fortnight back from some of the men: when I first took it, I could not see a morsel, I was quite blind. I was obliged to be led about like a child. I got Elrington[1] to look among my papers for that receipt [recipe] which you gave me. I sent it to the hospital and got it made up. I continued using it until I got a great deal better. I still use it, and will continue it until I am quite well, which I trust shall be in a short time. I shall, please God, be quite recovered by the time you receive this letter.

I have had great opportunities improving myself in the French language since I left England. Most of the better kind of people speak French, so that at first I could make myself pretty well understood by them. I am studying the Spanish language at present. I hope by the time I reach England I shall be perfect in it.

I have got a most beautiful garden behind my house. There are three or four plantains, and orange, and lemon groves, and all kinds of fruits. The things are getting much dearer in this place, at least they have been so to me, for I cannot live on the rations they serve out. This complaint prevents my eating salt provisions, and therefore I am obliged to live upon Mutton etc., which is very dear, and what's more, there is no way of getting money in this place, except the month's pay every 24th, and then they oblige us to pay 6d. in every dollar, besides the Income Tax; all of which does not make a dollar worth more than 4 shillings. They charge *two bintins* [*vintéms*] a pound for potatoes, which is about 3 pence English money, and 3 *bintins* or 4½d. for a loaf of bread made of Indian corn, very poor stuff, about the size of an English penny roll. I don't know any of the merchants, or I could get them to cash a draught upon Greenwood. I wish you could find out some way of giving me a check upon some of the banking houses in Lisbon, or of forwarding some money. It would

1. John Elrington. Ensign in 71st Highland Light Infantry October 1809, subsequently Ensign 3rd Foot Guards March 1811, Lieutenant and Captain 3rd Foot Guards May 1814. Served in Peninsula September 1810–June 1811, August 1812–June 1814. Apparently belonged to the Elrington family of Worcester.

be as short a way if you could insure it, and cut the notes in half and send two letters. I could get an English note changed in Lisbon by allowing the discount; speak to some of your banking friends in Wor'ster. I dare say Mr. Wakeman could put you in the way of it.[1]

My poney is getting on very well. In coming from Coimbra, I could get no forage for him, so I fed him upon bread and cheese and apples for two days. He used to stop when I was riding him and turn his head round as much as to say: 'I hear you eating, why don't you give me something?' When we were hutted near Coimbra, he used to stay about the hut continually. Since I have come to Lisbon I have heard the military speak very favourably of the state of our army. The French are very much in want of provisions. Our army has very good rations: 1 pound of beef, 1 pound of bread, and about a naggin [*sic*] of rum each day; men and officers take the same rations.

I hope that my father's health is mending. I expect to find him much better please God, when I return to England. It is very singular that I have never got any letters since I landed. I suppose it must be due to the negligence of the Post-Office here. I heard that the 4th Regt. disembarked on the 11th, and marched on to the army.[2] I am going to begin to draw a large map of the country, I hope I shall succeed.

You are enjoying comfortable fires in England. In this country the doors and windows are open, and we are drinking lemonade to keep ourselves cool: they have no fire-places in the rooms in this country, for they very seldom have occasion for fires, and when they do light a fire it is nothing but wood in a little pan in the middle of the floor. Elrington is very well, – don't tell Mrs. Elrington that I have sore eyes, or else she will think her son is also unwell. I don't find that I am unwell, indeed, I think it hard that they won't let me go to the army, but I trust I shall soon be there amongst the whole of them.

1. An 1829 history of Worcester recorded that 'The banking-house at the Cross, now conducted under the firm of Messrs. Farley, Johnson, Wakeman, Lavender, and Owen, was established as a house of regular business in 1798.' See Anon., *A Concise History and Description of the City and Cathedral of Worcester*, Worcester, T. Eaton, 1829, p. 197.
2. The 1/4th Foot, joining as reinforcements from Britain.

I hope that Miss Wakeman and all the rest of the family are quite well. I am afraid that she will quite forget me now that I am not present. The gaieties of Worc'ter are at their height by this time. Tell Miss W. that I expect she will do penance every assembly, by reserving herself one set. She must comfort herself with the supposition that I am sitting chatting with her. I shall certainly *reserve* myself the whole of any Portuguese assembly, for I don't think there is such a thing in this country. Give my love to all the belles in our neighbourhood.

I hope that Fanny's neck is improving, as well as Bessie's cough. The rest of our dear family I trust is in good health, not omitting yourself. I was never better; except my eyes are a little weak. I expect by the time I leave this place to be about the colour of a copper coal box. My love to my dear father and brothers and sisters, and let me continue as I ever have been –

> your dear son.
> John Vandeleur

[PS] Direct the next letter 71st Regt. in Portugal. Bellam [Belém], near Lisbon, 15th October 1810.

The 1/71st marched up to join the main field army in late September, arriving prior to Wellington's evacuation of Coimbra on 1 October. Vandeleur's account of their assignment is a little simplistic; their brigade formed part of the First Division under Lieutenant General Sir Brent Spencer, but the brigade itself was commanded by Major General Sir William Erskine. Known for his mental instability, Erskine was a bizarre choice for a field command and had been foisted on Wellington against the latter's wishes. In the event, he would soon be removed to a series of acting divisional commands, so that his interaction with the 1/71st would be short-lived.

The condition that cut short Vandeleur's first sojourn at the front was a souvenir of his regiment's first Peninsular campaign. Ophthalmia – the term is a catch-all for a series of infectious eye complaints – had been a problem within the British Army ever since the Egyptian campaign of 1801. The condition was contracted by large numbers of men during the retreat to Corunna – in which campaign the 1/71st were first exposed to it – and had proved difficult to eradicate thereafter. The nature of the cure looked up by Ensign Elrington is unknown, but remedies in use at the time included irrigation with various dilute mineral salts as well as bleeding and purges.[1]

Finally, this letter is the first to introduce the cornerstone of Wellington's strategy for the defence of Portugal, namely the Lines of Torres Vedras. Composed of two main lines of fortifications running from the Tagus to the Atlantic, along with a third inner line designed to cover an embarkation of the defenders if the outer lines were breached, these defences had been constructed to take advantage of natural terrain features, reinforced with fortifications. The Lines were manned almost in their entirety by Portuguese militia, leaving the field army secure behind them and able to respond to any attack. By this means, Wellington was able to render the area around Lisbon practically impregnable. In conjunction with a scorched earth policy outside the Lines, this strategy was designed to ensure that the French would be stranded deep within Portugal without means to support their army. However, the plan meant abandoning almost all of central Portugal and as a result was the cause of considerable protest and resistance. Continued retreat to the Lines, even after the victory at Busaco, was also unpopular within the army, and the coming months would see the emergence of numerous so-called Croakers who came to believe that the campaign had been a failure and that Wellington would ultimately be obliged to evacuate Lisbon. In the course of time John Vandeleur would himself for a while be amongst that number, but, as we shall see, not just yet.

1. Crumplin, Michael, *Men of Steel: Surgery in the Napoleonic Wars*, pp. 240, 249.

Bucellas, Nov. 1st, 1810[1]

My Dear Mother,

I am glad to hear from you at last. I suppose you have written more than one letter to me, but I never received any but this one dated 5th October. You complained of my not informing you what type of lodging we have. We have sometimes very good, sometimes very bad, and sometimes none at all. At present we are at Bucellas in houses, but as we are always on the move being a light regt., it is impossible to say whether we will be ½ an hour here or not.

We had a brush with some light troops of the enemy on the 16th at 10 o'clock at night. We fought all night firing at wherever we saw the flash of a gun. The men got tired of this playing as they call'd it, so they got orders to advance in loose light infantry order, and got within 5 yards of them before we were perceived. Several of them were bayonetted and shot. In the morning a flag of truce came to bury the dead, which was accepted. Our regt. lost very few men – not above 3 or 4, but there were as many as forty wounded – not any of the officers were the least hurt. Colonel Reynwell has a ball through his cap,[2] but he ran the fellow through who fired it. Our men are capital shots. I could see them pick the fellows off one at a time as day began to appear. Next night (Monday) they opened a battery of two guns upon us, which was taken by our Grenadier company in a very short time. They were obliged to retreat in a great hurry. We got a mule by it at all events.

You were very anxious to know how I carried my baggage and what I had. I can give you an inventory of them in a very small compass. I carry 2 shirts, 2 pr. of long worsted stockings, 1 pr. of stocking-net Drawers, 1 pr. of flannell, 2 flannell waistcoats, 2 Pockt.-handk. and a fur cap which I sleep in in lieu of a night-cap. I have had the good fortune to get an old

1. In the original text, pp. 12–26; the location is in fact Bucelas, ten miles north of Lisbon.

2. Thomas Reynell, major in the 71st but holding brevet rank as lieutenant colonel since March 1805. His Peninsular service January 1809–April 1811 was mostly on the staff, apart from a brief spell on regimental duty when the 1/71st first arrived in Portugal. Later commanded the 1/71st at Waterloo, and eventually married Denis Pack's widow.

jacket which serves as a second. I carry also my gt.-coat and a famous warm cloak and a good blanket folded up under the saddle of my horse. My jacket and the 1 pr. of grey trowsers I have are quite good yet – that is, they have not required mending yet. I have Gardiner's shoes on still. I don't think they will ever wear out, besides, I have got a very good pair set with nails in my havresack. I have no reason to complain for I am pretty well set out as to clothing. Whenever we are in the open fields if we have not tents we build huts. Every three of four build a hut to sleep in; we can get plenty of straw, so in general I sleep pretty warm.

I hope I shall see Col. Packenham[1] in a few days, perhaps not for 3 weeks. However, I shall take great care of the letter and deliver it myself if I have an opportunity; if otherwise I shall give it to some of the Aide-de-Camps to deliver for me.

There are two lieutenants in our regt. accepted companies in Col. Pack's Brigade of Portuguese, but their promotion still continues within the regt. so that is no advantage to me. I could have got a comy. in the same regt. by applying to Col. Pack but although it might be of great benefit to me, still it is an unpleasant way of getting promotion, particularly when I know it would be against the inclinations of both you and my father. I should like very much to go to High Wycombe when we return home. If my father could possibly get me on the list I should like to remain there two years or thereabouts. I should like very much to be employed on the staff until I get a comy., for you have no conception what an idle life a subaltern leads when he is at home, and what a slavish one when he is abroad. I am sure I would be glad of two years' study at Wycombe, and another thing it is near my home.[2]

You spoke of a great conspiracy which was discovered by an inhabitant of Lisbon. It is very true! The whole of the English who were billeted on the people of Lisbon were to have been murdered in one night, and there were several Portuguese large boats laden with straw

---

1. Colonel Edward Pakenham, then serving as Deputy Adjutant-General in the Peninsula – Vandeleur's paternal grandmother had been the colonel's aunt.
2. High Wycombe, in Buckinghamshire, was home to the Senior Department of the Royal Military College, a precursor to the Staff College.

which were to have been fired and cut adrift amongst the transports. One of the conspirators was to have been burnt for forging dollars. When he was on the scaffold he said if his life was spared he would make known to them a secret of great importance, so he was taken into the Justiciary, and there he gave a true account of everything. It was to have taken place on the following night – which was the night we lay in the Tagus. There were upwards of two hundred of the highest class of people in the city concerned. They were all seized and twenty or more of them suffered death – all the others were transported.

Lord Wellington is not at all afraid of them. He was never better situated than he is at present. He has thirty thousand fighting-men all British and about 30 thousand Portuguese troops that are, I think, just as good as the British. Besides, there is the Duke of Romana in the rear, somewhere about one hundred miles.[1] There are also a body of Portuguese troops in the rear in the possession of Coimbra, so that Massena has no communication with Coimbra or the country in the rear of that. He is very badly off for provisions. They have not had any meat for thirty days, so that if they do not fight or capitulate in some manner, they must all be prisoners of war, which will, please God, be the case. Massena offered to quit the field and march back with all the honours of war into France, but Lord Wellington told him either to surrender as prisoners of war, or else fight him. They want to fight, but Lord Wellington knows the situation they are in, so he wants to put it off till they are completely starved. There are as many on an average as 70 men desert to the English every day. Massena's army is computed to be 55 thousand.

Our regt. saw him as I did myself with my glass on a wind-mill prior to the engagement.[2] He gave the signal by waving a handkerchief. You would be surprised how well the Portuguese stood. I was in amongst some of them that stood firing all night with the greatest coolness.

1. Capitán-General Don Pedro Caro y Sureda, Marqués de la Romana, commanded the Spanish Army of the Left, of which two divisions were with Wellington behind the Lines of Torres Vedras, and the remainder – to which Vandeleur is presumably referring here – in Estremadura.
2. The 'him' in this context would seem to be Massena, who directed the fighting from a windmill above Sobral.

They charged too with the greatest courage and intrepidity; but they were seconded by our regt. We received thanks from Lord Wellington in the Public Orders which he ordered to be printed in the Portuguese gazettes in Lisbon. Elrington is quite well and in good spirits. I told him that I heard from home, and that his mother was well, which made him very glad.

I don't know in what part of the army the 83rd is; but whenever we should come near them I shall make it a point to be a friend to your cousin.[1] I am sorry to hear such a bad account of K_____ from home: he is led away by his own ignorance. I wish he was at home with his father; he will be the cause of his father's breaking his heart, or his mother's – if she was alive, at least. I know if it was the case with me, it would kill both my parents.

I hope that you won't say I am expensive in sending you double letters. You know that the back of your letter was torn through? You said that you thought Lieutenant Arthur would be coming home.[2] I should not think it unlikely, for the French cannot winter in this country, and if they come to action they are sure of being defeated and made prisoners. I really think that they will make some kind of terms, for they are starving. I have spoken to French officers who are prisoners; it was from them I heard the state of the army; besides, the poor fellows that desert from them say they are starved. Our soldiers have 1 pound and a half of good brown bread and a pound of beef each day, besides an allowance of either bacon or ham, and wood to burn. The French and English picquets are so near that they speak to each other, and even give time to the enemy. They are not allowed to fire; no more are we, nor allowed to engage unless attacked.

We have a great quantity of bugs, fleas, mosquitos, and what they call torpedos, a kind of black worm, with an innumerable quantity of legs;

1. The 2/83rd was in fact then serving in the Third Division. Vandeleur's mother was a Beattie by birth, but there is no officer of that name recorded as having served with the regiment so this unknown officer must have been a more distant relative.

2. No officer of this surname and rank served in the Peninsula: the closest match listed by Challis is Lt. Archibald McArthur of the 94th Foot.

it is covered with a hard shell. They give a very severe bite, something like the bite of a Mosquito, which is very painful. If we should come home before Christmas, I want you to get my father to ask for leave for three months from Col. Cadogan, who is now at our head.[1] Every ship has its regt. marked to it. Ours are two transports, the *Arethusa* and another. I am afraid we shall get a terrible tossing in the Bay of Biscay if we go back in transports.

I am very sorry to hear that my father's health is attacked with rheumatism, as I know from what I have already seen him suffer that it is very painful; but I trust in God that he will be better. Remember me kindly to our friends; I have not forgotten any of them yet. I wish I was comfortable settled for a few months in Barbourne. Nobody knows the comfort of home until they have seen some little hardship. I wish I was sitting down to as comfortable a dinner as you are, or your servants even. We live upon nothing but coarse bread, beef – the same as the men, only we have chocolate. I wish my canteen had been double, so as to have hung across a horse, for they are the most comfortable things we have. I was obliged to leave mine on board ship on that account; but then I shall have it when we go home. I wish you would send me out a note of about twenty pounds, as I will be able to get about eighteen for it in Portuguese dollars by getting some of our officers who are constantly going to Lisbon to change it at one of the banking-houses. I cannot draw my back pay in this country, or I would not trouble you. We have had no pay this month, for money is very scarce in this country. The great hoard of the regt., the pay-master, has but two dollars in the world. Our Colonel gave twenty dollars out of his own pocket for to relieve the sick by purchasing such little comforts as may prove necessary.

For fear of the French crossing the Tagus, they have planted gun-boats all up the river – about two or three hundred of them.[2] Well,

1. Lt. Colonel Hon. Henry Cadogan was commanding officer of the 1/71st September 1810–November 1812, after which he assumed command of the brigade in which his battalion was serving and remained so employed until his death at Vitoria. For his record in command, see also Bamford, Andrew, *Sickness, Suffering, and the Sword: The British Regiment on Campaign 1808–1815*, pp. 51, 79–82.
2. A tenfold exaggeration of the actual number!

I have told you all the news, the sum total of which is that the French army is in a very bad condition, and I think it probable that you will not only see the British Army soon back, but the French army too, with their hands tied behind them. Keep up your spirits, my dear mother. Trust in God's goodness and you will see me home in a short time. This is either the sixth or seventh letter; let me know how many you receive. Give my love to my father, brothers, and sisters, who I look to God to protect and take care of till I return. God bless my good mother, for in His power it rests that I should meet with such inestimable and loving parents.

J. Vandeleur

Seal your letters with wax, for the damp almost opened the last. You must excuse what mistakes and blunders: consider the time and place. Farewell.

The skirmish described by Vandeleur was part of the fighting that took place around the village of Sobral when Massena, having got over something of the shock engendered by his discovering the existence of the Lines of Torres Vedras, began to probe the allied defences to establish what chance there was of breaking through and taking Lisbon. Sobral lay forward of the main defensive position, and was manned by the outposts of the First Division. For several days the French reconnoitred the Lines, seeking a weak spot, whilst Lieutenant General Spencer incurred Wellington's wrath by evacuating Sobral. Thankfully, the village was swiftly reoccupied, only for the defenders to be cleared out by a French attack on 12 October in which the 1/71st was engaged and suffered casualties. Meanwhile, Massena sought a potential breakthrough closer to the Tagus whilst the allies established an outpost – manned by the 1/71st – some 300 metres in the rear of Sobral, covering the exits from the village. This outpost was attacked on 14 October, but was successfully held and the French driven back with some loss. The fact that even an outwork of the main defences was able to resist his troops helped convince Massena that the Lines could not be taken by force. It should be noted that Vandeleur's dates are rather off here. He has the action taking place on the 16th, but then says that the following day was a Monday. Since the closest Monday to these dates would be 15 October, it follows that he is actually describing events on the 14th.[1]

As for the grand conspiracy, there is rather more rumour here than hard fact, although to be fair to Vandeleur it was rumour that was widely held to be true by many in and around Lisbon. The siege mentality within the Portuguese capital seems to have led to wild fears of plots and treason, the more so since a not-insubstantial body of aristocratic Portuguese renegades – most notably the Marquis d'Alorna – had accompanied Massena's invasion. Ultimately, these fears led to the arrest of fifty individuals who were denounced as Jacobins: all were eventually exiled to the Azores, although the case against the majority of them was flimsy in the extreme.[2]

Vandeleur's letter perfectly captures the initial optimism created by the ease with which the French were repulsed at the Lines of Torres Vedras. However, it is easy to see that the fact that this did not lead to an immediate victory and the successful conclusion of the whole campaign – combined with an element of homesickness – led to disillusionment when events did not work out quite that way.

Lisbon, December 26th, 1810[3]

My Dear Mother,

I embrace this opportunity of writing to you, as I am at present in Lisbon, having brought down the sick of the brigade. We are still at Alcointrinha,[4] in advance about 12 leagues from Lisbon. We had two

1. Oman, *Peninsular War*, Vol. III, pp. 437–48.
2. Oman, *Peninsular War*, Vol. III, pp. 415–17.
3. In the original text, pp. 27–35.
4. Most likely Alcoentre, but definitely somewhere in the region of Cartaxo where the First Division was headquartered.

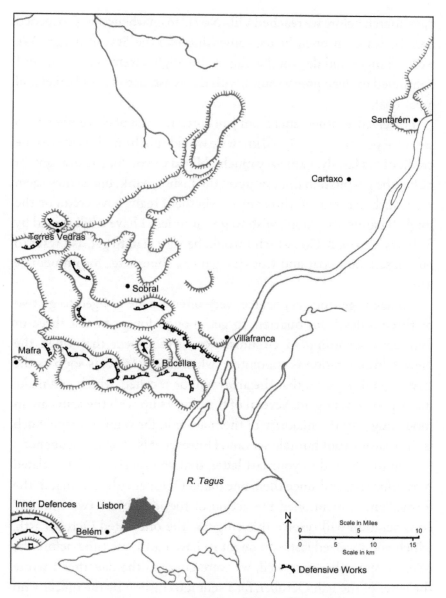

Map 1. Area around Lisbon, showing parts of the
Lines of Torres Vedras.

days' march before we reached Villa Nova,[1] from whence we proceeded here by water in open boats, something like the Severn barges. We were all night and day on the Tagus. The nights were very cold, but I continued to sleep pretty sound, with the assistance of my blanket and great-coat.

I received another letter from you dated the 21st of November. I am sorry for poor K_____. I well knew he would ruin himself as well as the credit of his family. I am very much obliged to you for the draught, or rather the permission to draw upon the Lisbon bank; but as they seem very much in doubt of who I am, or whether I really have credit on the English banks, they don't wish to give it unless I have a bill signed by Robarts, Curtis & Co., which I would be very glad to get, as I want to purchase a new coat and trousers, gaiters, shoes, etc., for immediate use.

Forage is getting very scarce; very often we are obliged to go two or three miles from quarters to get enough forage to last three or four days according to circumstances. We expect that when the New Administration is appointed (which is expected as soon as the Regency takes place) that the army will be recalled, which will make many people very glad. Several of the officers up with the army are in mourning, but the majority of them are not, for want of crepe. Such is the case for your humble servant. However, it is of no consequence.

You mentioned in your last letter, that you received a letter dated November 1st, and since then, one dated October 15th, and that in the former one, I mentioned the action of the 16th. Now, two minutes' consideration will resolve this enigma. The one dated October 15th, which you received last, you ought to have had some time before the other. I remember very well, we were engaged the day after I wrote the letter of the 15th October, for I sent it to Lisbon by the officer who took down the wounded men to the hospital. They left the regt. in such a hurry that I had neither time to open the letter or write a second. I wrote again on the 1st of November, and mentioned the action of the 16th, but it was the 16th of *October*. Now do you comprehend?

1. Vila Nova da Rainha, twenty-seven miles upstream from Lisbon.

I am really very sorry to hear that my father has been unwell, and as for that *rascal John*, I hope my father has no intention of receiving him again into the house; he has made mischief enough already. I hope you do not restrain your own little parties to Wor'ster on my account. I am getting on pretty well, and enjoy a good health and strong constitution, which I take great care of. I am glad to hear that Tom has taken the Red Cloth, and is on his way to College.[1] He will be very proud, as I was when I first hoisted the Red Flag. Elrington is very well and desires his love to everybody.

I still continue to write frequently to you, as you acknowledge what a comfort they are to you. Indeed, my dear mother, I assure yours are the greatest gifts that God Almighty can bestow on me. How I jump when I hear of a packet! I am always enquiring for letters. It makes me very happy to hear that you have got my little present, and I am assured that you esteem it dearly, not for its intrinsic value but for the love and affection which you bear to the donor. You tell me that the Dean is still loitering and dragging over his time in the idle amusements of Cheltenham. I would like to see him march 4 or 5 leagues in such a country as this, with a heavy havresack across his shoulders.[2] I hope all the family are well. You did not mention Robert had made up a resolution to what line of Business to pursue. You should get him to make up his mind at once, and not let him lose so much time, for the sooner he enters the studies of whatever profession he chooses to follow the better, for this is a time, above all others, he ought not to lose. God forbid he should lead such an idle and lazy life as the Dean.

The people in Lisbon say there is a fleet coming out with 15 regts., and large detachments to each regt., amounting to almost 18 or 20 thousand men, under the command of Genl. Blake.[3] You will be able to

1. Thomas followed his brother as a gentleman cadet at Marlow.
2. The Dean of Worcester at the time was Arthur Onslow, who was sixty-four, which perhaps makes this a slightly unkind imagining.
3. Possibly a confusion of the fact that reinforcements were due from England, from which in due course were formed the Seventh Division under Major General William Houston, and of the preparation of a Spanish force at Cadiz under Teniente General Joaquín Blake y Joyes, for operations in southern Spain.

tell from the papers how much of this is true. I hope it is not, for that will make our stay in this country more certain. Bread is very scarce, but beef very plenty. However, we are supplied with good English biscuit from the ships, which I like better, and is more convenient to carry than immense loaves. The French – they say they have plenty of provisions, but I can scarce believe it. I heard the Commissary-Genl. say that he cannot tell where their supplies come from, for they have drained the country most completely. I think we are likely to remain in the same place for some time to come; we are afraid to attack the French, they have got possession of such a strong position, and they are afraid to attack us for the same reason. However, we are a good distance from each other, so we are both pretty safe.

It draws near to Christmas Day. I suppose it will be over when you receive this. I have my eye on a good fat Turkey and some good old hens that are near the place. I think they will grace our table on that famous day. The boys and girls are now at home for their holidays, warming their cold feet and hands over the fire. I have never felt even the want of a fire. Although it is now the coldest time in this country it is as warm as any day in April, or May in England. Well, goodnight, mother, I am just going to enjoy a famous feather-bed, which I, by chance, am billeted upon in Lisbon, where I intend to remain for some days, laying in stocks of provisions for the officers of the regt.

Since I wrote the above part of the letter, Col. Pack came to Lisbon very ill with ague; of course when I heard of his arrival I waited on him. I mentioned to him how much I was in want of some money. He was very kind to me and put me in a way of getting as much as I wanted. I drew out a little bill upon Greenwood & Cox[1] which he had the kindness to countersign, and therefore his name was a sufficient security to the merchants, who immediately cashed my bill. We are all making grand preparations for Christmas. I have got a great quantity of currants and raisins to make plum puddings for Christmas Day. We are very comfortably situated for the winter in Alcointrinha, where we have built fireplaces in the corners of our rooms. We receive regular

1. A well-known firm of regimental agents.

supplies of all sorts of good things from Lisbon, by sending an officer down once a fortnight. With mules we have got our canteens and other necessary appendages from Lisbon. The French are lying in Santa Rem [Santarém], which is a great distance from this, and we are very far on the advance. Everything is going on very quiet and settled, the same as if we were in quarters at home. Genl. Pack says he thinks it very probable that we will remain two years longer in this country, unless recalled by the death of the king.

Do you think it is *possible* for my father to have sufficient interest to get me on the staff of some general, either at home or abroad? It would be a very comfortable thing if he could. I am already quite sick of campaigning in Portugal. The inhabitants are so very uncivil and unfeeling. I have got a letter for Elrington which I got in the Lisbon post-office. I hope it bears good tidings of my family. He is remarkably well himself, as I am also, thank God. I hope my father's health is improving. Always in your letters be so good as to number the corner, commencing with the next, because then we shall be able to see how many letters there are due or miscarried. I shall begin by numbering this letter No. 1, the next I write No. 2, and so on in rotation. I have received but two of your letters since I arrived in Portugal. I am sure several must have been lost.

I wish you could possibly continue to send me a few necessary articles from England by some officer you may hear of coming here, directing it to be left at Senor Edward de Lonza's, Merchant, Lisbon, at the same time giving him a note which he will put in the office in Lisbon for me. I want another jacket and wings, a pair of grey overalls, a pr. of short gaiters bound about one inch round the bottom with strong black leather, some long flannell drawers and shirts of do, some newspapers, a good but small English saddle, some Windsor soap, pr. of spurs, and a new cap of very light felt covered with blue cloth – the first wet Solomon's cap got, all the pasteboard gave way and got as heavy as possible – a good curb and bridle for a mule, and what other articles you may think requisite. Pack them in a couple of boxes of equal weight and size so that they can be carried by a mule. You may stuff a piece of anything into the corners by way of ballast, such as good ham, or a small tub of butter, anything would be acceptable, for none of these things can be had in Lisbon.

Give my dearest love to my good father and family, and believe me,

> Your ever dear child.
> J. V.

It would be a sweet comfort to me if you would write oftener.

Give my love and respect to Miss Wakeman and family, the Parkers, General Gore, etc. etc. etc., in fact to every one.[1] How do the girls get on with the music etc. etc? I have had this letter in my pocket, which unfortunately I forgot to put in the post when I passed through Lisbon. Adieu, adieu, my dear mother.

> J. V.

There is much of interest here, although the sense is not always apparent without the context. Insofar as the petty scandals of Worcester are concerned, that understanding remains lacking along with the identities of 'K_____' and 'that *rascal John*'; otherwise, however, much of what Vandeleur writes makes rather more sense when taken in context of the French withdrawal from before the Lines of Torres Vedras, and the recognition that George III's mental illness had become so pronounced as to require the formation of a regency under the Prince of Wales. Since the Prince had traditionally espoused the politics of the Whig opposition, it was expected by many that once the regency was formally established – which would in fact not be until 5 February 1811 – the current administration would be turned out and replaced by one composed of the Prince's political friends and allies. This, in turn, was expected to result in the withdrawal of British forces from the Peninsula. Vandeleur's reference to mourning crepe would seem to relate to the death on 2 November of Princess Amelia, the King's youngest and favourite daughter, whose loss has generally

---

1. Presumably acquaintances from Worcester – for the Wakemans, see p. 12.

been seen as a key factor in the decline of George III's mental health.

Interesting for rather different reasons is the list of items that Vandeleur requested to be sent out to him, for they help resolve some issues surrounding the attire of officers of the 71st at this time. The regiment was unique in combining elements of light infantry and highland dress, with the former being represented here in particular by the 'wings' mentioned by Vandeleur as decorating the shoulders of his jacket. Overalls and short gaiters make admirable sense for a winter campaign, and again add useful detail, but the most interesting piece is the 'new cap of very light felt covered with blue cloth'. The implication would seem to be that officers of the 71st were adapting their headgear in a similar manner to the regiment's rank and file, who had retained their traditional blue knitted bonnets but blocked into the same shape as the light infantry shako. Possibly this was a short-lived experiment, particularly bearing in mind the recorded fate of Vandeleur's first cap, but his request provides an additional nugget of detail for studies of Napoleonic uniformology.

In the atmosphere of political uncertainty that is apparent throughout Vandeleur's letter, it was therefore all the more depressing that Massena had neither dashed his army to destruction against the Lines or Torres Vedras, nor seen it fall apart through starvation. Certainly the French situation was bleak, but those who hoped that the French were in such dire straits as to be compelled to surrender, or negotiate terms as Junot had been obliged to do after Vimeiro two years previously, were engaging in marked over-optimism. On 10 November, Massena did order a withdrawal, but only as far as Santarém on the Tagus, fifty miles northeast of Lisbon. Here, he hoped that sufficient food and forage could be brought in to keep his army fed through the winter, pinning Wellington within the Lisbon Peninsula until French reinforcements could be brought up. Beginning on 14 November, under the cover of heavy fog, Massena successfully disengaged his forces and began to fall back. Wellington, unsure of the French intentions, sent only the First, Second, and Light Divisions in pursuit, along with some cavalry and Pack's Portuguese. The last-named, along with the First and Light Divisions, were to have attacked the French rearguard on 19 November, but, in the event, the poor state of the ground and the strength of the French positions caused the cancellation of this operation, the circumstances of which are discussed in more detail in the next letter. Had Wellington correctly grasped the French dispositions, he could well have crushed the French II Corps before Santarém, but instead he delayed until he was certain of what the French were about. By then, Massena's position was secure, and so Wellington elected to put his army into winter quarters, leaving the Light Division and Pack's Portuguese to man the outposts, with the First Division – including Vandeleur and the 1/71st – around Cartaxo to serve as a link with the main body of the army.[1]

With no obvious end to the campaign in sight, and Pack's 'two more years' no doubt ringing in his ears, it is easy to see how the prospect of Christmas away from home could provoke the evident homesickness that is apparent from this letter. Equally, the fact that Wellington's campaign seemed to have bogged down in stalemate rather than ended in the hoped-for triumph was no doubt responsible for the rather gloomy summary of the positions of the two armies. Still, for all the tendency towards croaking, Vandeleur's plans for the future, and in particular his arrangements to equip himself for further campaigning, suggest that he was resigned to staying the course and making the best of things.

Alcointrinha, January 29th 1811[2]

My Dear Mother,

I have just had the happiness to receive a letter dated 30th December from you. You said that you were very happy to hear I was enjoying such

1. Oman, *Peninsular War*, Vol. III, pp. 461–78.
2. In the original text, pp. 36–43.

good health; I am glad to have it in my power to say that I am still very well, and, thank God, I have had a good share of health since my arrival in this country. Elrington received a letter by the same post from his mother, he is very well and happy and desires to be remembered to you. You desired me not to mention to any of my brother-officers, my wish to go home. I am not the only one in the regt.; the whole of them wish it, even the heads of the regt.; but we never mention it publickly.

I am sorry to hear that the English papers speak so unfavourably of Sir B. Spencer, saying he was petrified; I assure you it has been no small annoyance to him and his staff. He is a brave old fellow, but he is very prudent and does not like risking men's lives when there is no occasion! Well, he might be petrified! When the division was to pass, there was a defile that could not be avoided, which was defended with several heavy guns at the end; one of which, loaded with canister shot, would have carried away a whole compy. at a time; besides the roads leading to it must have been mined, we knew not otherwise. It was a very lucky thing that Pack could not get his artillery up. The captn. that commanded the gun lives within a stone's throw of where I live at present at Alcointrinha, where we have been for some time and I think we shall remain for some time yet: for we never can think of attacking the enemy at Santarem, which is built on a hill, something like Gibraltar; very steep and high, with batteries all down it, and to the right and left.

The first march that we make will be back to our old quarters at Tobvero.[1] We are very comfortable at present. We had the good luck to find several useful articles in the house where we are, such as, *matrasses*, some Indian corn, chairs, tables, a few odd plates and cups, which with our canteens we continue to live very comfortably. We have all built chimneys in our rooms, and made grates with old hoops which are very comfortable. We are quartered within pistol-shot of a fine fir-wood, so we are well off for fire. We have just found that pine-apples or fir-apples (I don't know what denomination they fall under) are very good substitutes for coals, for there is no such thing in this country.[2]

---

1. Unidentified location.
2. Presumably Vandeleur means pine cones.

Portugal is a very miserable place; the inhabitants have no idea of any kind of comfort, they have not even a fire place in their houses.

I wonder very much that K_____ could have the face to return to Wor'ster, after such a disgraceful downfall as he had previously sustained. I am very glad that Miss Wakeman thinks about me so seriously as to send her love, all that I can do in return is send mine to her, and all her kind family. Miss Roper's marriage made me laugh very much. I regret much that J_____ D_____ was not drowned, he is an infernal vagabond. In your next letter let me know the result of that elopement. Who is the lady? I suppose she is an heiress, but what kind? You remember the old Irish song:-

> 'She an heiress that's clear
> For her father sells beer.'[1]

I am glad that Robert is so good a shot, there is capital shooting in Portugal. Such quantities of hare, rabbits, partridges, woodcocks, snipes, plovers, and swans, that we almost subsist upon them. There are four officers in each compy., so that those four in general mess together. We have got an old Spanish gun that we plundered, which produces as much as we can eat each day, together with our rations of fresh beef. We live famously. We have two dishes of beef every day, dressed in various shapes. We make mince-scallop, beef-steaks, beef-soup, beef-hash, beef-fry. We very often get a bullock's heart or tongue by being friends with the butcher of the compy.! We have also found a way of making soft bread out of the king's biscuit, by steeping it in water and then toasting it.

We have likewise a way of making stirabout out of biscuits or out of Indian corn. We are very conveniently situated within a few

---

1. The refrain is from a comic song in George Colman's *The Review; or the Wags of Windsor*, in which Looney Mactwolter declares his love for the publican's daughter Judy O'Flannikin. Oxbery, W., *The Review; or the Wags of Windsor. A Musical Farce by George Colman*, London, W. Simpkin, 1820, pp. 18–19. The editor of the original text having disguised the identity of 'J_____ D_____', it is hard to know what local scandal this refers to, and whether or not the heiress in question had rather more to inherit than the play's Judy. It may be that this 'J_____ D_____' and the previous letter's 'rascal John' are one and the same person.

leagues of the Tagus, therefore we are enabled to get up provisions, etc., from Lisbon and send our mules to the water to bring them up. We get everything almost that we want: such as butter, cheese, onions, spirits, mustard, and spices, grey cloth, and everything necessary for our own comfort, but it is expensive. Salt butter half-dollar a pound, sugar very dear, onions three-halfpence a piece, and every other article dear in proportion. In your next letter I wish you would send me a few references from that valuable cooking-book you possess; but I must first acquaint you what items we are obliged to do with and what without. We have beef, rice, onions, and cabbage; also flour, butter. No eggs, nor milk, tea, coffee, chocolate, etc. Put the beef into as many shapes and forms as possible, with onions and potatoes.

We live very comfortable at present. We are a good distance from the French – about eight or ten miles – but our cavalry are lying close upon them, so that they cannot give the least move but that we know it in the course of fifteen minutes by telegraph, which we have in all directions. Whenever they think of moving we know it directly, and move back to our old position, which extends from Mafra to Villa Franca[1] – there we are snug. The longer they stay where they are, the stronger the position grows, for the Portuguese are working under our engineers continually. All the roads are undermined ready to blow up directly we pass. There is not a hill in the whole chain but has a fort of five, six, seven, or eight pieces of heavy cannon ready. The chain is just like one immense long battery from the sea to the river Tagus.

I don't think a banker's life, or the profit he gains by so much drudgery, is worth that two figs. I think what would suit Bob best is a commission in our own county militia, for there is no fatigue or picquets or long marches etc. Besides, as he is so delicate, he would have the opportunity of being at home very often. I am glad to hear that the girls are improving. I expect to find them much improved in every way when I return to England, as well as the young men. I did as you told me concerning the money, but they would not give it to me, for they had no proof of what or who I was. I mentioned the circumstance

1. Vila Franca de Xira.

to Genl. Pack and he was good enough to put me in the way of getting it from another man, but I was obliged to pay at the rate of twenty per cent. exchange money, so I lost as much as four pounds or better. I drew upon Greenwood & Co., and got my bill countersigned or indorsed (I don't know which term to use) by the Genl. Sir W. Erskine has left our brigade, and we expect Pack to get it: it is the wish of the whole brigade, for Pack is a brave fellow.

We have got a famous little wild goat that gives us as much milk for breakfast and supper as we can consume, and when we march he follows the regt. in company with the other goats. I am exceedingly concerned to hear that my father's health is so indifferent, but I hope he will soon be better. I am a little tired of so much beef day after day, but, thank God, we get enough and that is everything. Vegetables are very dear. Potatoes as much as 6d. per lb., but nevertheless I find them so very fattening, that I eat some lbs. each day. We make puddings, pies of potatoes – in fact we are getting very fat, keeping ourselves in good health. Always up by daylight, and fast asleep by eight o'clock in the evening.

Well, my dear mother, God bless you and all our family; with my love and affection to my dear father, and brothers, and sisters; also remember me kindly to Mrs. Elrington, and the Parkers. Young El–n. is at home I suppose. Elrington is perfectly well, and is growing up and handsome. You never mention anything about the stock, the farm, etc. Is Neptune and old Squib still in the land of the living? I was promised a nice pug in Deal by Mrs. Dan's which she is to keep for me till I return. If it's very handsome, I'll take it to Barbourne. Adieu, my dear mother, always trust in God for my protection, as I do for yours and my father and family.

> Your ever dear and affectionate child,
> J. Vandeleur

By implication, since he does not mention it until this letter, Vandeleur must have left his battalion prior to the abortive attack of 19 November on the French near Santarém. His account of it is, however, a sound one, and his defence of Sir Brent Spencer largely valid. In particular, it should be stressed that Spencer had orders to go forward only if Pack and Craufurd made progress on his flanks, and this neither was able to do. Whatever criticism may have been passed at home, Spencer's actions were entirely proper.[1] This aside, there is little in the letter that requires further elaboration, for in the main it serves as an excellent account of life in winter quarters. Perhaps as a result of being so settled, the writer also appears to be in rather better spirits; certainly, there is little croaking now in the summing-up of the merits of the Lines of Torres Vedras. Only one bit of disappointment awaited the 1/71st; their wish to get Pack back as their brigadier was another false hope. Erskine did indeed leave the brigade, taking acting command of the Fifth Division with effect from 6 February, but Pack remained with his Portuguese brigade and Erskine's replacement was Major General Kenneth Howard.[2]

The letter of 29 January seems to have been the last that John Vandeleur sent home from the Peninsula during his service with the 1/71st. On 5 March 1811, the French finally abandoned their position at Santarém and began to evacuate Portugal. During the course of the following month, Wellington's forces – weakened by the detachment of a sizeable corps to operate in southern Spain where the French under Soult had mounted an offensive against Badajoz, but nevertheless amounting to 37,000 men – harried Massena's rearguard all the way back to the Spanish frontier. With his army short of food and deficient in cavalry, Wellington could pursue no further, so that by mid-April the Armée de Portugal was regrouping around Salamanca, having left garrisons to hold the captured fortresses of Almeida and Ciudad Rodrigo. The former place, the last French military presence on Portuguese soil, was blockaded by the allies, and Massena, having obtained reinforcements in the form of the IX Corps and also the loan

1. Oman, *Peninsular War*, Vol. III, p. 473.
2. Oman, *Wellington's Army*, p. 353.

of a detachment of cavalry from the Armée du Nord, mounted a new offensive intended to relieve the beleaguered garrison. Wellington, in one of the riskier moves of his career, elected to give battle with his back to the River Côa, placing his army in an extended position behind the Dos Casas brook, facing east against Massena's 48,000-strong army.

The key to Wellington's position – if only because of the dogged persistence with which Massena attempted to capture it – was the village of Fuentes de Oñoro, whose narrow streets and stone walls turned it into a makeshift fortress. The village was initially held by a collection of detached light companies, but after the initial French assault on 3 May additional battalions were thrown into the street fighting. One of these was the 1/71st, which successfully drove the French from the village on the afternoon of the 3rd, and held it thereafter until forced out by a French flanking movement two days later. This new offensive, reopening the fighting after a day's lull, was a major effort to turn Wellington's right flank, but although the allies were driven back a new line was formed, at right angles to the old, with Fuentes de Oñoro as the hinge. This new alignment rendered the village all the more important, and the 1/71st, along with the 74th and 1/88th, were able to retake it for a second time and hold it until the conclusion of the fighting. Having been so heavily engaged, losses in the 1/71st were naturally high, with 4 officers, 4 sergeants, and 22 rank and file killed, and 8 officers, 6 sergeants, 3 buglers, and 100 rank and file wounded. Two more officers, and an unspecified number of men, were taken prisoner.[1] Amongst the wounded officers was Ensign John Vandeleur. Invalided home on sick leave, his first spell of Peninsular service thus came to an end.

1. Hildyard, *Highland Light Infantry*, pp. 80–1; for two eyewitness accounts, see Anon., *Journal of a Soldier of the 71st, or Glasgow Regiment, Highland Light Infantry, from 1806 to 1815*, pp. 132–40; Anon., *Vicissitudes in the Life of a Scottish Soldier*, pp. 151–65. The last mentions an officer of the 71st with a severe bayonet wound, which may be a reference to Vandeleur – since Vandeleur's own account gives no mention of the nature of his wound, however, this remains supposition.

Chapter 2

Return to the Peninsula

~

Not surprisingly, John Vandeleur's convalescence was a lengthy one, spent back at home, with only the news of his promotion to lieutenant – gazetted on 3 June 1811 – to serve in some way to sweeten the pill. That promotion was as a result of dead man's shoes, being granted without purchase to replace Lieutenant John Graham, killed at Fuentes de Oñoro. In the normal way of things, as a junior lieutenant Vandeleur would have been posted, once fully recovered, to the 2/71st which was now serving on the south coast of England. Instead, whilst still on sick leave, he was able to secure a transfer, without purchase, to the 12th Light Dragoons, this new posting being gazetted on 13 July. At this time, an infantry lieutenancy cost £550 if purchased, and its cavalry equivalent £997 10s; to obtain the transfer without paying the difference between the two commissions was therefore quite a coup, albeit with the caveat that a commission obtained without purchase could not subsequently be sold.[1] As a result of this transfer, Vandeleur exchanged the red jacket of the infantry for the blue jacket and Tarleton helmet of the light dragoons.

The 12th Light Dragoons at this time had three squadrons on active service in the Peninsula, where they had been since June 1811, with the other two forming the regimental depot at Radipole Barracks in Weymouth. Prior to this deployment, the regiment had served in the Walcheren Expedition of 1809, which followed a lengthy period in which it had been brought back up to strength on

1. Relative prices from Glover, Michael, *Wellington's Army in the Peninsula*, p. 76.

the home station following extensive service in the Mediterranean and Egypt during the French Revolutionary War.[1] It was therefore to Radipole that Vandeleur went when he joined his new regiment in September 1811, having still been on sick leave at the time of his appointment. He was evidently not fully recovered even then, however, and was again on sick leave from January to March of 1812. Thereafter, with his health restored, Vandeleur returned to duty at Radipole and remained there until assigned to a reinforcing draft being prepared for service in the Peninsula. Composed of three officers, three sergeants including the 12th's sergeant major, one trumpeter, thirty-three rank and file, and ninety-four troop horses, the draft sailed in early September 1812. The other officers were Lieutenants William Hay and William Dowbiggen, both of whom, like Vandeleur, had previously served in the Peninsula as light infantry officers before transferring to the 12th. Hay, after his poor start at Marlow, had bucked up his ideas sufficiently to obtain a commission in the 52nd Light Infantry with which regiment he had served through the 1810 campaign and into 1811 before going home on sick leave. His memoirs, written much later in life, leave us with an interesting comparison between Vandeleur's very immediate impressions, both bad and good, and Hay's rather more rose-tinted recollections of active service.

Niza, 28th September 1812[2]

My Dear Mother,

You must be rather disappointed at not hearing from me at Lisbon, but the great hurry and confusion which the disembarkation of a number of troops caused such constant trouble and bother that I hardly knew what I was doing. We had a very long and pleasant voyage, but wanted the greatest of all comforts, which was society, being all three

1. The Napoleonic service of the 12th is detailed in Bamford, Andrew, *Gallantry and Discipline: The 12th Light Dragoons at War with Wellington.*
2. In the original text, pp. 43–8; location in fact Nisa, close to the Spanish frontier approximately thirty-five miles east of Abrantes.

in different ships, on account of each ship holding but a few horses; the two largest carried forty-two horses each. It was rather fortunate that we were but seven days at sea, or I should have gone melancholy mad, having no person to speak to but the old Scotch captain. It was a pleasant thing for me that I was well supplied with books, which I found very amusing.

We marched from Lisbon on the 18th inst. to Sacavem,[1] where we foraged a young pig (in other terms, *made it*), which lasted us two days. On the 19th we marched to Villa Franca;[2] we got nothing there except the produce of the country – bugs and fleas. We met two thousand French prisoners on the march to Lisbon, who were taken at Salamanca. On the 20th we arrived at Azembiya,[3] which was in a very shattered condition, and nothing to be got but potatoes and onions, which made a good dinner when boiled up with the remainder of the pig and some ration pork. It is a most extraordinary thing, that this village, when I passed through it before, was quite perfect, not a stone unturned, and now there is not a whole door or window in the place. The French never were in this village except when they passed through to Lisbon six years ago. It is the peasantry that destroyed it for the sake of plunder, when the British troops left it, when the French retreated.

On the 21st we entered Santarem,[4] the headquarters of the French, for a long time, very strongly fortified. It is a fine town, situated on the top of an immense hill, strongly fortified all the way up by the French. Hay contrived to pin a turkey, which we stuffed with garlick and made a famous dinner and breakfast. 22nd marched to Golligam,[5] a miserable little village, some of the largest houses burnt, there were a few inhabitants who subsisted entirely upon bread and salt flesh with a little rice.

1. Sacavém, on the Tagus approximately seven miles north of Lisbon.
2. Vila Franca de Xira, a march of eighteen miles.
3. In fact Azambuja, a march of a twelve miles.
4. A march of sixteen miles from Azambuja.
5. In fact Golegã, a march of twenty-three miles.

On the 23rd we entered Vinette[1] and on the 24th that famous city, Abrantes,[2] which checked the French so much all the winter before last. 'Tis an immense town, strongly fortified, more by nature than by art, it is on the left bank of the Tagus, on a hill that is almost perpendicular. The road into Abrantes winds up the hill like a serpent. Abrantes is a beautiful city at a distance, but like all other garrison towns extremely filthy, the streets are narrow and the houses very high. In fact it is the dirtiest place I ever was in. Here I halted a day to shoe the horses but marched out again on the 25th to Gaveon,[3] which is on the opposite side of the Tagus, and we crossed at the wooden bridge of boats by Abrantes. Gaveon is a very small place, but to our surprise there was a kind of shop that sold coffee ready made, and porter, a bottle of which made the ration beef more palatable than any we had had since Lisbon. On the 27th we arrived at Niza, a very nice village in the Alentejo, where the French had never been; here we halted two days and tomorrow, which has made the horses quite fresh again. Ratler is as well as possible, and as fat. The mare is very well and so is Taffy, who is admired by everybody. There is a great scarcity of money in Portugal, the troops have not had a farthing these three months. I bought a very nice little mule for ninety dollars, which as yet has given me great satisfaction. That pack saddle of Gibson's and the hussar saddle are the best for horses' backs that I ever saw.[4]

The heat is so intense we are obliged to march by night, and generally our march is over by six o'clock. This side of the Tagus is twice as hot as the other, and less cover – few trees – the country here is a barren heath of sand and weeds. Poor Windsor was exchanged some time ago and is now quite well at his regt.; so I heard from one of his brother officers.[5] There is a Commissary here who has invited Hay and I to

1. Unidentified location.
2. Consistently given as 'Alrantes' in the 1894 text, which I have assumed to be a Victorian typographic error and corrected accordingly.
3. In fact Gavião, a march of nineteen miles.
4. Messrs Gibson and Peat were employed as saddlers to the 12th Light Dragoons.
5. Lieutenant Edward Charles Windsor, 1st Royal Dragoons, taken prisoner at Maguilla, 11 June 1812. Promoted to captain whilst in captivity. Vandeleur's

dinner, which we look forward to with much pleasure, for those fellows always live well. I saw young De Bath yesterday, he is a capt. in the 94th Regt.; he looks very well, and was glad to see me.[1] Lord Wellington is on the other side of Burgos, which is not far from France. I am afraid the French will be driven out before we get up. We shall go through Ciudad Rodrigo, Valadolid [Valladolid], and Salamanca in a row. I am very badly off for a map, I cannot purchase one for any money. I trust you will write to me regularly as I shall to you.

> Your very affectionate son,
> J. Vandeleur

Vandeleur's travels up through Portugal place in stark relief the state to which much of the central part of the country had been reduced by the measures taken to resist the French invasion of 1810. Much of the destruction was indeed at the hands of the Portuguese themselves, but not, as Vandeleur rather unkindly states, 'for the sake of plunder', but rather as part of a deliberate scorched earth policy. Even with the French driven from Portugal, the country was still in a poor way, and its people greatly impoverished by the invasions of 1807, 1809, and 1810; only the southern part of the country had not been touched by war. Nevertheless, as the various acquisitions of Vandeleur and his party make clear, there was still food to be had if one had a good purse – or, better still, light fingers. Hay's memoirs, it should be noted, make little mention of the privations that the party shared, but he did give some further detail on the composition of the detachment – remarking that it 'was a large one, consisting of remounts for nearly every dragoon regiment employed' – before going on to complement Vandeleur and their fellow-subaltern William Dowbiggen whom he described as 'most excellent men and thorough soldiers'. Hay believed that all three officers 'knew, as old campaigners, the best

---

informant seems to have been in error, as Windsor was not exchanged until March 1813. He was killed at Waterloo.

1. Captain William Plunkett de Bathe, 94th Foot.

mode of taking care of ourselves where little or nothing was to be had for love or money'.[1] Evidently, John Vandeleur had made a good first impression with his fellow officers upon joining the 12th; indeed, he is one of the few officers that Hay ever refers to by name in the course of his memoirs.

This first letter also serves to bring up to date the story of the war since Vandeleur's wounding at Fuentes de Oñoro over a year previously. The loss of that battle had seen the Armée de Portugal again forced back to its base at Salamanca, where the defeated Massena found himself relieved of his command and replaced by Marshal Marmont. The only positive notes for the French were that they had managed to extricate their garrison successfully from Almeida, preserving the troops but losing their last toe-hold in Portugal, and that Marshal Soult had opened up a new front in the south with his capture of Badajoz. The loss of this vital fortress, which controlled the southern road into Spain, would distract Wellington for nearly a year after Fuentes de Oñoro, as he fought a mobile campaign up and down the Portuguese border trying to win himself a window in which he might assault either Badajoz or its northern sister, Ciudad Rodrigo, before the French field armies could concentrate against him. Not until January 1812, after a sudden winter campaign, was he able to take Ciudad Rodrigo, and it took a further three months after that, and the cost of over 4,000 lives, to restore Badajoz to allied hands. Capture of the fortresses, however, allowed Wellington finally to advance against Marmont, whose army he defeated in open battle outside Salamanca on 22 July 1812. After the victory, Wellington was able to occupy Madrid, and then turned north against the combined forces of the Armée de Portugal and Armée du Nord. The next obstacle to face him was the castle of Burgos, blocking the Great Road leading to the French border, but although Vandeleur's informant was technically correct in saying that Wellington was beyond the fortress, this was only true insofar as his outposts –

1. Hay, *Reminiscences*, pp. 64–5.

including the 12th Light Dragoons – were pushed past it to screen his besieging forces. The main field army, less a powerful corps left to hold Madrid and keep a watch on Soult, was still bogged down before the castle walls of Burgos, and Vandeleur's fears that they would get to France without him were altogether far from the mark.

Calsada de Don Diego, 13th October 1812[1]

My Dear Mother,

As yet I have received no letter from you but that is owing to my not being with the regt. I expect to get a few letters when I arrive there. I believe I wrote last from Niza in Portugal. We crossed the Tagus, back again, and marched on the 29th inst. to Vilha Velha,[2] the worst march without exception that I ever had in Portugal, it was about twenty miles, and when we got there we found but three or four houses which were in a wretched state and only held eight or ten horses. It was a very rainy cold night and every one wished to be one of the ten, therefore, to prevent any discontent, I slept out myself with my horses and they all did the same. We had no sort of cover nor a single tree to make a fire with. We marched very early next morning to Sondas,[3] a very wretched place, where we got nothing but a little honey, which we find better than bad butter which we should have to carry. The place was full of people with the fever, so that we were glad to get off next morning, the 1st instant, to Castel [Castelo] Branco, a fine town, where everything was to be sold.[4] The people here were very disaffected, and shewed the French a great deal of civility, which is the cause of the town being in such a good state. We drew rations here, and halted one day to refresh the horses. I happened to get a good billet here upon a padre, or priest's

1. In the original text, pp. 48–54. Location in fact Calzada de Don Diego, fifteen miles west of Salamanca.
2. Vila Velha de Rodão, on the north bank of the Tagus and only an eleven-mile march north from Nisa.
3. Sarnadas de Ródão, a march of nine miles.
4. Another march of nine miles.

house, who shewed me a great deal of attention. He bought 2lbs. of tea pretty cheap (an English officer cannot purchase anything here so cheap as the inhabitants, the shop-keepers ask double very often). Tea is not to be had in Spain, the people never take it except as a medicine; therefore I have carried a good stock of that commodity up the country. Sugar is always to be had at large places.

We continued our march on the 3d instant to Pena Maior,[1] where we got rice, potatoes, wine, and milk to buy. We were quartered on a house where a Portuguese, who formerly was a captain in the Guirillas, lived. He was a fine, noble fellow; he had but little, and that he welcomed us with. He said he was sorry he had nothing, but that he could go and shoot for us. We offered to accompany him, which we did. He conducted us up some very steep high hills, covered with heath, where we found plenty of rabbits and hares. I shot one rabbit, being no great sportsman, Hay shot a hare, and the Guirilla shot two rabbits and one hare. He cut the two hares up and made a sort of stew with rice and oil, which made an excellent dinner. He insisted on our carrying away the three rabbits, which we did without much persuasion.

We marched next morning, the 4th, to St. Miguel,[2] which is very much destroyed by the French. Here we got quarters on a very patriotic old fellow, who had plenty of old wine in his house. We asked him for some, but he denied having any. We saw he was of a good-natured turn, so we got out a canteen which was full of our ration-rum. We offered him a glass which he drank, Hay telling him that it was English liqueur. We then offered him a second and a third, which made him quite tipsy. He then gave us a key of a cupboard, telling us the wine was there, and to take as much as we wanted. We took him at his word, and began to fill all our canteens, bottles, etc. with the wine, and he was so drunk that he did not know what we were at. When we were finished, we put

1. Probably Penamacor, but this would have been a march of thirty-seven miles which seems rather extreme. However, since the next location listed lies between Penamacor and Castelo Branco, it would seem that Vandeleur has his sequence mixed up here and the march was done over two days, with an overnight halt.
2. São Miguel de Acha, twenty miles from Castelo Branco and seventeen from Penamacor.

the key in his pocket and made his servant take him away to his bed. We marched off early, with the wine, next morning, the 5th, to Memoe,[1] a small wretched village, a great part of it burned by the French. A long march, but a good road. On the 6th we went to Sabujal [Sabugal], which was a fine town. It has the remains of an old Moorish castle, it is built on the Coa, about two miles below the ford where the Light Division gave the French such a drubbing on their retreat.[2] The town is terribly destroyed. I was in it before, but it was dark, and a great many houses on fire, when the French passed thro'. We halted here a day – the 7th.

We marched on the 8th to my old quarters, Albergaria, a frontier town in Spain, where I expect to be welcomed by the people whom I was billeted on before;[3] but to my astonishment I found their house, which was a good one, totally destroyed by the French and the people fled; it was the same with about half the village, which when we were there was so beautiful. We marched on the 9th to Ituero;[4] on the 10th to Ciudad Rodrigo, where I saw the spot where my cousin was wounded.[5] I went all over the place; saw the two breaches and the remains of the battering forts and parallels, which were erected by Lord Wellington. It is a very large town, and must have been very difficult to take – nothing but the greatest courage and intrepidity could ever force it. The Portuguese are erecting other works on the hills near it, which will make it doubly strong. They would not allow the troops to enter the town, but quartered us in the suburbs outside the town, in an old church that had the whole of the roof off. Here it rained all day and

1. Meimão, a march of twelve miles.
2. The Battle of Sabugal, fought on 3 April 1811, was one of the major clashes between the French rearguard and their allied pursuers during Massena's retreat from Portugal. A march of eight miles from Meimão.
3. La Alberguería de Argañán, a march of eighteen miles from Sabugal. The 1/71st was stationed here prior to the Battle of Fuentes de Oñoro; see Anon., *Scottish Soldier*, p. 148.
4. Ituero de Azaba, a march of eight miles.
5. A march of fourteen miles. The cousin in question was Major General John Ormsby Vandeleur, who had been wounded in the storm of the lesser breach during Wellington's recapture of the fortress, whilst commanding an infantry brigade in the Light Division.

night without ceasing. The rainy season has unfortunately set in, but will not last long.

We proceeded on our march on the 11th to Puentas de Castelegos,[1] a very long and tedious march, with rain; but we got into a nice clean Spanish village, where we got famous dry beds, which we have got everywhere in Spain. The 12th we marched to Texadillo,[2] a clean, comfortable, village; but nothing to be had but a little milk and honey. The 13th to Calsada de Don Diego, where this letter must be closed. To-morrow we march to Salamanca, about four leagues, where we expect to halt about a week to shoe up the horses. I shall put the letter in the post there. I shall commence my next letter with the best description I can give you of Salamanca. The Spaniards are undoubtedly a noble-looking people – fine, straight, tall, well-made fellows. Their houses are remarkably clean, they give us beds every night, and shew a good deal of blunt civility. The Spaniard will not submit to be ill-treated. They are extremely tenacious of everything, and jealous to the greatest degree. However, I have not seen enough of them to form an opinion as yet.

I hope that my father has had no more attacks of shivering since I left. I am very anxious to hear from you; it is now two months since I got a letter at Portsmouth, and I am very anxious to know whether my father has seen into the mistake which caused me so much anxiety and trouble. I have often thought since what could have possessed his mind with such an idea; but, thank God!, there is a Judge that sees thro' all our actions. I hope my brothers and sisters are well. How does Tom like the new college? Ratler is as fat and fresh as ever, and so is Taffy and the mare. They are not quite so smooth, but that is owing to the cold and dirty stables.

May God bless the whole of you is the constant wish of your most affectionate son.

John Vandeleur

---

1. Unidentified location; other contemporary accounts give it as Fuentes de Castelegos, but neither name appears on modern maps; possibly the modern Fuente de San Esteban.
2. Tejadillo, a total march of twenty-nine miles from Ciudad Rodrigo.

For the most part this travelogue speaks for itself, although it is refreshing to see – in the account of the rainy night at Vila Velha – direct evidence of an officer being so willing to set an example and share the discomforts of his men. That said, the fact of the officers of the 12th's detachment being billeted on a priest, and doing well out of it, may not have been quite the coincidence that Vandeleur implies. Hay, in that passage of his memoirs detailing this march, wrote that:

> In this unfortunate country – as indeed in all Catholic countries – the priests lead and the flocks follow, and each priest had at the time found his way back to his residence in the villages along our line of march, where it was the parishioners' business to put to rights, or rebuild, his casa before attending to their own; and not only was this done, but all his wants liberally supplied, and his cellar well filled.
>
> His house, to look at from the outside, was generally the worst in the place, so as not to attract the attention of the soldier officers passing and searching for quarters; but, to those who knew the secret, it was, from being so well stored within, a most desirable resting-place, especially for a tired and hungry man, so that you will not be surprised to hear that one of us three knowing ones of the 12th always contrived to find himself in the padre's house at the end of a day's march.[1]

Such means of making the best of things notwithstanding, Vandeleur's account largely reinforces the theme, picked up in the previous letter cataloguing his journey up from Lisbon, of a nation badly ravaged by war.

So far as family news, it is unclear what the difference between Vandeleur and his father was about. However, as we shall see, Vandeleur senior had an unfortunate – if well-intentioned – tendency to interfere in the careers of his sons without first checking the

---

1. Hay, *Reminiscences*, pp. 65–6.

propriety of his actions or considering their consequences, and it may well be that something of that sort had occurred prior to Vandeleur having come out to the Peninsula.

Villa de Porco, Nov. 25th 1812[1]

My Dear Mother,

It is now three months since I landed, and I have not had a single letter from you, which is very extraordinary, particularly as the two other officers who came out with me have had several letters. Thank God I have joined the regt. at La Seca some time back,[2] during the time Lord Wellington halted on the Duro [Duero]. The regt. remained but two days at La Seca, when the whole army retired and our brigade covered the retreat. They let us off that day very quietly to Nava del Rey,[3] where we bivouacked; and the next day we saw nothing of them until the evening, when they shewed their pickets. They followed us very close, but did no mischief till we got near Salamanca, where the whole army except the Light and 5th Divisions were encamped. The outposts were two leagues and a half in front of the city. We watched the left of the line, and Generals Long's and Slade's brigades watched the right, on the other side of the Tormes; but these gentlemen between them contrived to allow the whole of the French cavalry and a large body of infantry to cross the river.[4]

We crossed lower down to Salamanca, and drew up for battle nearly on the same ground, but the rascals would only skirmish with the cavalry, as it was nearly dark. We remained standing to our horses all night, and fully expected a general action in the morning. Very luckily

1. In the original text, pp. 54–9. Location in fact Vila Pouca da Beira, forty miles east of Coimbra.
2. South of the Duero between Salamanca and Valladolid, eight miles north of Medina del Campo.
3. Twelve miles southwest of La Seca, in the direction of Salamanca.
4. Major General Robert Ballard Long and Major General John Slade, two of the most controversial officers to serve with Wellington's cavalry contingent, were then commanding the two British brigades of Lt. General William Erskine's 2nd Cavalry Division.

I was mounted on Ratler, but to our disappointment at day's dawn we perceived large columns of cavalry moving away along our front in the direction of Ciudad Rodrigo, which caused the whole of our army to retreat on that road. It was a very wet day. We were all wet to the skin, and had to skirmish with those fellows all day long, and the same thing for five successive days – out the whole of every night in the most severe, cold, rainy weather, and often without a morsel of wood to cook our ration of meal, which we were as often without as with; and entirely without bread, or corn for our horses.

We got into this village four days ago, where our poor horses got under cover. We are in the rear of Ciudad Rodrigo, about four leagues, therefore they dare not come to us. The horses had not the saddles off for six days, neither had we a clean shirt to our backs, and continually wet thro'. However, thank God!, I was never better. I only wish I had enough to eat to keep me in health; but I assure you I have not as much as a grain of sugar to drink with my tea, which is the only thing I've got, and that with a bit of dry biscuit is my breakfast.

All the other officers are living well with their comfortable bread and butter, tea and sugar, etc.; but I have not a single halfpenny now to pay for anything. I have about £30 in Greenwood's hands, but no person will give me money for a bill unless it is fifty pounds. The army have had no pay for these four months. I have not had sixpence of mine since I landed, and I cannot afford to pay the immense usury of 30 per cent. upon money which I already pay ten per cent. for in England. I would lose nearly half my income. I drew £50 in Lisbon, but my mule cost 90 dollars out of that, and the remainder barely supported me up the immense journey which I travelled. Every common necessary of life is such an immense price. When I had money the first time I travelled thro' Salamanca, common brown sugar of the coarsest kind was two shillings a pound; butter is now in Ciudad Rodrigo 4 shillings a pound.

Times are very different now to what they were when I was in the country before: the army was well paid, and I always lived comfortably on mine. But now the British army that did so many wonders are destitute of their pay; badly clothed and most completely crippled, the number of dead I saw lying on the roads very far surpassed that of Marmont's [Massena's] army when they retired from Santarem. I have heard officers say who were on Sir J. Moore's retreat, that this equalled it in every way, except that we were starved, and they always had plenty of Spanish bread. The Spaniards treated us badly on the retreat; they would give us nothing – not even as much as a bit of fire to light a pipe; and their rascally army have deserted upon every opportunity. We had no business in Spain, but we can keep Portugal. The French have retired into Salamanca. Their outposts are five leagues on this side, therefore we are at a good distance. We are relieved from the outpost duty, and are going a good way in rear of the infantry to the low country.

I have seen General Vandeleur in Salamanca. I dined and slept there. He told me always to come. He promised to introduce me to Lord Wellington. I gave him the two letters, and I have not had an opportunity of seeing him since. We shall be in quiet for some time, I hope, for now we are at home in our own country, as we call it. I hope you are all in good health. I assure you I am very anxious to hear how my father is, for 'tis a long time since I heard about him. Give my love to him and the whole of the family; and believe me, my dear mother, ever to remain, your affectionate son.

John Vandeleur.

The dating of this letter represents a large gap from the time of the two previous missives, with much hard campaigning having filled the interim. As Vandeleur had predicted in his letter of 13 October, the remount detachment pressed on through Salamanca in the direction of Valladolid. As the component parts began to separate, Vandeleur took charge of those horses and men going to join the regiments of Anson's Brigade, these being the 11th, 12th, and 16th Light Dragoons; Hay, to his chagrin, was left to supervise unfit mounts at a temporary cavalry depot. By this stage, the failure of siege operations at Burgos and the growing pressure of the regrouped and resurgent French armies had forced

Wellington to retreat lest he be crushed by superior French forces. Calling up Lieutenant General Sir Rowland Hill with the troops left in Madrid, Wellington had originally hoped to hold the line of the Duero, but was instead compelled to fall back on Salamanca. Joining his regiment for the first time as these operations were in progress, Vandeleur would have found the 12th in a greatly weakened state: the regiment had been marching and fighting almost without a break since January, and its horses, men, and equipment were all showing signs of wear. Hay, who finally joined the regiment near Salamanca, described how 'The men's clothes were actually in rags, some one colour, some another; some in worn-out helmets, some in none; others in forage caps or with handkerchiefs tied round their heads; the horses in a woeful state, many quite unfit to carry the weight of the rider and his baggage.' Like Vandeleur, however, Hay thought that the men were still full of fight.[1]

This was all to the good, for the French were now closing in on Salamanca. Having assembled a force of 75,000 men – some 20,000 of them Spanish, and the remainder his Anglo-Portuguese veterans – Wellington sought to make a stand on the same ground where he had defeated Marmont back in June. The French had by this time combined their forces to put 90,000 men in the field under the nominal command of Joseph Bonaparte and the actual command of Marshal Soult, but Soult – doubtless with Corunna and Albuera in mind – was wary of attacking the allies and chose instead to turn Wellington's lines and compel him to retreat. Wellington, for his part, had not the numbers to make an attack on the French, and was thus obliged to fall back towards Ciudad Rodrigo. The army had already suffered considerable privations on the road from Burgos, and nearly all its units were as worn and attenuated as the 12th Light Dragoons. Combined with the awful weather conditions and shortage of food described by Vandeleur, discipline in many regiments fell apart. Possibly because they

1. Hay, *Reminiscences*, pp. 72–7.

were in close contact with the enemy for much of the retreat, the 12th held together relatively well, but there was no denying that Vandeleur's new regiment, along with the army as a whole, would need a substantial amount of time to rest and recuperate before it would be fit to make a renewed advance.[1]

Corregal, near Coimbra, Christmas Day 1812[2]

My Dear Mother,

The enclosed letter, which I wrote at Villa de Porco, near Ciudad Rodrigo, I have not had an opportunity of sending before. We were about ten days on the march from Villa de Porco, from whence we marched the day after I wrote. Capt. Sandys promised to take the letter for me, as he is going home on leave, which is the cause of the delay, for he remained with the regt. waiting to hear the answer made to an application of Capt. Erskine's, which has terminated to his satisfaction; and they both march to-morrow morn for Lisbon.[3] General Vandeleur is now in Fuentes d'Onore, where he expects to remain for the winter. He wrote to me and wished me to go and stay with him as long as possible; but I am sorry it will not be within my power, as almost every officer in the regt. who is senior to me wishes to obtain leave to go to Lisbon, Oporto, etc., to see different friends.

We are very far in the rear, and have no duty to do except forage. My horses have withstood the campaign, altho' *short*, uncommonly well. Almost every officer in the regt. has sustained some loss on the retreat. My capt., Andrews, lost all his luggage and his second horse,[4] Bertie

1. Divall, Carole, *Wellington's Worst Scrape: The Burgos Campaign 1812*; see also Oman, *Peninsular War*, Vol. VI, pp. 1–180.
2. In the original text, pp. 59–65. The location seems to be Carregal do Sal, which is some forty miles northeast of Coimbra.
3. Both men mentioned were officers of the 12th. Captain Edwin W. T. Sandys served in the Peninsula June 1811–April 1814, with a gap December 1812–April 1813; Captain George Francis Erskine had similar service but was absent on leave December 1812–June 1813.
4. Henry Andrews: cornet in 12th Light Dragoons June 1808, lieutenant March 1809, captain July 1812. Served with the regiment throughout its time in the Peninsula.

lost his first charger,[1] Goldsmith lost both his horses;[2] Dr. Robinson lost a mule,[3] the Vet. lost a mule,[4] Col. Ponsonby, a horse,[5] Calderwood, a horse.[6] We were blessed with a very bad Commissary, who has been dismissed in gen. order.[7] There is another remount on their march of fifty-four horses. We have lost 198 horses this last year, so you may calculate the ware and tear of cavalry regts. on service.

All the new clothing has come out except the caps, which we expect every day, also the new saddlery, which is to be hussar. We are to wear dark brown overalls with two stripes of yellow down the sides, the officers to wear two stripes of silver. In fact our neat little uniform is changed to that of the most foreign look.

We expect to see the Horse Guards, Hussars, etc., in a short time. We also expect to be brigaded with a hussar regt. to teach them the out-post duty. It is generally thought that this year will settle the business, for the immense force of cavalry which we expect to have ready by spring, and the numerous force of Spaniards that are organising by the Cortes, together with the Army of Galicia, the Army of Valencia, and of Andalucia, it is computed we shall bring into the field, one hundred and fifty thousand men! We include the

1. Lindsey James Bertie: cornet 12th Light Dragoons October 1811, lieutenant May 1812. Served in the Peninsula April 1812–April 1814.
2. Albert Goldsmid: cornet 12th Light Dragoons May 1811, lieutenant February 1812. Served in the Peninsula May 1812–April 1814.
3. Benjamin Robinson, surgeon of the 12th Light Dragoons since October 1803. Served with the regiment throughout its time in the Peninsula.
4. The veterinary surgeon of the 12th Light Dragoons was James Castley, appointed August 1809 on transfer from the 15th Hussars. Served with his former regiment in the Corunna campaign, and with the 12th throughout its time in the Peninsula.
5. Lt. Colonel Hon. Frederick Cavendish Ponsonby. See commentary following letter.
6. James Calderwood: cornet 12th Light Dragoons June 1811, lieutenant March 1812. Served in the Peninsula May 1812–April 1814.
7. The post of commissary with the 12th had been temporarily filled by Lt. Matthew Willock, 103rd Foot, serving as Acting Deputy Assistant Commissary-General, who was dismissed for 'great neglect of duty' by General Order of 4 December 1812.

cavalry, which, with the new regts., etc., will amount to 7500 men, besides Don Julian's Lancers, 2000.[1] Mina's cavalry, 1000,[2] and other detached Guirillias will bring a force of about 10 or 11,000 cavalry. You may depend on it that if they ever meet us again they will get as severe a milling as ever man got.

I have bought a French horse to carry my servt. and corn and saddle-bags, for I found when I lost the genl. mare that it was not possible to do without it, for my second horse was never fresh, but more fatigued if possible than the other. He is a fine, strong, hardy, horse, and I got him very cheap for 91 dollars, which, at 4s. 6d. per dollar, is £20, 9s. 6d. I got some money through the kind interference of my captain from the paymaster. 90 dollars, at 6 shillings per dollar, the rate of exchange now going, which is £27. I took the liberty of drawing it on Mr. Stuart. I hope you will allow him to honor it, and charge from my next year's allowance. I was paid by Greenwood up to the 24th Aug., since which time I am in arrears four months' pay, which I cannot touch until issued by the Paymaster-General. He issues one month's pay the 24th Jan. it is expected, which will pay us up to Sept.

Thank God I am going to sit down to a comfortable dinner with the other officers of the squadron which is detached here. We have a turkey, which cost 3 dollars, a suckling pig, rice pudding and potatoes – what I call a good blow-out. Things are cheaper here than in Spain: bread, 1s. a pound, brown sugar 11½, salt pork, 1s., fresh pork, 1s., 6d., wine, about 4d. a bottle, but not very strong – one could drink three bottles and feel not the least effect, as we have tried. Capt. Sandys says he will bring out anything that I want as far as Lisbon; he will write to you when he is going to return. He is to join his regt. on the 24th Feb. in this country, so you must lose no time. Everything that I want you can

---

1. Julián Sánchez, leader of a partisan band operating around Ciudad Rodrigo 1810–12, subsequently incorporated into the regular army as two regiments of Lanceros de Castilla which served under Wellington in the Salamanca and Vitoria campaigns.
2. Francisco Espoz y Mina, commanded the guerrillas of Navarra 1810–13, his men then being incorporated in the Spanish regular forces serving with Wellington.

get in Worcester. Pack them in two deal boxes of equal size and weight and tie them together. I give you the list in the margin.[1]

I have no news at present. I wish you all a very happy Xmas. I was near neglecting to acknowledge your letter. I received it on the march. It made me very happy to find that my father was better. Thank God I enjoy the best of health and spirits, and only want to hear from you a little oftener to complete my happiness.

Here are the necessaries I am much in need of:– one plain saddle with cloak straps in front, very strong crupper and three cloak straps, 4 sets of girths for other saddles, 2 very strong head collars, 1 curb bridle, very strong reins, leather for making a second one, the reins etc. of which are rotten, one curb chain, 2 pair of short boots (Wellington),[2] 2 pair of stout shoes, a sufficient quantity of lamblet to make a cover for my head to annex to my cloak, map of Spain and Portugal – a good one – 4 or 5 lbs. of canister tobacco, which you had better get from London in two-pound canisters, and two or three hundred cigars, a new tube for my pipe, for I unfortunately lost the other. Some tea, a basket of English salt, mustard, writing paper, pencils and brushes, three knives and plated forks, 3 spoons, two plated cups – small – some blue cloth, sufficient to make a waistcoat, a sketchbook – I have filled the other one – a ham or two, with any other little comfort you think necessary for to begin a campaign with will be accepted. I wish you a very happy Xmas. Write to Mr. Sidley to send my cap which he has in store to you to send me.[3]

Give my love to all the family, and may Heaven bless you is the wish of your ever affectionate son.

John Vandeleur.

1. In fact included in the letter text below.
2. This must surely be one of the earliest recorded uses of the term – after all, Arthur Wellesley had only been ennobled as Lord Wellington three years previously – and yet the fact that Vandeleur could use it to his mother suggests that it was already generally understood.
3. Richard Sidley, then holding the warrant rank of Troop Quartermaster and serving at the regimental depot; later promoted to commissioned status as Quartermaster.

This letter captures very well the battered state of Wellington's forces after the conclusion of the retreat from Burgos. An official report by the 12th's brigade commander dated the day previously – reproduced as Appendix I – indicates just how bad things had become, but also emphasizes the fact that measures were now in hand to set matters right. A particular problem had been the non-arrival of new uniforms and equipment, caused in part by the fact that the light dragoon uniform had undergone a substantial change during the previous year. This new uniform had been formalized in a Warrant of 12 March 1812, but it took time for the new items to be produced and issued to the men in the field. What was more, because the change had been mooted for some time, there had been no re-issue of the older uniform, with its braided jacket and crested Tarleton helmet. The new uniform, with a shako, plainer jacket with facing-coloured lapels, and overalls for campaign service, was not at all popular, in the main for the reason that Vandeleur highlights – that it was too foreign. More particularly, and potentially seriously, it meant that there was now very little difference in silhouette between the British light dragoons and the *chasseurs à cheval* who made up the bulk of the French light cavalry in the Peninsula. Vandeleur's assertion that the overalls were brown is interesting, as they should by rights have been grey. Possibly this represents the use of locally-procured items, as the 12th's commanding officer had been an early proponent of overalls for wear on active service, even before the official changes to the light dragoon uniform.

Since he has a major part to play in much of the rest of this narrative, that commanding officer is worth properly introducing. He was Lieutenant Colonel Hon. Frederick Cavendish Ponsonby, second son of the Third Earl of Bessborough. By the time that Vandeleur joined the 12th Light Dragoons Ponsonby had been in command for less than a year, but he had already made his mark on the regiment through his inspired – and inspiring – leadership. Although quite the man of fashion, having obtained his first commission as a cornet in the 10th Hussars thanks to the patronage of the Prince of Wales, Ponsonby was also by 1812 an experienced cavalry officer with three years' service in the Peninsula under his belt. He had come out to Portugal as a major in the 23rd Light Dragoons, and taken part in that regiment's disastrous charge at Talavera. When the 23rd were sent home due to their heavy losses, Ponsonby transferred to a series of staff posts and distinguished himself at Bussaco and Barossa before being appointed to command the 12th. Not much older than most of his junior officers – he would not turn thirty until July 1813 – Ponsonby was a popular head of the 12th's officers' mess. At the same time, his liberal views – the Ponsonbys were a leading Whig political dynasty – led him to espouse a paternalistic and sometimes even indulgent attitude when it came to regimental leadership, refusing to work his men hard unnecessarily and doing his best to eliminate the use of corporal punishment in the 12th. A lesser man might have found such a stance taken advantage of, but Ponsonby's obvious skill and bravery in action assured him of the respect of his whole command.[1]

Vandeleur was quite correct about the planned reinforcements. The Household Brigade, composed of the 1st and 2nd Life Guards and the Royal Horse Guards, joined the army in the Peninsula in late 1812, followed by the Hussar Brigade – 10th, 15th, and 18th Hussars – in April 1813. The 7th Hussars joined later. In return, Wellington was obliged to send home four cavalry regiments that had been badly worn down by long service. Although Vandeleur's idea of brigading the new regiments with veterans had merit, and

1. Biographical sketch from Collins, Major R. M., 'Colonel the Hon. Frederick Cavendish Ponsonby, 12th Light Dragoons', *Journal of the Society for Army Historical Research*, Vol. XLVI. No. 185 (Spring 1968), pp. 1–5; Ponsonby, Major General Sir John, *The Ponsonby Family*, pp. 115–25; Salmon, Philip, 'Ponsonby, Hon. Frederick Cavendish (1783–1837)', History of Parliament Online, at http://www.historyofparliamentonline.org/volume/1820-1832/member/ponsonby-hon-frederick-1783-1837; Stewart, Capt. P. F., *The History of the XII Royal Lancers (Prince of Wales's)*, pp. 64–5.

was eventually put into practice by pairing the 18th Hussars with the 1st KGL Hussars after the former regiment proved particularly badly disciplined, the 12th Light Dragoons remained under Major General Anson's command along with the 16th Light Dragoons. The third unit of the brigade, the 11th Light Dragoons, was one of the four regiments sent home during the winter, the brigade having only two regiments thereafter. Although Wellington did not care to see veterans replaced by new troops, he could at least keep the seasoned horses of the regiments that went home, and use them to remount his remaining regiments. With veteran regiments thus brought up to strength, the new arrivals, and the Spanish regular and semi-regular cavalry enumerated by Vandeleur, the 1813 campaign would see Wellington field the most formidable mounted force ever deployed by the allies in the Peninsula.[1]

Carragal, 25th January 1813[2]

My Dear Mother,

I felt a great deal of joy and pleasure at receiving your letter last night, numbered three, in which I am surprised you mention not hearing from me. However, you must have received two letters, one enclosed from Capt. Sandys, who left this place on the 26th December. He promised to secure a franck to send them in. Your letter amused me very much; the idea of a man in his senses going to marry the youngest Miss Langley is quite ridiculous.

I am just going to set out on a shirt and blanket expedition to cross the Estrella mountains and travel up to Fuentes in Spain,[3] about twenty-two leagues from this. The mountains are covered in snow. I must make it in four days. I start on the 1st and return on the 24th. The General wishes me to go there in order to be introduced to General

1. Changes to the cavalry order of battle summarized from Oman, *Wellington's Army*, pp. 365–7.
2. In the original text, pp. 65–9; location as above, although the spelling is correct this time.
3. Fuenteguinaldo, fifteen miles southwest of Ciudad Rodrigo.

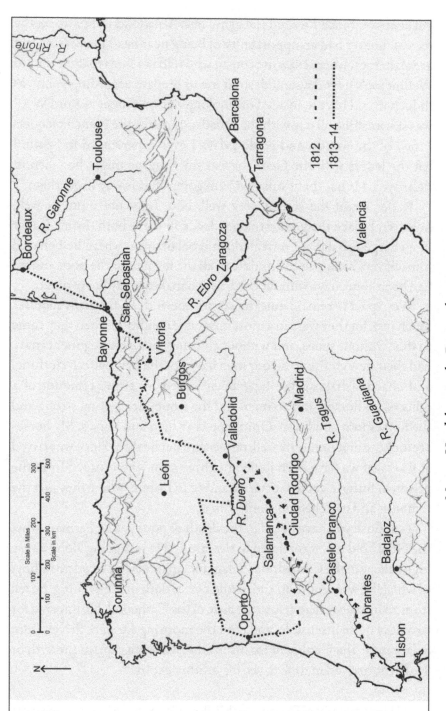

Map 2: Vandeleur in the Peninsula, 1812–1814.

Packenham. Since I joined the army near Valadolid in Spain, on the retreat, I never had an opportunity of being near headquarters, except at Salamanca, where I saw my cousin who told me I was to dine at Lord Wellington's next day, and desired me to prepare accordingly; but, as ill-luck would have it, instead of enjoying a good dinner at Lord W's, I was skirmishing all day with the squadron against the French picquets – one of the wettest and coldest days I ever experienced in Spain. I left the letters with the Genl. for fear my baggage might be taken or destroyed. He has them still, and I am going all this way to get them.

Ratler stood the retreat very well, butt Taffy not quite as well; however, I place the greatest dependence in them both. I rode Ratler in a charge the day we retreated from Salamanca, where he behaved himself very steady in the middle of all the firing; but the poor animal had been some days without corn, which makes every horse quiet.

We expect to remain quiet for some time; indeed, the army requires much rest, for they were in a most miserable condition when they came to this, without shoes, and without clothing; but most regiments have had their new clothing; all our men have got the new pattern clothing, and chacos [shakos]. We have been joined by a fine remount of 2 officers, 40 horses, and 20 men, and the troops are getting strong and the horses into condition. Our troop is 37 men and horses. My horses are looking uncommonly well, rather thin but healthy. Since we arrived at Carragal we have been joined by three men who escaped from the prison in Burgos, got to Corunna, and so to Lisbon, where they met the remount and marched up along with it.

I suppose you have heard of the death of poor young Ferman, who, the Genl. told me, was related to the family. He was going along a very high gallery in the Cathedral at Salamanca, part of which had no railing, of which he was ignorant, and, being rather dark in the evening, he fell from an immense height into the aisle of the Cathedral. He lingered for two days quite insensible, and died the morning we were driven from Salamanca. The Genl. sent for his brother, who is a capt. in the 87th or 83rd, who arrived in time to see his brother expire.[1]

---

1. 2nd Lieutenant Walter Firman, 3/95th Rifles, killed by accident 15 November 1812

The genl. has been most unfortunate. I see by genl. orders that he has lost a beautiful brown horse which he wanted to sell for 100 guineas. The army are paid up to Sept. with golden guineas, half-guineas, and seven-shilling pieces, the first of which the people of Portugal are obliged to take for 4½ Spanish dollars and 9 pence, the others in proportion. There exists in Portugal, near Lisbon, a very fierce banditti. They attacked the money as it came up last month, but were driven away by some German infantry who composed the guard.

I am very sorry to hear that George has the hooping-cough I hope by this that the poor little fellow has recovered from it. Tell Tom that he had better be quick with Miss Blackbourne, for perhaps we may not remain here much longer. The Portuguese are of the opinion that the French are leaving Spain for France. There is a very strong report among the inhabitants of this nature, some of them go so far to say that Lord Wellington's baggage is going to Lisbon to embark – poor ignorant animals. I heard Colonel Ponsonby say that if there was another campaign, which he doubts, it will finish the business one way or the other. I am sorry I have no news to tell you. This is a stupid time. I hope my father has got over this winter well. I was sorry to hear that he had been unwell. Give my love and duty, and allow me to conclude this uninteresting epistle.

> I remain, dear mother, ever your affectionate son.
> John Vandeleur

PS I forget the numbers of the letters I wrote by Capt. Sandys; in your next letter I would thank you to correct me. Is Miss Fanny St. John married to Mr. St. Aubin, and is Miss Langley fortunate enough to ensnare the unlucky young man?[1] Adieu.

---

in the circumstances described. The brother was Captain Brook Firman, 1/82nd Foot. Major General John Ormsby Vandeleur's mother was born Elinor Firman, hence the family connection.

1. Miss Frances St John married the Rev. Richard Thomas St Aubyn in January 1813; see Burke, John, *A General and Heraldic Dictionary of the Peerage and Baronetage of the British Empire*, London, Henry Colburn, 1833, Vol. II, p. 387.

Fuente Guinaldo, 9th Feb. 1813[1]

My Dearest Mother,

You may perceive by the date of this letter that I have arrived at the General's. I am happy to add that he is in excellent health and spirits. I am to return to my regt. on the 24th. I am to pass thro' Frenada, the head-quarters, and to dine with Lord Wellington, at the same time to present my letter. Genl. Packenham is further down the country. I mean to call there on my journey, as the Genl. recommends, and introduce myself with my letter. Young Armstrong[2] is very well, but is rather disappointed in not receiving a plain saddle from Gibson's along with two hussar saddles and bridles which he has just received. I certainly ordered them for him at the same time. It was only a few days back that the genl. got all those things which were ordered from Gibson and Farmar. He is much pleased with them. I have dined off his plate twice; he keeps a very good, respectable table, always entertains two or three officers of the brigade.

The whole of the horses have turned out remarkably well that you sent out, but most particularly the mare. The Genl. always rides her; she has become as tractable as a lamb. The little mare that you sent to Armstrong has improved very much, but the poor dragoon that brought them out is nearly dead with the ague. When you send me a saddle by Capt. Sandys I wish you would also send a plain one to Armstrong, with a pad and straps for a cloak. I have no information of any kind to impart except that I was at a ball given to the Spanish ladies of this place by the brigade. The Genl. partakes of every amusement with his officers, and appears to be very much beloved by every one. He desires me to give his love, and kind enquiries after poor little George, who, I hope, has recovered his illness. Give my love to my father and the family, and believe me, my dear mother, ever the same, your affectionate son.

John Vandeleur

1. In the original text, pp. 70–1.
2. Lieutenant William Armstrong, 19th Light Dragoons, served as aide de camp to Major General John Ormsby Vandeleur in the Peninsula September 1811–April 1814, and again during the Hundred Days.

For the most part these two letters form an unexceptional account of a dull, or, in Vandeleur's words, 'stupid' period, with the army in winter quarters at a substantial remove from the enemy. It does, however, begin to set the scene for the campaign of the following year, both in terms of the operational situation and Vandeleur's increasingly close connection to his relation, the general, who was back in command of his brigade in the Light Division after recovering from the wounds he had taken at Ciudad Rodrigo. This relationship would grow far closer during the year to come. Insofar as the military prospects for the new year were concerned, things were beginning to take a turn for the better. Although those reports claiming that the whole of the French were evacuating Spain were false, substantial numbers of veteran troops were being drawn off in order to replace the losses that Napoleon had sustained in his disastrous Russian campaign. Combined with the influx of reinforcements for the British, which included additional infantry as well as the cavalry reinforcements already accounted for, this shift in the balance of forces would ensure that the campaign of 1813 would give the allies the lasting upper hand that they had been unable to secure in 1812.

Chapter 3

From Portugal to the Pyrenees

~

The campaign of 1813 marked a new departure for operations in the Peninsula. One of the consequences of the previous year's battles had been to force the French to evacuate much of southern Spain, concentrating their armies in the north – where a bitter guerrilla war had flared up along the Biscay coast – and centre of the country. Wellington, for his part, therefore no longer needed to maintain a detached corps in the south, but could instead concentrate all his forces into a single field army. With 39,000 Spanish troops under his command as well as 81,000 Anglo-Portuguese, Wellington could put a total of 120,000 men into the field. Joseph Bonaparte, who had relocated his capital to Valladolid, had 140,000 men in the Armées de Portugal, du Midi, du Centre and du Nord, but the last-named was fighting the insurgents in the north, and the remainder were dispersed. Had Wellington advanced into central Spain by way of Salamanca, as he had done the previous year, the French would likely have had time to concentrate against him, but the British commander preferred not to give them the chance. As his troops completed their winter of rest and recuperation, Wellington began to move an increasing proportion of his army into northern Portugal; from there, in due course, would be mounted the main offensive of 1813, intended to outflank the French armies and force them either to retreat or to face battle on unfavourable terms.

Barcellos, May 2nd 1813[1]

My Dear Mother,

I had the pleasure of receiving your letter of March 7th, on the march 28th April. I wrote to you dated the 24th or 5th from Agenda.[2] We marched very unexpectedly on the 26th, when the regt. broke up their cantonments, and proceeded on the Oporto road to Albergaria Vilha (or Old Albargaria),[3] 3 leagues as the right squadron commanded by Capt. Stowel marched a day before the other two.[4] We halted there on the following day, to allow them to come up. We marched on the following day to the neighbourhood of Oliveira de Saymaise, 3 leagues, a fine village, very large and remarkably clean for a Portuguese village.[5]

We started again the next day (29th), and marched into the suburbs of Oporto, which I mentioned before as being a beautiful town, regularly built, everything so plentiful. The houses are principally built of stone, the streets wide and well built. It beats Salamanca in every particular, except the Roman Catholic Cathedral of the latter place, which, altho' not a large building, is more richly carved and decorated than anything I ever saw. We dined at the English hotel, where we got a most elegant dinner, and went to the opera more for the sake of seeing it than for pleasure. The performance was miserable, the house very small, about the size of the Worcester theatre, and very badly lighted. I left it rather soon, fatigued from walking over the city all day, gaping with my mouth open at all the fine buildings, shops, etc., not forgetting the bar and the harbour, the latter of which is very fine, but the former very dangerous in blowing weather.

1. In the original text, pp. 72–7; location in fact Barcelos, on the River Cávado fifteen miles west of Braga.

2. Agueda, between Coimbra and Oporto; this letter does not seem to have survived, which means that Vandeleur's account of the first stage of the 12th's march northwards from their cantonments is missing.

3. Albergaria-a-Velha, a march of ten miles.

4. Captain Samson Stawell served with the 12th in the Peninsula June 1811–April 1814, apart from the period April 1812–January 1813 when he was ADC to Lt. General Christopher Tilson-Chowne, commanding the Second Division.

5. Oliveira de Azeméis, a march of twelve miles.

I spent nearly all my cash in Oporto, buying little comforts for the campaign, such as tea, sugar, coffee, a pair of boots for overalls, etc., etc. We received a month's pay very *seasonably* at Oporto. I saw Genl. Packenham's aide-camp there, who started the next morning for Cea, the headquarters of the 6th Division.[1] We marched the next day, the 5th inst., at seven o'clock; we then crossed the Duero (which runs between Oporto and its suburbs) over a bridge of boats. We were all in our best for the occasion; the inhabitants were truly grateful, giving bread, wine, etc. to the soldiers and officers. The young girls threw roses and laurels under our horses' feet, every one, old and young, shaking our hands and kissing them, some pitying us, others exulting at our departure to expel their enemies. We had hardly got out of Oporto, when one of the most dreadful showers I ever encountered blew right in our faces and wet our new coats and hats, to take the glaze off.

We had a long wet march that day to Sta. Tysere, five leagues, where the right squadron were posted, in a convent of the Benedict order.[2] We were received with great hospitality by the monks, who live more like kings than recluse, in this convent. They immediately paraded a breakfast of tea and hot bread, and at six, gave us a very good dinner, and a fine old port wine. However, out of respect to the Father of the convent who dined with us, we left table at about half-past eight, and went in to see the mass by torchlight, which was truly solemn, and I can say almost terrific. Conceive about 120 or 30 bare-headed monks singing in a low, but hoarse voice, which echoed thro' every arch in the convent. They never admit women, except at public mass. We proceeded to Barcellos, which is about 4 leagues on the next day, the first of May, but we erred on the way, and took a round of nearly 8 leagues, about 32 miles. Barcellos is a fine large town built on the river Cavado, to the north of Oporto, 3 leagues to the left of Braga, which is at present the headquarters of the brigade.

1. Major General Pakenham had acting command of the Sixth Division 26 January–22 July 1813 in the absence of Lt. General Henry Clinton; see Oman, *Wellington's Army*, p. 369. Headquarters were at Seia.

2. Santo Terso, a march of nineteen miles; the 'convent' was the Benedictine Monastery of São Bento, founded in the eighth century.

They say that the 3rd, 4th, and another division are to join us, but it is difficult to say. Some say that Genl. Hill is to have command of the Alicant [Alicante] army, which is to be strengthened by some of his present corps, if not all. You asked me if I had met Col. Sherlock? Very fortunately I did not, but I should have gone to see him in the winter, had I not been warned against him in a former letter. I should be very happy to know why I am not to know him, and whether he has behaved disrespectfully to any part of the family. It is but right that I should know the cause; why would you conceal it from me? You know whether to trust me.[1]

I am very much surprised you never heard from Sandys, he must have forgot writing in the hurry that he left England, for a man must leave very suddenly that only has two months' leave. However, I am sure Philips will not forget.[2]

You ask me how I like the Spanish ladies? I like them very much, and would like them much better if they would leave off smoking and eating garlic, both of which they consume in large quantities.

If this letter overtakes you before you go to Weymouth, let me advise you to go somewhere else in preference, for above all places in England, Weymouth is worse for ague cases. I know it well from the number of men constantly in the hospital from that complaint. However, I suppose Dr. Wilson has been at Weymouth and knows better concerning those things of course; but at all events our house at Barbourne is a very unhealthy place for ague, for it is built completely on the edge of a marsh, so therefore my father must go somewhere. Certainly, if he goes to Weymouth, I beg you will shew every civility possible to Phillips, who is a very quiet good man in every respect.

1. Lt. Colonel Francis Sherlock, 4th Dragoon Guards; the cause of the family's dislike of Sherlock is unclear, but may stem from his past service in the 8th Light Dragoons which successively brought him into contact with Vandeleur's father, late uncle Thomas, and the future Major General John Ormsby Vandeleur.
2. Lt. Joseph Philips was the Riding Master of the 12th Light Dragoons, and one of the stalwarts of its regimental depot.

I am very anxious to hear the result of the Catholic petition.[1] I should like to see M'Mence's book. I have no doubt that this upstart thinks himself uncommonly clever.

I am exceedingly sorry to hear that my father has the ague, it is a very unpleasant condition, but not dangerous. It is very prevalent amongst the troops at all seasons in this country from so much lying out.

My unfortunate mule has arrived here with great difficulty. I was obliged to carry my baggage on Taffy, who does not relish it at all. Pray what has become of Capt. Elrington?[2] I have no other news to tell you therefore I must close my letter with a thousand blessings on the family.

> Your very affectionate son.
> John Vandeleur

PS I believe we are to halt here some days; this is the opinion of the Col. who has just arrived. M.-Genl. Baron Bock, who commands the cavalry in the absence of Sir S. Cotton, continues his headquarters in Oporto.[3]

Apart from some interesting details of the places through which the writer passed, the main point of note in this letter is the fact that it emphasizes how the purpose of Wellington's movements, and the nature of his plans for the coming campaign, remained a

1. Relating to the Roman Catholic Relief Act, 1813, which removed many of the restrictions on Irish Roman Catholics living in England.
2. Given as 'Elsington' in the 1894 text, which I have assumed to be an error of transcription. Vandeleur's friend John Elrington was still only an ensign, so this would seem to be a reference to Captain (Brevet Major) William Sandys Elrington of the 11th Foot, born Low Hall, Worcestershire, who had returned home from the Peninsula in January 1813.
3. Lt. General Sir Stapleton Cotton was the nominal commander of the British cavalry in the Peninsula, which had been reorganized into a single division for the 1813 campaign. However, he had been on leave during the winter to recover from a wound received at Salamanca, and in his absence was replaced by the senior brigade commander, Major General Eberhard Otto Georg von Bock of the KGL.

mystery even to his own army, never mind the French. Vandeleur in fact references two of the operations intended to distract the French from Wellington's main offensive, but confuses and conflates them into a single entity. Lieutenant General Sir Rowland Hill, who Vandeleur speculates is to take command of the Anglo-Sicilian forces operating on the east coast of Spain, was in fact to lead the southern wing of Wellington's forces in an advance on Salamanca. By accompanying this operation himself, Wellington hoped to convince the French that it was his main effort for 1813, distracting the French from the main thrust out of northern Portugal under the superintendence of Sir Thomas Graham. That said, the east coast army under Lieutenant General Sir John Murray was to play a distracting role of its own, tying down the French troops in Catalonia and Valencia. Murray, more by accident than design, had got the better of the French under Marshal Suchet at Castalla on 13 April, and was now making preparations for an offensive against Tarragona. Although ultimately descending into farce, these operations would ensure that Suchet had no troops spare to aid Joseph. No doubt Hill would have made a better fist of things than the lacklustre Murray, but Wellington had need for his trusted subordinates close at hand.[1]

Monforte, 20th May 1813[2]

My Dear Mother,

I begin this letter with an account of our march up the country, which I will insert as often as opportunity occurs. As we are now on the move it makes it quite uncertain what day the packet leaves the army, therefore it often happens that a letter does not go for five or six days after it is wrote; however, to remedy this evil, when I close my letter I will date it at the bottom, and when it is delivered to the orderly I will date it on the outside.

1. Oman, *Peninsular War*, Vol. VI, pp. 275–321, 488–521.
2. In the original text, pp. 78–88. Location is the Castelo de Monforte, eight miles east of Chaves, a fortification dating back to the twelfth century.

But to proceed with our movements. We remained in that famous town, Barcellos (from whence I last wrote), until the 13th inst., we remained much longer there than we expected, the route arrived in the middle of the night, and we marched at daylight to Braza [Braga], the largest city in Portugal next to Oporto. Here the Archbishop lives, who is the Senior Primate on the Continent. This day, the 13th, happened to be the birthday of the Prince Regent of Portugal (John), the A.-bishop's palace (which bye-the-bye is much inferior to the Bishop's palace at Worcester) was illuminated in a most paltry way, there were a few rockets fired and a few squibs, with a miserable band of one fife and two drums. However the whole population of the city assembled to gratify themselves with a spectacle so grand, some of them had so great an opinion of their lamplighters that they actually asked us if we knew how to put so many lights together in England.

After we had satisfied our curiosity outside the house, we marched in expecting there would be some amusement inside also. We proceeded up stairs into a long range of rooms which were illuminated with wax candles; but were greatly disappointed in our expectations, for instead of a party of pretty girls or a ball, we found the old Bishop in the middle of the lamplighters and oil pots with his sleeves tucked up above his elbows, and so busy that we were several minutes in the room before his reverence was apprised of our visit. When he discovered us he arranged his apparel and received us very kindly. He took a candle in his hand and led us to his library, where he showed us prints of old George, Prince of Wales, Marquis Wellington, Beresford, Graham, Ballasteras [Ballesteros], Mina, etc. etc., the taking of Badajos, battle of Albuera, etc., and a hundred other patriotic prints, which are the refuse of every shop in Paternoster Row. However we kept our countenance and admired them greatly for their value.

It happened unluckily that none of the party (which was Bridger, Calderwood and I)[1] could speak a word of the language except myself,

1.   Having been promoted to major in December 1812, James Paul Bridger arrived
     in the Peninsula February 1813 to act as Ponsonby's second-in-command, and
     served in that capacity for the remainder of the war and again in the Hundred

and they insisted upon my asking the old fellow to produce wine and a desert. I thought this a rather barefaced question to ask an A.-bishop, but I hit upon an old expedient of mine, which was to tell him we were all Irishmen, he consequently asked us if we were Catholics, which we answered, 'Certainly, of course', he then embraced us, and said how happy he was to see us, and what terribly wicked people the Protestants were. We said they were terrible dreadful people and ran them down as much as possible. After a long discourse upon the excellence of our supposed religion he offered us some of the best port wine I ever tasted, some fine preserves, and other delicacies, which we most greedily devoured to the great astonishment of the Archbishop, and plied his wine so heartily, that I am sure he wished we had never entered the house. We wished the old gentleman good-night and walked into the street, which by that time, nine o'clock, was exceedingly thinned. We remained there about half an hour, but, unfortunately, a heavy shower of rain put an end to the evening's amusement by drowning all the lights and driving the populace to their homes. So thus ended the holiday about half-past nine.

We got excellent quarters in Braga, which we left at five next morning, the 14th, and marched to a miserable village called Perdecieras, 3 leagues.[1] On the 15th we had a terrible march, though only 4 leagues; we were on horseback nine hours. The roads were very bad and uncommonly hilly. One of the guns, a six-pounder, upset down a precipice and hurt two of the horses so badly that they were obliged to be immediately shot. One of the riders had his thigh broke and otherwise so dreadfully hurt, that he is given over. Several of our horses fell, but none hurt. We have repassed the river Cavado, and entered the province of Tras os Montes, which literally signifies Cross over Mountains, and well it might be called so, for in all my life I never

---

Days. Previously, as a captain, he had commanded the regimental depot. For Calderwood, see p. 59.

1. Most likely Cerdeirinhas, a march of sixteen miles; nowhere else in the area comes close to the name given by Vandeleur.

beheld such mountains or such roads. We arrived at Rivaens,[1] worse, if possible, than the former village, thatched houses built of mud, nothing to buy but milk and Indian corn bread. This place is 4 leagues from the former. We continued our march on the 16th to Alturas,[2] five leagues, a bad road, and bad village. On the 17th we marched 3 leagues to Boticas,[3] which was rather better than the former places; here we were able to get some white bread and eggs for breakfast.

The people, seeing us in the new dress, took us for French Dragoons, and the greatest part of them fled to the neighbouring mountains, of which there was no *scarcity*. We were ordered to halt in this village. On the 18th, unfortunately, some of the inhabitants left their wine-houses open, which was soon found out by the 12th, who lost no time in conveying it away in camp kettles, canteens, earthen pots, etc., they all got rather intoxicated in the course of the evening. On the 19th we marched again to a most beautiful town, or rather a city, called Chaves, or in English 'Keys'.[4] This town was fortified by the Moors, they strengthened it considerably. It was retaken by the Portuguese a short time after, who added very much to its strength and beauty by building a castle, which I explored by permission of the Governor. Neither the Moors or Portuguese shewed much judgement in fortifying this place, for it is commanded on two sides by hills, from which you may batter it to pieces without the least resistance.

We marched the next day, the 20th, to Monforté, which signifies a strong mountain. This place is small, but well situated. I have got into a priest's house, who has given me a fowl and some ham, with potatoes, milk, and eggs. He was rather rusty when I first entered the house, and asked me 'what business he had to get me dinner', and asked me 'how I always provided myself with a dinner.' I answered I had a friend who always took care of me, and shewed him my sword which was rather sharp. This had such an effect upon him that he immediately procured

1. Ruivães, a march of twelve miles.
2. Alturas do Barroso, a march of nineteen miles.
3. A march of eleven miles.
4. A march of fourteen miles.

these things which are now in the pot. My dinner this day consists of an Irish stew made of beef and potatoes, a roast fowl and some ham. I wish I had the company of some of you to help me, but not in this country.

Excuse me for not acknowledging the receipt of your letter of the 7th of March. I don't know whether I received it before I closed my last or not. The last letter I wrote was written on a piece of paper similar to this, and dated from Barcellos. I hope you received it as it contained just a rough description of our march to that place.

There is some baggage in Oporto for almost all the officers, but no names were specified, who accidentally saw it. However, the Col. has ordered the Commissary[1] to send some mules to Oporto for the purpose of bringing it up. I hope my boxes are there, for I am much in want of them, and if I don't get them now, perhaps I never shall. The whole of the heavy baggage of the army is gone to Corunña [*sic*]. I suppose we shall get supplied for the future from that port.

We are very far north; the French are in Astorga, Benavente, Zamora Zoro, Valadolid, Salamanca, Legovia [Segovia], Madrid. We are to join the Galeirian [Galician] army at Bragança on the 23rd ultimo. Our army in this part will then consist of the 1st, 3rd, 4th, and 5th divisions. Our force in this, part including the Spaniards, will be about 65,000 men commanded by the Marques himself.[2] The Hussars with the 6th and Light divisions, I believe, are on the march to Salamanca under Hill. The 14th Light Dragoons are to join us at Braganza. I suspect three such regts. as the 12th, 14th, and 16th were never better brigaded. The Hussars said that the Light Brigade did not understand the outpost duty, which was the reason they were sent out, but now it is pretty clear we have the post of honor in the British army. The unfortunate Blues are reported unfit for service; I hope not, but such is the report.

1. After the removal of the unsatisfactory Willock, Deputy Assistant Commissary-General William Myler was assigned to the 12th Light Dragoons. Accompanied on campaign by his wife, he was described as 'a very excellent commissary and a great favourite with everyone' in Hay, *Reminiscences*, p. 119.
2. That is to say, Wellington.

I was very sorry to hear of the death of poor Mrs. Mairs. I heard from Armstrong a short time ago, dated the 6th, the Light Division had not at that time moved from Fuente Guinaldo. The Genl. was, I am happy to say, in good health. He mentioned the death of Mrs. Mairs, but said he had heard no particulars relative to her property. His regt. is gone to America,[1] but by the H. orders no aide-de-camp is obliged to go out with his regt. when ordered on service, providing he is actually serving in a foreign clime with his Genl. The Genl. told me that he intended next winter to apply for leave for two months, to return to England. If he really will return at the end of his leave, I should like to go home with him, and also return at the same time as he does; but before I ask him I wish to know my father's thoughts on the subject. Ponsonby would apply, and so would the Genl. It will be necessary to know your mind soon, as there are 3 or 4 of the officers who mean to ask Ponsonby to apply for them also.

I was obliged to buy another mule from the Veterinary Surgeon for 120 dollars (£30), as my poor little mule is done. I was killing my horse by carrying baggage on him. Since I came to the regt. I got some money at 6s. per dollar, which amounted to £27. I lost £4 5s. by discount that is paid. I bought a French horse for I think £23; I lost £3 11 8 on that. I got £17 5 from Hay, paid; I lost £2 8 6 on that, so in all by discount alone I have lost £10 5 2. The allowance you were so kind to give me was 25th April. My father was so good as to make me a present of £30. Mr. Phillips credits to me, you say, £25. These three sums make £80. The amount of the other three was £67, 5, 0. Therefore there is a balance in my favour of £12, 15, 0, and £10, 5 of discount, which is £23. But as I am ignorant whether the £25 for horse, although credited to my account by my father's orders, is meant as a gift, or to be repaid, I took the liberty of giving a bill for mule on my father for fear Greenwood had not this £25 in his possession, and my bill might have been protested. However, if this money has been lodged, and you would be so good as to lodge the discount money, Greenwood will then have £90, 5 0, but I owe him £67, 5 0, therefore he will be my debtor £23. Since I joined the army for my subsistence and clothing I have drawn only £44, which I got

1. The 19th Light Dragoons had embarked for Canada, arriving in May 1813.

from Chatterton and Hay, as above, this includes the discount.[1] I have been here 9 months; but I have been unfortunate with a mule, and I was obliged for my own comfort to buy the French horse to carry my tent and corn in the field. I hope this account is £ clear. I wish to know about the £25. My father, of course, will stop the next quarter's money, which will pay the bill, as the discount is more than £5.

I beg, my dear mother, that you will never put a black seal on a letter again without letting me know the reason previously. I am very happy that George has recovered, and also that my father is better. Give my love, and believe me, my dear mother, your very loving son.

J. Vandeleur

This letter shows the steady development of Wellington's plan of operations; even without leaving Portugal, the lead units of his army were already deployed to the north of the greater part of the French forces in Spain. The intention was quite clearly to win the campaign by hard marching rather than hard fighting, and although the long haul across the Tras os Montes was every bit as taxing as Vandeleur describes, for the most part the army held up well. The unfortunate incident at Boticas, as well as confirming the un-wisdom of uniforming the British light cavalry so like their French counterparts, does also reveal the regrettable tendency towards mass drunkenness that remained the bane of the British Army on active service in this era. It is telling, however, that this incident took place after several hard days on the road, just as did Vandeleur's own rather direct means of getting a meal out of his host the padre. Whilst the exertions of the march by no means excuse any of this behaviour, they do perhaps go some way to explaining it. Certainly, officers and men were well advised to get what rest and refreshment they could, for there was more hard marching to come.

1. James Chatterton: cornet 12th Light Dragoons November 1809, lieutenant June 1811, served in the Peninsula June 1811–April 1814. Hay, of course, is William of that ilk, the future memoirist.

For some of the newest regiments, this proved quite a test, and both the Household and Hussar Brigades went through quite a steep learning curve as they adapted to active service. The Blues, notwithstanding Vandeleur's report, seem to have fared better than the two regiments of Life Guards in this respect, but the performance of the three hussar regiments would prove mixed to say the least. Considering that these regiments had adopted for themselves all the fashionable accoutrements of crack European light cavalry, but had seen no active service since Corunna, there must have been a certain grim satisfaction amongst their drabber brethren in the veteran light dragoon regiments, confirming that it took more than a busby and a pelisse to make an outpost soldier. Certainly, this rivalry between the two types of regiment would continue throughout the Peninsular War, and re-emerge during the campaign of Waterloo. Vandeleur was incorrect, however, in his belief that the 14th Light Dragoons – which had been brigaded with the 12th and 16th prior to July 1812 – would again serve alongside them. Impressive as such a concentration of veteran light cavalry would have been, the 14th remained in the brigade of Major General Victor von Alten.[1]

Another point that is worth discussing, since it features heavily in the closing passage of this letter, is that of finances. A cavalry officer was expected to have a private income – £150 per annum, over and above pay, was believed to be the minimum desirable by General Sir James Steuart, regimental colonel of the 12th – and in the case of a young man like Vandeleur, this naturally took the form of an allowance from his father.[2] As is no doubt often the case with such arrangements, a great deal of wrangling seems to have taken place as to what was a gift and what was to come out of the allowance, particularly when it came to equipment for campaign. The strains of extensive overseas service put just as much pressure on officers' private equipment and resources as they did on those

1. Oman, *Wellington's Army*, pp. 360, 365.
2. Bamford, *Gallantry and Discipline*, p. 43.

Captain Vandeleur
served at
Waterloo.

2

An early photograph showing John Vandeleur in later life.
The description of him as Captain Vandeleur does not fit the
likely date of the portrait, and may have been added later.

'Great Marlow. The Royal Military College', 1817 engraving.

'Troops bevouack'd near the village of Villa Velha, on the evening of the 19th of May, 1811', aquatint by Charles Turner after Thomas Staunton St. Clair.

'The village of Pombal in flames, as evacuated by the French Army . . . on the morning of the
11th of March, 1811', aquatint by Charles Turner after Thomas Staunton St. Clair.

'Battle of Fuentes D'Onor, taken from the right of the position occupied by the 1st, 3rd and 7th Divisions
on the 5th May, 1811', aquatint by Charles Turner after Thomas Staunton St. Clair.

'Distant view of Ciudad Rodrigo ... with a troop of Spanish guerrillas',
aquatint by Charles Turner after Thomas Staunton St. Clair.

Lt. Colonel (later Major General) Frederick
Cavendish Ponsonby, watercolour and pencil
by Thomas Heaphy, *c.* 1813.

'12th – the Prince of Wales's – Light Dragoons,
c. 1812', watercolour by Reginald Augustus Wymer,
depicting an officer in the new-pattern uniform
issued at the end of the 1812 campaigning season.

'City of Coimbra', aquatint by Charles Turner after Thomas Staunton St. Clair.

'The Battle of Vittoria, June 21st 1813', aquatint by Thomas Sutherland after William Heath.

Sir John Ormsby Vandeleur, oil on canvas
by William Salter, *c.* 1835.

'Major General Sir Denis Pack, K.C.B., Lieutenant
Governor of Plymouth &c. &c. &c.',
mezzotint by C. Turner after Saunders.

'Attack on the Road to Bayonne', watercolour by W. Heath, showing the action during the
Battle of the Nive witnessed by Vandeleur.

'1814', detail from a water-colour by Richard Simkin, depicting uniforms of the 12th Royal Lancers at various dates.

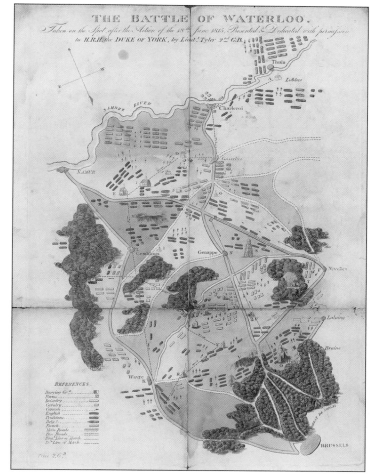

'The Battle of Waterloo', 1815 map after Lt. Tyler, showing positions of the three armies on the 16th, 17th, and 18th of June 1815. Note that the map is oriented with north at the bottom.

'View from Mont St Jean of the Battle of Waterloo', aquatint from the 1816 *Campaign of Waterloo*, published by Robert Bowyer, depicting the scene around 7.00, with the cavalry of Vivian's and Vandeleur's brigades massing on the far right of the image.

'Chasseur de Lord Wellington faisant ses adieux à une modeste', a contemporary cartoon recognising the impact of the new light dragoon uniform on the ladies. Engraving by Rulhières, after 'D. J.'

'10th (the P. Wales's own) Royal Regiment of Hussars', lithograph by C. H. Martin, after L. Mansion and L. Eschauzier; No. 1 in a series entitled 'Officers of the British Army'.

of the Army itself, and the need to be fully equipped for campaign, and replace any losses sustained, meant that expenditure soared as a result.

Barbarina, June 19th 1813[1]

My Dear Mother,

I last wrote to you from Monforté, if I remember. A packet has arrived here, but no letters from you have arrived. We have been sadly knocked about since I wrote, harassing marches, but no fighting. The Hussar Brigade have the out-post duty of the main body of the army; we act upon their left flank, that is, on the enemy's right. We have the 1st, 3rd, 4th, 6th divisions of Infantry, and the 1st division of Cavalry, commanded by Bock, composed of the 10th, 15th, and 18th Hussar Brigade, 12th and 16th Light Brigade, 3rd, 4th, and 5th Dragoons Heavy Brigade, three regts. of heavy German drgns., 1st, 11th, and 12th Portuguese Light Dragns., making four brigades. The first commanded by Col. Grant,[2] 2nd by Genl. Anson,[3] 3rd by M-Genl. Ponsonby,[4] 4th by Baron Birlow,[5] 5th, or Portuguese, by M-Genl. Baron Davembj.[6]

1. In the original text, pp. 88–98. Location in fact Berberana, some twenty-five miles west of Vitoria.
2. Lt. Colonel John Colquhoun Grant, 15th Hussars; not to be confused with Major Colquhoun Grant, 11th Foot, the noted intelligence officer.
3. Major General George Anson; having previously served as a brigade commander under Wellington June 1809–December 1811, Anson had returned to the Peninsula and taken command of his current brigade in July 1812.
4. Major General Hon. William Ponsonby, a cousin of the 12th's Frederick Ponsonby; note that the final regiment was in fact the 5th Dragoon Guards, not the 5th Dragoons.
5. Lt. Colonel Johann von Bülow, 1st KGL Dragoons, commanding Bock's Brigade whilst Bock had the division; note that this brigade contained two regiments, not three.
6. In fact Brevet Colonel Benjamin d'Urban, serving as a brigadier in the Portuguese service. It can only be inferred that 'Baron Davembj' represents a Victorian effort to untangle a particularly scrawled or faded passage of the original letter.

I shall now continue my route, so get the great map out. You left me at Monforté, a little better than half-way between Braga and Braganza. We left it on the morning of the 21st May, and reached Val d'Armeira,[1] 3 leagues; very bad road, and very bad village. The 22nd we marched 4 leagues into a very good Portuguese town, Vinhaes;[2] has a convent, where upwards of 200 nuns are confined and deprived of liberty, but not prevented seeing their friends in the presence of the lady abbess. We all put on our best shirts, and made a formal visit. They had tea and coffee waiting, with all sorts of preserves of their own making.

Next day,[3] the 22nd we marched in the direction of Braganza, where we expected to halt; but we were posted three leagues in advance, which made our march rather severe, being seven leagues. In passing thro' Braganza, we were looked at by Genl. Graham, Genls. Ponsonby, Anson, and Pack. As soon as we had ranked by, I fell to the rear to see my friend Pack, who brought me to his own house to breakfast. Genl. Ponsonby came in at the same time, and without any introduction shook me by the hand, and said that he had heard, or he had wrote, I forget which, to or from you. Pack wanted me to stay to dinner; but as Ponsonby, my colonel, was going home, I objected on that account, not knowing the way. Pack told me whenever I was near there was always a seat at his table; he spoke with the greatest kindness possible. I got to the regt. about six o'clock in the evening, to a neat little village, called St. Julien,[4] on the road to Benevente [Benavente]. We halted here on the 24th and 25th, and destroyed an immense quantity of pigeons for food – in fact, for nearly a week afterwards there was nothing but roast, boiled, stewed, broiled, etc., and in every way. On the 26th we marched 3 leagues to a wood near Tayo,[5] where we bivouac'd. We had a fine night. We marched at daylight the next morning, passed

1. Vale de Armeiro, a march of twenty-one miles from Castelo de Monforte.
2. Vinhais, a march of fourteen miles.
3. This must have been the 23rd; either that, or previous and subsequent dates in the letter are in error.
4. São Julião de Palácios; ten miles past Braganza, and a total of thirty miles from Vinhaes.
5. Unidentified location.

the river Sabore into Spain,[1] to a village in the province of Zamora, where the Genl. and all the other big-wigs were put up, but we were all bivouac'd in a wood near.

On the morning, 28th, we commenced our march with an advanced guard. In a most dreadful shower of rain, we arrived at a large forest near Tabora [Tábara], which the enemy immediately quit upon our appearance. The whole of their infantry had retired some days before. We remained in this forest. On the 29th, Genl. Ponsonby's brigade was up; Erwin of the 5th Dragns. [*sic*] came and dined in my tent.[2] He invited me to dine in his next day, but the right squadron was sent to the front next day on piquet. Here I was ordered to patrol with two men, to feel where the enemy were. I found them to the amount of near 250 with 4 guns on picquet at the north side of the bridge at Benevente. When I got within two miles of them I halted my two men and went on myself, relying on Ratler until I got close up to their vedettes, and saw all that I wished to know. Two of them being rather dubious as to who I was, rode after me at full speed. I turned about and went back at a canter, letting those fellows keep pretty close. I allured them away about half a mile, but they got too cunning. If I could have got them as far as my two men, we certainly should have taken them. I was extremely fortunate, for on my way home I met a Spaniard going towards the French to sell them some fine fresh trout which I did not scruple to take from him (but mind ye I paid him, not what he asked, but what I considered enough).

During these last few days there has been constant heavy rain. It was a very unfortunate time to commence lying out, it has not improved the looks of the horses. But to continue, we got an order to march between 11 and 12 that night. We arrived at daylight in the morn, about two leagues above Alemandra,[3] to ford the Esla. The heavy Germans and Portuguese lost 3 men and 5 horses in crossing the

1. Vandeleur is in error here: the River Maças forms the Spanish–Portuguese border; the Sabor is further west.

2. Captain William Irwin, 5th Dragoon Guards. Served in the Peninsula September 1811–April 1814, and was promoted to major a few days after his dinner with Vandeleur.

3. Alemandra seems in fact to have been Villamandos.

ford. The rain had made the river (which at best of time is dangerous to cross) so excessively rapid, that it was deemed a dangerous thing to allow our brigade into the water at that place. All this time the river was rising higher and higher, so much so that the last squadron of the Germans was ordered to remain with us. The Hussars were ordered to ford the river at Almendra, the regular place, where the French had a subalterns piquet of 16 men. The advanced guard of the Hussars crossed unperceived, formed up, and rattled up at the piquet, which by this time, was formed. It gave them a fire which did no mischief, and then turned about, but the great superiority of the English horse there proved itself, for every single man of the piquet was either cut from his horse or taken alive. This was the 16th French Heavy Dragns.

Our brigade, which was waiting at the other ford to pass, determined to obey the orders in crossing. However, as good fortune would have it, Genl. Graham sent an A.-D.-C. full gallop to counter-order his former command. We were then ordered down to the other ford, which was two leagues down the river. We had already matched 5 leagues. The sun was tremendously hot, everyone fatigued and hot and sleepy. However, we continued our march, crossed the river, marched back the two leagues on the other side and arrived at a little village at 8 o'clock that evening, which concluded a march of 9 leagues (about 36 English miles) that was performed in the space of 20½ hours, over a terrible hilly country. We imagined to have a day's halt here, but we were mistaken. We marched at the usual hour, 4, next morning, the 1st of June, to Toras,[1] a very good village, over a fine flat country, without a tree to be seen, but covered with rich grain, barley, upon which we fed our horses. On the 2nd, we marched to Vez de Marban,[2] two leagues and a half from Zamora. Here we received a month's pay.

The Hussars made two hundred and fifty prisoners of the 16th French H. Dragns. at Toro (not Toras), the whole of which regt. is totally annihilated. As yet, we have had no opportunity of signalizing

1. Toro, as Vandeleur in fact corrects himself in a later paragraph. Situated on the north bank of the Duero, twenty-one miles east of Zamora.
2. Vezdemarbán, a march of ten miles.

ourselves, but patience, we have the outpost of the left flank, the Hussars the right. We have very hard duty, always a squadron of the brigade on piquet, sometimes two. There being but two regts., we are constantly on some duty or other, observation duty, patrols, carrying confidential letters, etc. etc. A subaltern officer of cavalry has more duty than any other officer of the army. A capt. of cavalry has no duty whatsoever, but piquets.

But to my detail. We marched on the 3rd of June to Villa Fradas,[1] a good sort of place enough. On the 4th we marched to Villa Bracana,[2] on piquet again the right squadron, but there was no trouble. The piquet entered the place two hours after the rearguard of the French. We took two French hussars (or rather found them). We are much stronger this year than they are, that is, counting Spanish and Portuguese cavalry, which is better this year than ever. We spent the king's birthday on top of a hill, looking at those rascally French hussars, and very hot weather to comfort us.

On the 5th we passed thro' Rio Seca,[3] a fine large town, as large as Worcester almost. The people received us with the greatest possible joy. They hung out silk and damask quilts from the windows, which is a triumphal signal, brought the men out wine, cheese, etc., and almost pulled the officers from their horses, kissing our hands and calling us their deliverers. I never saw such beautiful girls as there are here, but we were not favoured with a halt in this place. However, I got leave to remain there some hours to buy some meal, French brandy, etc. The head-quarters were in this town. We went on two leagues to the front as usual, to a village called Castel Mow,[4] which signifies a dirty castle, where we put up for the night. Next day, the 6th, we entered Pedraca del Campo on the Valencia Road.[5] We have a Col. and two squadrons on

1. Villardefrades, a march of ten miles.
2. Villabrágima, a march of ten miles.
3. Medina de Rioseco, site of Marshal Bessières's 1808 victory over the Spanish armies of Blake and Cuesta.
4. Unidentified; possibly Vandeleur has taken a description for an actual name.
5. Pedraza de Campos. Vandeleur is here – and after – confusing his spellings; the 12th were on the way to Palencia, not Valencia.

piquet to-night, from the brigade. The enemy shewed us a strong front this morn at daylight, but retired quietly.

I expect we shall enter Valencia [*sic*] in two days hence, not Valadolid. I suppose you heard that the Light Divisions made 500 prisoners in Salamanca. Don Julian made prisoners 30 dragns. and two officers this morn, a piquet.[1]

We are now on the direct road to Burgos. The 4th division have lots of new scaling ladders, there is a train of 24 guns, twenty-four pounders, on the road from Corunna. Thank God the cavalry don't storm forts.

We are now in the thick of the business, horses saddled every night at dusk, and remain so all the night, but we are all as happy as possible. We have got a month's pay, plenty to eat and drink, horses in good condition, and an enemy flying before us. What can we desire better.

A packet arrived last night but no letter for me; this is the second time I have been disappointed since I left Barcellos. I hope my father is better of the ague. Poor Louis Gordon has gone home, ill with a similar complaint to my father's.[2] The other is also ill at Oporto. I must conclude my letter as it draws near dinner. I have a roast shoulder of mutton and sheep's head, so I am well off, the only comforts we are destitute of are vegitables. Give my love to the family, and believe me, dear mother, your ever dutiful son.

John Vandeleur

PS Pedraca, near Valencia [*sic*], 6th June 1813. The regt. is now 336 effective horses strong – all mounted.

Before moving to more serious matters, it might be noted that Vandeleur's comments on the state of the nuns in the convent visited by the officers of the 12th are quite typical of the time. Nuns seem to have been the focus of not inconsiderable interest and fantasy amongst British officers, who as a body seem to have convinced themselves that Spain's convents were full of young

1. That is to say, Julián Sánchez.
2. Unidentified – Challis lists no officer of that name.

women forced to take the veil against their will and only awaiting rescue by some dashing wearer of the red coat. It may safely be said that this belief was a mistaken one, but hope prevailed and, in the meantime, officers continued to visit convents on a social basis.

The powerful screen of cavalry detailed by Vandeleur provided near-impenetrable cover for Graham's column of the allied army. With only scattered French forces available to oppose this part of Wellington's advance, progress was held up primarily by the terrain. The lack of enemy attention allowed the infantry divisions to remain well closed up and concentrate on their own forward movement. More dangerous than the enemy was the terrain, and the crossing of the Esla in particular represented quite an ordeal that cost the lives of several infantrymen who were swept away in the current. The most significant French force initially opposed to Graham's troops were the 16e Dragons, whose discomfiture and near-destruction – which were inevitable considering the odds against them – took place much as Vandeleur describes, with only the arrival of infantry support allowing the surviving French troopers to escape. Vandeleur gives credit where it is due to the Hussar Brigade, but this early success for the newly arrived rivals must surely have stung for the officers of the 12th and the other light dragoon regiments.[1]

Vandeleur's comment 'Thank God the cavalry don't storm forts' reflects one of the key appeals of mounted service. Whilst cavalry officers were no doubt pleased to be left out of the preparations, the siege train that Vandeleur witnessed on its way to the front represented a far more professional approach to the mooted siege of Burgos than had been the case in 1812. Wellington had learnt his lesson well, and had his army well supplied with all the necessary materials to reduce the fortress that had thwarted his efforts the previous year. In the event, the speed of the allied advance forced the French to evacuate Burgos without a fight, but

1. Oman, *Peninsular War,* Vol. VI, pp. 322–33.

the siege materials would be put to good use at San Sebastián and elsewhere, later in the campaign.

Field Near Vitoria, June 22nd 1813[1]

My Dear Mother,

We have had a very severe action near this place, and most completely routed the enemy. We have taken 87 guns, the military chest, and I believe not less than 2000 prisoners. We charged a solid square of infantry, which made a most desperate resistance. They killed the adjutant, Hammond of Ours,[2] and Lieut. Thullitson, 16th;[3] wounded St. Arnold, 16th,[4] and their adjutant.[5] Poor Hammond was shot very near me, he is much regretted, and leaves a wife and 4 children. The plunder is immense, but as yet we have had but a small share. They have lost the greater part of their baggage and nearly all their artillery. Col. Cadogan, 71st, is killed and the regt. suffered much. It is impossible for me to give you an account of the losses on either side, genl. Vandeleur and Armstrong are safe, and thanks be to God for His goodness in preserving me also. I was never under such fire before. I hear we are to follow them up the Bayonne road, the two other columns on the Pamplona road. Poor Ratler escaped unhurt; I shall never part with him. It is generally thought the French will never attempt a halt until they cross the Pyreneese. They cannot come to a general action, as they have lost their guns and, consequently, cannot fight in position. I hope you are all in such health and spirits as I am. We have a cold night before us, and no baggage. The killed and wounded French are

1. In the original text, pp. 98–100.
2. Cornet Abel Hammon, recently awarded a combatant commission after years of meritorious service as Quartermaster. His post as Adjutant of the 12th was a temporary one; the previous incumbent had recently been promoted, and his replacement not yet arrived from the depot; see Bamford, *Gallantry and Discipline*, pp. 191–5.
3. Lieutenant Hon. George Thelluson, 11th Light Dragoons, who had remained in the Peninsula attached to the 16th after his own regiment was sent home.
4. Lieutenant Robert Arnold, 16th Light Dragoons.
5. Lieutenant and Adjutant Joseph Barra, 16th Light Dragoons.

immense, they are burying them as fast as possible. Give my love to all, and believe me, dear mother, ever the same –

      Your affectionate son.
        John Vandeleur

Excuse this scrawl, 'tis nearly 12 o'clock and I am terribly fatigued. We have a *good fire* of gun carriages, wheels, etc.

This brief note represents a break in the chronological order of things, being dashed off in a hurry on the field of battle in order to get quick word home that the writer remained fit and well. As such, we are as well to return to Vandeleur's account of the march to Vitoria before considering the battle itself.

      Villa Franca, on the Bayonne Rd, July 12th 1813[1]

My Dear Mother,

Since my last there has arrived another packet, which makes the 3rd, since I have had the happiness of hearing from you. We have been marching every day since I wrote, except this, which is only the second halt day we have had since we marched from Barcellos. I had the pleasure of seeing my worthy cousin the Genl., at Pena del Campo.[2] I went out and dined with him, but I could not stay the night, as I had to mount picquet in the morning. I am sorry to say that Armstrong has been very ill, and I am afraid, is still so, with that nasty complaint, the ague, but the Genl. is in good health and fine spirits. He says my father never writes to him.

Such are the uncertainties that at the moment I finished the last sentence, the trumpet sounded the alarm. The enemy who attempted to drive in our picquet at Parades del Campo,[3] the place where I commenced this letter, did not succeed. The regt. marched the same night, about a mile from the town, and encamped on a disagreeable

1. In the original text, pp. 100–10; unidentified location.
2. Unidentified location.
3. Most likely Boada de Campos, twenty miles west of Palencia.

plain, without baggage or cover. On the 7th instant Colonel Ponsonby drove their picquets thro' Valencia [Palencia], about 3 in the morning, and encamped in a wood in front of the town. The next morning, the 8th, we commenced our march, not upon Burgos as expected, but to the left of it to Bercerril.[1] The towns begin to be much cleaner and better. We marched without interruption to Amuseo,[2] on the 9th; to Fromista,[3] a large town, on the 10th; to Osomo,[4] on the 11th; to Hijoso,[5] the 12th; halted on the 13th; to Amaya, 14th;[6] on the 15th we commenced our march at ½ past 12 at night, marched 8 leagues, across the most terrible mountains, without our artillery or baggage, and arrived at St. Martin,[7] where we crossed the Ebro, and encamped immediately we got across. The men and horses we fatigued to such a degree, that we could not ascend the mountain on this side. The infantry did not get in till 2 o'clock next morning, so they were on their legs from half-past 12, or 1 o'clock one night, until 2 o'clock the next. We marched at 5 again, and marched 6 leagues to Villa Cayo,[8] the distance was nothing, but the mountains we had to cross were terrific.

These two days' march fagged the troops very much, but by this movement which astonished the enemy, we forced them to abandon Burgos. On the 17th, we had a short march of 3 leagues, passed Medina and encamped at Salinas.[9] On the 18th, we fell in with a corps of the enemy near Barbarina.[10] I was on picquet with the advance. I patrolled to Osma, where, just as I arrived, I saw about 12 dragns. coming towards us. I had but three men, we halted and they halted, I took them for Spaniards, but they fired a shot and retired. Col. Ponsonby came up

1. Becerril de Campos, nine miles northwest of Palencia.
2. Amusco, a march of twelve miles.
3. Frómista, a march of eight miles.
4. Osorno, a march of twelve miles.
5. Hijosa de Boedo, a march of seven miles.
6. A march of seventeen miles.
7. San Martín de Elines, a march of thirty-eight miles.
8. Villarcayo, a march of twenty-nine miles.
9. Salinas de Rosío, by way of Medina de Pomar; a march of ten miles in total.
10. Berberana, a march of twenty-five miles.

with the remainder of the picquet, and ordered me to skirmish, which I did with them for 2 hours, supported by Capt. Webb,[1] who had his horse wounded. They retired about half-a-mile into a thick wood, where they had a number of sharpshooters concealed. I followed no further than the edge of the wood. The col. then ordered up the German riflemen, who drove them back on the left.[2] It then became an infantry business; the 3rd division beat them back, and night put an end to the business. The ground is so very strong, that it becomes impossible to drive them back very fast, as they take advantage of every favourable spot to make a stand.

The next morning, the 19th, they were all off, and we marched quietly to Vitoriano,[3] on the 20th, we marched to Rotaria,[4] where we came up with their rear-guard, and skirmished a little. The next day, the 21st of June, we gained the ever-to-be-remembered battle of Vitoria. You have had a better description of it in the newspapers than I can give you, therefore excuse me calling again to my memory such an event, where I lost so many friends, and to recall such a sight when our regt. charged the infantry and cavalry. The death of the adjutant so exasperated the men, that they spared nothing, but cut and slashed about them like madmen. The col. with all his coolness and intrepidity could not check the impetuosity of the charge, but charge upon charge was continued as long as we had light, and had not it failed us so soon, we should have massacred every soul of them.

On the 22nd we followed not the main body, but a convoy, which we failed to take on the Bayonne road to Alegria.[5] The other two columns followed the enemy to Pamplona. During the last two or three days we had very rainy weather; but in spite of it we continued our march on

---

1. William Webb: lieutenant 12th Light Dragoons October 1804, captain August 1812, served with the regiment in the Peninsula June 1811–May 1812, April–September 1813.
2. The 1st and 2nd Light Battalions of the KGL, a portion of which were rifle-armed.
3. Bitoriano, a march of some thirty miles from Osma.
4. Retana, a march of fourteen miles.
5. Alegría (in Basque, Dulantzi), a march of ten miles.

to Salveterra,[1] the 23rd, where we again bent our course to the left, and the following day, the 24th, arrived at St. Adrian,[2] which we passed, and endeavoured to pass a mountain, that took us from 2 o'clock p.m. until past 11 at night to get to its summit, where we were obliged to halt from the excessive darkness of the night and the badness of the descent, which was bad enough next morning to get down. We passed thro' a cavern of great extent, which was perfectly dark and dismal, and one of the greatest curiosities in this province. However, as we marched quietly along the road, we overtook some of their rear guard, which was entirely composed of infantry, who soon stopped us from the nature and strength of the ground. However, our infantry came up and drove them back to Tolosa, but not without some loss on both sides. The ground in this part of the Pyrenees is very woody, and consequently not a cavalry country. You can form no idea of the stupendous height of the mountains; but it is a most extraordinary thing that the pass from Yrun into France thro' these mountains is one of the best roads in Spain. It is a regular made road along the bank of a river, and as hard and level as most roads in England; but the bye roads are hardly passable for a goat.

However, after beating them well thro' Tolosa, we halted for some days until the 1st of the month, when we marched to Belmonte, which is to the left of the high road.[3] Next morn, the 2nd, we assembled next morn at Ernani and marched out in the direction of Yrun,[4] which is the last town in Spain. Here our squadron was on picquet. When we came up to them they fired a few shots and retired quietly along the road. The whole of the British cavalry and infantry had gone back to the ground they occupied the night before, and left us there for three or four hours in their front without any support. However, the British infantry came up during the night, and attacked the enemy at daylight

1. Salvatierra (in Basque, Agurain), a march of eight miles.
2. The Ermita de San Adrian, a church high in the mountains of what is now the Parque Natural Aizkorri-Aratz.
3. Monte Belkoain.
4. Hernani, five miles south of San Sebastián; Irun, where the Great Road between France and Spain crosses the Bidassoa, is a march of fourteen miles.

in the morning, and very gallantly beat them back from two heights in front of Yrun, and forced them to take up a position on the other side of the river Bidassoa, which divides France and Spain. There was a wooden bridge over the river, and a very strong bomb-proof stone building, with holes to fire thro'. They defended this all day long, but burned it, along with the bridge, during the night, and drew their picquets to the French side of the river, and there they are *in status quo* at this time. The picquet went home next day, but Capt. Andrews and I remained and rode to Fuenterabia,[1] where we crossed the river in a row boat at a short distance from their picquets and actually landed in France; but mark, we immediately stepped into the boat again and went back; but we can say that we were the first two men of the allied army that landed in France.

We then went quietly home, where I was told to my great astonishment that Genl. Vandeleur was appointed to the brigade, and that Anson was going home, all which was realised on the 6th by his riding in with a servant and a pair of saddle-bags, without bag or baggage, all of which has since come up. He immediately wrote to Sir T. [*sic*] Cotton to get me appointed A.D. Camp. He has not yet received an answer, but there is no doubt I will get the appointment, as Genl. Anson had an extra A.D. Camp also. I am now living with him, and I trust it will make you and my father very happy to hear of my success. Armstrong is quite well, but still rather weak.

We have laid siege to St. Sebastian, which, altho' a small fortress, is very strong. The town will easily be taken, but I am afraid the castle, which much resembles Burgos, will be a difficult job. They began to batter yesterday with 18 and 24 pounders, of which description of guns we have got plenty. As soon as it is taken we move into France and leave a Spanish force to blockade Pampeluna [Pamplona]. The genl's orders this morning caution us to behave in the most humane way to the French peasantry, and to recollect that we are not at war with the inhabitants, but with their ruler; that all provisions, forage, etc., etc., are

---

1. Fuenterrabía (in Basque, Hondarribia), four miles downstream from Irun at the mouth of the Bidassoa.

to be paid for by the commissaries in the same manner as in Spain and in Portugal; that all private property is to be respected. The orders also cautions us to take care and not straggle from our camp, etc.

All this indicates that we shall enter it shortly, and thanks be to God, I hope victorious. If J. Bull would but send out a few thousand militia, we would walk straight to Paris. The French have 2,500 men in St. Sebastian. We have a fleet of transports sailing opposite, ready to take them away, and a fleet of frigates commanded by Admiral Collyer.[1] There are 4000 men in Pampeluna. Joseph Napoleon is at St. Jean de Luz.[2]

Provisions are rather scarce, but they are forming depôts on the coast. In Tolosa they ask 3s. a 1lb. for coarse sugar, 5s. for butter, and 16 dollars a pound for tea, which is only to be bought in apothecaries' shops, where they use it as a medicine. Every body drinks coffee. Tea 16 dollars, or a pound of silver! But we shall soon get everything from England. I gave 9 dollars a yard for grey cloth to cover my nakedness. Our horses, from the rest they have had, are in most beautiful condition, and the men very healthy; indeed, the army was never in better health or discipline than it is at present. The climate here is very like what it is in England. We frequently have balls, and are constantly in the society of the most beautiful girls I ever saw. In this province Guipuzco [Guipúzcoa] the women are more beautiful than any other in Spain. Their hair, which is jet black, reaches very nearly to their heels and is very neatly platted and ornamented with ribbons etc., etc. They speak the Biscayian language, which is the harshest and most unintelligible lingo in the world. The people from other parts of Spain cannot make themselves understood; but fortunately the better kind of inhabitants speak the Castilian language, which fortunately I understood.

I suppose you got my letter from Vitoria. I hope you are all as happy and in good health as I am. Give my love, which is conjoint with the

1. Captain Sir George Ralph Collier, RN.
2. Joseph Bonaparte was in fact at Bayonne after having been relieved of his command.

Genl.'s, to my father and all the family. We have moved back a few leagues for the convenience of forage. Your affectionate son,

John Vandeleur

Lieut and A.D. Camp

Even after contact had been made with more substantial bodies of the French forces, the scattered nature of Joseph Bonaparte's armies meant that the allied advance was impossible to resist. The French were repeatedly forced to abandon good defensive positions – first the castle at Burgos, then the line of the Ebro – because they had already been outflanked by the hard-marching allies. Symptomatic of the French confusion is the fact that fight at Osma on 18 June 1813 that Vandeleur outlines in his letter was brought about by a substantial French contingent blundering into British forces whilst still on the line of march. Along with a second action fought the same day at San Milan, this fighting forced Joseph to concentrate his available troops around Vitoria from where they could cover the evacuation of his forces – and the huge convoy of baggage and plunder that they were escorting – from Spain. It was here that Wellington finally brought the French to action on 21 June, putting 82,000 allied troops into the field against 60,000 French.

Joseph had deployed his forces in three successive lines blocking the passage up the valley of the Zadorra, using that stream to anchor his right flank. Wellington made his attack in four columns, one on the right under Hill to draw off the French attention, two in the centre under his own direction to deliver the main blow, and one on the left under Graham to turn the French flank by crossing the Zadorra further upstream and thereby threaten Joseph's rear and line of retreat. Anson's Brigade, along with Bülow's KGL dragoons, formed the cavalry component of Graham's command, which also included the infantry of the First and Fifth Divisions, and an attached force of Spanish troops. During the morning, Wellington's plan unfolded as intended, although Hill's infantry paid a heavy price for their capture of the heights of La Puebla, with Vandeleur's old battalion taking substantial losses. Henry Cadogan, who had stepped up to lead the whole brigade, was mortally wounded at the head of the 1/71st. With the French attention drawn off, however, Wellington was able to break Joseph's centre with attacks by the Third, Fourth, and Light Divisions, and in doing so bring about the collapse of the French positions.

Although Graham's cavalry were required during the morning to screen the infantry advance, it was only late in the day – after a bitter struggle by the Fifth Division to capture the village of Gamarra Mayor and its bridge across the Zadorra – that the horsemen came into action. By the time that Graham had his troops across the Zadorra, the French had regrouped on the far bank, and it seemed as if there would be a continuation of the bitter struggle that had characterized the earlier fighting. However, the French elsewhere on the field were by this stage falling back in defeat, so that the troops facing Graham were now tasked with forming a rear-guard and keeping open the line of retreat. Anson's two regiments were sent forwards, led by a squadron apiece from the 12th and 16th Light Dragoons, and found themselves facing two regiments of French cavalry. After an initial attack was beaten off by the superior French numbers, Anson put his whole brigade into line and ordered a second charge, which is the one in that Vandeleur describes. This attack also failed, for, unbeknownst to Anson and his officers until it was too late, there was a regiment of French infantry drawn up behind their horsemen. Although French musketry caused a handful of casualties at this point – notably the unfortunate Cornet Hammon – it was really the surprise of finding the infantry on the field that caused the British troopers to rein in. Only once the French began to retire could Anson's Brigade resume its advance, allowing some measure of revenge to be obtained for the earlier discomfiture. Limited though it was, this series of attacks represented one of the most effective uses of allied cavalry in the whole battle. Many of Wellington's mounted troops were never engaged at all, whilst the

Hussar Brigade, who did get into action, allowed themselves to be distracted by the lure of the abandoned French baggage train. Many fortunes were made, and numerous trophies acquired that still grace the messes of the modern successors to the hussar regiments that captured them, but Anson's Brigade missed out on the plunder, being left with only the cold comfort of the moral high ground.[1]

Captain Stewart, in his history of the regiment, made use of an original 1894 copy of the Vandeleur letters for his Napoleonic chapters but questions Vandeleur's version of events at Vitoria, suggesting that the 12th were less heavily engaged and accusing him of employing 'the exaggeration of youth' in his account.[2] It is true that this was Vandeleur's first general action as a cavalry officer, and the exhilaration of taking part in a mounted charge for the first time may have caused him to form a more dramatic and impressionistic version of events than might have come from the pen of a more experienced officer, but, even so, there seems little in either of the two letters relating to Vitoria that cannot be corroborated. The very obvious awareness of the horrors of battle inherent in the second letter also argues against a desire to present a deliberately dramatized or romantic view. Whilst it does seem to be the case that Anson's Brigade as a whole did not mount a second charge after the appearance of the French infantry, there is plenty of evidence to suggest that elements of the brigade did continue to attack and harry the French rear-guard. Since Vandeleur does not mention taking part in the earlier cavalry fighting, it may be inferred that his squadron was still fresh at this point, and in a position to continue the fight whilst those of other eyewitnesses, such as Hay, or Captain William Tomkinson of the 16th Light Dragoons, were not.[3]

1. Overview of the Battle of Vitoria from Oman, *Peninsular War*, Vol. VI, pp. 384–450.
2. Stewart, *XII Royal Lancers*, pp. 84–5.
3. Hay, *Reminiscences*, pp. 113–14; Tomkinson, Lt. Col. William, *Diary of a Cavalry Officer in the Peninsular and Waterloo Campaigns 1808–1815*, pp. 250–6.

The confusion and lack of order that had characterized allied actions in the later stages of the Battle of Vitoria continued during the pursuit that followed. Several units moved without orders, some ending up on the wrong roads, and it took time – and a flare of Wellingtonian anger – to set matters aright. The bulk of the troops that had fought under Graham remained under his command and drove north-west, as Vandeleur describes, in pursuit of the French. Actual fighting – for the cavalry, at least – was relatively limited, as the main French concern became one of getting their surviving forces intact over the frontier. Joseph Bonaparte, having been driven from his kingdom, was stripped of his command of the remaining French forces, which were placed under Marshal Soult as head of a new and unified Armée d'Espagne. On the face of things, it seemed as though the stage was now set for a rapid advance into France, and Vandeleur was by no means alone in his enthusiasm for a swift finish to the campaign. However, with the fighting in central Europe still undecided and with the fortresses of San Sebastián and Pamplona still in French hands, Wellington elected to secure his position rather than to push straight through the mountains. The need to reorganise the army's logistical systems, shifting from Lisbon and Corunna to the Biscay ports, as described by Vandeleur, also argued for consolidation rather than a rapid advance. These delays, and a rapid French military resurgence that served to prove the wisdom of Wellington's cautious strategy, meant that there were several months of fighting still to come.

Chapter 4

Into France as an Aide de Camp

~

Since the remainder of Vandeleur's Peninsular service would be spent as ADC to his relation, it is perhaps time that we took a closer look at Major General John Ormsby Vandeleur. It will be remembered from the Introduction to this work that he was the son of Richard Vandeleur, whose brother, also John Ormsby, was the grandfather of the writer of these letters. Born in 1763, the future general began his military career in 1781 as an ensign in the 5th Foot. Rising steadily through the ranks, he remained an infantryman until 1792 when, by now a captain, he exchanged into the 8th Light Dragoons. Two years later, he was promoted to the rank of major in that regiment, with which he served throughout the Flanders campaigns of 1794–5. In 1796 he went with the 8th to the Cape of Good Hope, and two years later was promoted lieutenant colonel and took command of the regiment, which remained in southern Africa until 1802 when it was transferred to India. Serving under Lieutenant General Sir Gerard Lake in the later stages of the Second Maratha War, Vandeleur held local rank as a colonel and functioned as a brigadier of cavalry.

In 1806, Vandeleur returned to Britain with a brevet promotion allowing him to retain his full colonelcy. He exchanged into the 19th Light Dragoons, and served as the regiment's commanding officer until promoted to the rank of major general on 4 June 1811. In his new rank, he was placed on the staff of Wellington's army in the Peninsula where he was given command of an infantry brigade in the Light Division. He briefly had acting command of the division during the storm of Ciudad Rodrigo, after the mortal wounding of its commander Major General Robert Craufurd, but, as we have already seen, was then himself wounded and forced to relinquish his command. He was back with his brigade for the fighting at Salamanca, and thereafter served with distinction during the Vitoria campaign before being reassigned to the cavalry under the circumstances described at the end of the previous chapter. It should be stressed that his being ordered to relieve Major General Anson came about as a result of a long-standing desire on the part of the latter to return home to attend to private affairs. There was certainly no connection between Anson's departure and the relief of several unsatisfactory brigade commanders around this time, and the associated re-jigging of the cavalry order of battle, beyond the fact that all these changes required the approval of Wellington's chief of cavalry, Lieutenant General Sir Stapleton Cotton, who only resumed his command a few days after the Battle of Vitoria.

Aside from his day-to-day military duties, John Ormsby Vandeleur was one of a relative minority of officers who had given serious thought to the theoretical aspects of his profession. In his 1801 publication *Duty of Officers Commanding Detachments in the Field*, Vandeleur drew both on his own experiences in Europe and Africa and on the work of others who had served in North America during the 1770s and 1780s to produce a primer on the effective use of light cavalry on active service. In an age when most cavalry treatises dealt primarily with the mounted charge, Vandeleur's book instead focussed its attentions on picquet, patrol, and outpost work. A selection of Vandeleur's brigade orders from 1815 relating to this aspect of service are reproduced as part of Appendix III, along with those issued by Lieutenant Colonel Ponsonby: they together represent the distillation of experience gained through several decades of cavalry service across three continents.

Not only, however, was the general a thoroughly competent soldier, well versed in both the theory and practice of the military arts, he was also by all accounts an excellent comrade and a thoughtful and considerate superior. George Napier thought him, 'a fine, honourable, kind-hearted, gallant soldier and an excellent man', and went on to comment that 'I never knew him to say or do a harsh thing to any human being.'[1] Certainly he quickly endeared himself to his new aide, and John Vandeleur seems to have developed a close bond with his relative and new superior officer.

Camp Near Yrun, on the Frontier
and on the River Bidassoa, 4th Aug. 1813[2]

My Dear Mother,

There has been two or three packets lately up to the 10th July, but as usual I have had no letter except a sort of a one, we'll call it a note, such a note as you would write to an old maid to invite her to tea, not longer I'm certain, however it was short but sweet. You said you were all going to Weymouth; I hope now that you are there that you will like it. There is always an abundance of amusement and fish. My father will be delighted to see the dragoons cutting 5 and 6, etc., in the barrack yard, it will remind him of former times.[3]

There has arrived at Belbao [Bilbao] a very strong remount for the regt., 107 horses and 70 men. We have sent off a capt. and sub[altern] to assist in bringing them up to the regt. I have now more hopes than ever of seeing my saddle and things whatever they are. I suppose there is no butcher in England that rides in so bad a saddle as I do, but the Genl. often tells me that it is very fortunate that there is so strange a contrast between the butchers of this country and of England. In the

---

1. Quoted in Haythornthwaite, Philip J., *The Waterloo Armies*, p. 70.
2. In the original text, pp. 110–16.
3. Cavalry troopers were trained in a number of different cuts and parries, which were practised dismounted in the first instance. Since Vandeleur's father had once commanded a cavalry regiment, this would of course have been a familiar sight.

latter place they always ride excellent horses, but here they invariably walk. The Genl. has applied to Sir S. Cotton to make application to Marshal Wellington to appoint me as extra aide-de-camp. He has not yet received an answer, but expects it every day, but *ad interim* Col. Ponsonby has ordered me to do duty as an extra aide-de-camp with the Genl. as he says there is no doubt in the case.

The last letter (not note) that I wrote you was from Lascona near Villa Franca,[1] since then we have been moved up to nearly the same ground as before. The siege of St. Sebastian is going on very badly. I saw at first from what little knowledge I have of fortification, that the place was uncommonly strong, and would take a long time to take, which must be done by sheer battery. We have a great plenty of heavy guns up for that purpose, but it appears to me that there is a want of ammunition. The guns effected a very good looking breech, which was to be attacked by signal yesterday morning. In cutting one of the trenches a few days ago, our people discovered a tunnel that had formerly conveyed water into the town. This place was entered by our miners, who got to the other end of it, where there was a strong iron gate. Our people immediately thought of blowing the whole town up. Accordingly the place was filled with 36 barrels of gunpowder. The French fellows found this out and very properly took away all the powder thro' the grating except two or three barrels which were at the end next to the French. The enemy did not even wait for us to fire it, but did it themselves at two o'clock in the morning. It exploded near our trenches without doing any mischief.

This explosion, which was not *properly* to have taken place until day light, was the signal to attack. However, our gallant but unfortunate men marched or leaped into the ditch and charged into the breach, but as fast as they got up, they were either shot or rolled over into a second ditch twice as deep as the former, which was full of burning wood that was rolled over by the French from the walls of some houses that had been set on fire by some shells. Every man that fell into that ditch was either burnt to death or crushed to atoms by immense flags or stones, that were also pushed over the ramparts. The 1st regt. or Royals took 4 companies

---

1. Unidentified location.

to storm, the Grenadier company brought a sergeant and 3 men only out of the ditch alive; the Light company 5 men; the other two 10 or 12 between them. There were 21 officers that led on these 4 companies, 5 of them came back only. One of these was Lieut. Armstrong,[1] a cousin of young Armstrong; from him I learnt this horrible account. Probably you will see the dispatch as soon as this, but you will find my account perfectly true without garnish. There were upwards of 400 men lost in that breach alone, besides the other casualties, and, mark me, this place is every bit as strong as Burgos. Besides the great want of ammunition which there appears to be, I think our artillery is not so well served as it might be. However, in a few days you will see the result of all this, and whether my ideas are right or not.

Communication has been effected with Lord Wellington and I am happy to say that the Army of Soult has suffered a most severe defeat; he attempted to relieve Pampeluna [Pamplona] after drawing Genl. Hill from the pass at Roncevalles [Roncesvalles]. Lord Wellington met him at a league's distance from Pampeluna, and offered battle. Soult attacked 4 times, and was as often repulsed. He then retreated on the Lanz road,[2] but his column was headed by the Light division; the others came up and were engaged in a running fight for 3 days. We took upwards of 3000 prisoners, not including the whole of the wounded, which is not a trifling number.[3] A few days afterwards the Light division again came up with them, and took the whole of their baggage, including Marshal Soult's, and made 300 men, the escort, lay down their arms.[4] Soult's army is retreating in the greatest confusion and disorder. We expect to cross the river[5] by force tomorrow or the next day.

1. John Armstrong: ensign 1st Foot February 1807, lieutenant April 1809. Served in the Peninsula with 3/1st from November 1810 onwards. Wounded at Vitoria.
2. Lantz; the road ultimately allowing a return to France either via the Maya pass or by way of Santesteban and Vera.
3. Vandeleur is here describing the First and Second Battles of Sorauren, fought 28 and 30 July 1813.
4. Vandeleur is here describing the action near Yanci on 1 August 1813.
5. The Bidassoa.

The Genl. takes me out each morning at 4 o'clock; he rides very hard and a great deal. He has desired me to get another horse, as I am now allowed to keep three, as extra A.D. Camp. Poor Armstrong is again attacked by that ague. I am afraid he will be obliged to go to England; the Genl. told me he would send him home if he did not get better. He does not know this; be careful, and do not mention it to his friends. The Genl. is in good health. He always gets up at 4 or 5 o'clock; rides 4 leagues, and comes home to breakfast, which is two eggs, tea, and dry toast. He always writes letters, etc., in the heat of the day, dines at 3 o'clock, drinks very little wine, eats some soup and plain beef or mutton, never meddles with made dishes, stews, etc. he keeps a very neat and gentlemanlike table, always sits down eight. He mounts his horse after dinner, rides till half-past 7 or 8, returns, takes his coffee, smokes a cigar, and goes to bed at 9.

I send this by Col. Gibbs, a friend of the Genl.'s who goes home with the supplementary dispatches.[1] You must excuse the hurry. I conclude my letter for fear it will be late. I received your letter, dated 9th, from Worcester, a fortnight after the one you wrote from Weymouth. I have had no account of the boxes. I will give you an account in my next letter of the regts. that compose the different divisions of the army. Give my love to my father, and tell him to give me an answer about a horse. I think I could buy one from some person in this country. Adieu. Believe me, dear mother, your ever affectionate son.

John Vandeleur

Other than giving an interesting potted account of a day in the life of a Peninsular brigadier and his staff, this letter is primarily a second hand re-telling of the dramatic series of events that took place in the weeks following the Battle of Vitoria. Wellington had deployed the bulk of his army to hold the Pyrenean passes whilst Graham oversaw the siege of San Sebastián and a Spanish corps maintained a blockade of Pamplona. However, the first

1. Lt. Colonel Edward Gibbs of the 52nd Light Infantry; his regiment had formed part of Major General Vandeleur's former brigade in the Light Division.

attempt to take San Sebastián by storm, at dawn on 25 July, failed with heavy losses much as Vandeleur describes. He is, however, incorrect – although no doubt reflecting contemporary gossip – in his assertion that the mine whose explosion served as the signal for the attack to begin had been fired by the French. In fact, the French were momentarily shocked by the explosion – which was rather more substantial than even the British engineers had expected – so that a brief window of opportunity existed in which the place might have been taken at the rush. However, inadequate preparations for getting the attacking troops from their trenches to the breach meant that the French had time to recover, and the assault was met with a stiff resistance that wreaked havoc in the ranks of the would-be stormers. The 3/1st Foot, at the head of the column, suffered extremely heavy losses as Vandeleur describes.[1]

Meanwhile, Marshal Soult had thrown himself into the task of reorganizing the French forces that had been defeated at Vitoria. In the space of a fortnight, he was able to restructure, re-equip, and re-inspire his command to create a unified Armée d'Espagne of 79,000 effective troops With this force he mounted an offensive intended to relieve the besieged garrisons south of the Pyrenees. The initial actions of the resulting Battles of the Pyrenees saw the allies pushed back from the mountain passes, and it was not until the retreat had carried them almost to Pamplona itself that a stand could be made. Then, however, there followed a series of French defeats as the allies recovered their balance and first held their ground and then counterattacked. By 30 July, Soult had lost over 10,000 men and was in full retreat, and the allied position was once again secure.[2] Nevertheless, although it yet again seemed as though the French were on the run and the time ripe for crossing the frontier, Wellington remained cautious and the hopes of those like Vandeleur who expected a rapid advance were to be

1. Oman, *Peninsular War*, Vol. VI, pp. 578–82.
2. Oman, *Peninsular War*, Vol. VI, pp. 587–740; on these and later operations, see also Robertson, Ian C., *Wellington Invades France: The Final Phase of the Peninsular War*.

disappointed. For Vandeleur, too, there would be disappointments of a different sort, as the next letter reveals.

Usurbril, 18th August 1813[1]

My Dear Mother,

I have not heard from you since I was at Astigaira,[2] which is a good while. I am afraid that your letters are gone round by Lisbon, in which case I shall not receive them for a length of time. Since I wrote last I have been very ill of a fever and ague, which stuck to me for some time, but now, thank God, I am perfectly recovered and getting strong. It is a very extraordinary thing, that during the most unhealthy time of year in Portugal and Spain, that I have escaped this malady, and now I have had it in the healthiest part of the year and climate, where I have had nothing to do, and a good bed every night; but now that I am well I will take more care of myself, and not expose my person quite so much to the inclemency of the weather. I actually got so indifferent to the rain, that I never by any chance used to put my cloak on until night came, which I think was the sole cause of my indisposition.

You know that genl. Vandeleur applied to get me appointed on his staff as extra A-D-Camp, but to the surprise of everyone, Lord Wellington refused and said 'he could not comply with a request so irregular', altho' only a few days before he granted the same request to M. Genl. Ponsonby, a junior officer who commanded a brigade that never was or is intended to be on outpost duty, and another thing, the very officer who the Genl. succeeded (Anson) was allowed an extra, altho' he never gave them anything to do, but always employed and used the regimental officers upon every service of difficulty, and pampered his two A-D-Camps in the most shameful manner. However, the Genl. has no particular interest, therefore he is refused everything he asks, and has no redress, but this refusal only makes the difference of my receiving no bat and forage money, £90 a year, for the Genl. makes me

1. In the original text, pp. 116–21. Location in fact Usurbil, seven miles southwest of San Sebastián.
2. Astigarraga, four miles inland from San Sebastián, on the River Urumea.

act as extra A-D-Camp altho' I do not get the allowance.[1] I live at his table and sit at the foot of it, Armstrong at the head.

The town and castle of St. Sebastian is not yet taken, nor is there a probability of it. The fellows had the impudence the other night to make a sally, but they all got bayonetted by the 59th,[2] not one that came out escaped; they received no quarter. There is a report that a flag of truce has arrived at Yrun, from Bayonne, proposing an armistice. The people in this part, and the army in general, expect a general peace. Don't be surprised if we are all home by Xmas. The army are all in camp, except the cavalry. Since I wrote last we moved up to Yrun, where it is expected we were to have dashed across the ford and attacked them in position. However, after remaining in a wood a few days, we were moved back here, where we have nothing to do but eat and drink, and give balls to the girls, who are truly beautiful in this part of Spain. They all say they will go home with us. I hope they will not insist on it, as it may be disagreeable.

I hear a great many people in England are mad at our victories, but a great many have reason to be sorrowful. Poor Vandeleur of the 87th has died of his wounds at Vitoria,[3] and Col. Fitzgerald is taken prisoner.[4] The Genl. wrote to Lord Wellington to beg to have him exchanged if possible, for we took a great quantity of prisoners, but he has not yet had an answer on the subject.

I have never had any account of my saddlery. I very much fear it is lost. If you paid the postage and booking, surely you can recover

1. Bat and forage allowance was an extra payment to cover the keeping of animals required to carry out a duty, in this case, to enable an ADC to be properly mounted so as to be able to accompany his general. Of course, as a cavalry officer, Vandeleur was already well-mounted, so the money would have been a useful extra income.
2. 2/59th Foot, in Robinson's Brigade of the Fifth Division.
3. Captain Frederick Vandeleur, son of Crofton Vandeleur and second cousin to the writer.
4. Brevet Lt. Colonel John Forster Fitzgerald, 5/60th Foot, was taken prisoner during the fighting in the Pyrenees, whilst in temporary command of the Second Division brigade that had previously been under Cadogan. Released at the end of the war, he later rose to be field marshal.

the value of the boxes. We expect a remount every day of 176 horses, perhaps it may find its way with them. I have written to Lisbon to enquire whether they came there, but I have not heard anything of them. The Genl. has received a pair of boxes containing books, maps, etc., with a very correct miniature of Mrs. Vandeleur.

Bye the bye, I wish you would write to Col. Ponsonby to get me leave for a couple of months this winter, to go home along with the Genl. and return at the same time. It would be the greatest service to me, as I want a new rig-out of almost everything. I have worn out most completely my pelisse and jacket, so that I only have one in wear, and am very badly off for boots, flannels, drawers, saddles, and bridles, etc. If by any chance there should be a peace, I shall have time to talk about it more seriously.

I hope my father has received benefit from the Weymouth air – you have I'm certain. I shall direct this to the post office, as I don't know your address. Give my love to my father and the family, not forgetting to remember me to my old friend Nash.[1] Have you got acquainted with any of the Weymouth people?

God bless you, my dear mother –

> believe me, your ever affectionate son.
> John Vandeleur

Pray write a little oftener, I am afraid you have forgotten me.

For the first time since his return to the Peninsula in 1812, there can be seen here the beginning of a recurrence of the homesickness that marked several of the letters home during Vandeleur's time with the 71st around Lisbon. With a bout of illness to contend with, military operations bogging down, and autumn coming on, not to mention the disappointment of the blocking of his promised appointment as an extra ADC, it is easy enough to see why Vandeleur could be feeling a little sorry

---

1. The Nashes were an established Worcester dynasty, but it is unclear exactly which member of the family Vandeleur is here referring to.

for himself, and the lack of word from home evidently was not helping. The attempt to self-justify the lack of letters as being due to the relocation of the army's supply lines is probably an accurate one, but, considering that the previous letter began with a rather chiding complaint about his mother's brief note, this was still evidently a sore point. The idea of the parents enjoying themselves at Weymouth while the son shivered his way through a bout of ague in the foothills of the Pyrenees was no doubt not an image to inspire confidence that an extensive correspondence was in the post.

Insofar as the refusal of Vandeleur's appointment to his relation's staff is concerned, there is no written record in Wellington's *Dispatches* or *Supplementary Despatches* that touches upon this decision, although Major General Vandeleur was not an officer of particular influence and there may well be some truth in the assumption that he was unable to employ sufficient 'interest' to have the appointment confirmed. In the event, Lieutenant Colonel Ponsonby's generous agreement to allow Vandeleur to serve unofficially as an ADC meant that Wellington's veto had only the effect of preventing him receiving the financial perks of such an appointment. The financial loss must have stung, though, but it would at least not be long before – as the next letter reveals – a resumption of communication with his family gave Vandeleur something to feel more positive about.

Renteria, 1st Sept. 1813[1]

My Dear Mother,

I have just had the happiness to hear from you from Capt. Brian, 39th,[2] who left Weymouth when you were there. I am sorry to say that

---

1. In the original text, pp. 121–5. Location is Rentería (in Basque, Errenteria), seven miles east of San Sebastián.

2. Captain James Brine, served in the Peninsula with 2/39th July 1809–July 1811, returning home after being wounded at Albuera. Challis dates his return to active service with the 1/39th as being September 1813, but the date of Vandeleur's letter would suggest that he actually arrived in Spain in late August.

I never heard from you, from what account I cannot conceive. The last letter I had from you was written at the moment before you entered the coach for Weymouth, which was just four lines.

I am happy to have the pleasure of saying that my good friend Genl. Pack has quite recovered his wound.[1] He says now that if the ball had struck any other but an Irish head, it would certainly have broken it. I am sorry to say there were lots of broken heads yesterday, 1st at St. Sebastian, and latterly about the centre of the lines near Lazarte. I saw the 1st place stormed and carried, that is the town, I hope after which the castle will soon surrender. The French fellows made a most determined resistance. They had a mine ready to blow up our people, but by some mistake before they were away from the top, it exploded and killed upwards of 200 of them. I never saw anything so dreadful as the unfortunate French fellows in the air, with their legs and arms flying about. However, as they intended the mischief for us, I did not much pity them. John Armstrong of the 1st Foot was shot though the thigh in the breach, where he lay for some time before he was taken away. However, I am happy to say that it is only a flesh wound, and very slight. He is a cousin of William Armstrong's.[2]

There was a disturbance also at Yrun, as I mentioned before, yesterday morning. Marshal Soult (who is always doing what he can to annoy us) continued to pass 3 divisions of his army across the Bidasson river, under cover of the night (which was as dreadful a one as I ever saw) immediately in front of the Spaniards, who did not discover it until morning. The Portuguese and Spaniards immediately attacked, but unfortunately were driven back; they tried it again and repulsed the enemy with the bayonet, killed a great many, and drove 300 of them into the river where they were drowned. The Spaniards lost either two or 3 genl. officers, and a col., with 300 men killed and wounded. There were no British troops engaged except one small picquet. This is the whole of the news in this

1. Pack, now a major general commanding a brigade in the Sixth Division, had been wounded during the fighting around Sorauren.
2. John Armstrong's wound may have been more serious than Vandeleur reports, for he shortly afterwards returned home. He was back with his battalion in the Hundred Days, only to be killed at Waterloo.

part. Our brigade was sent for from Andaya,[1] about 8 leagues on the road, where we were for forage, but now they are all ordered back except a squadron. The infantry are all encamped in the same position where they have been since we first came to this part of the country.

The doctors have recommended me to bathe in the sea, which I do every morning along with the genl. I am now, thank God, nearly as well as I ever was in my life, the bathing has made me quite strong again. I mean to ask leave to visit the old ground at Vitoria, where I understand everything is to be bought. I want to clothe myself again with a pelisse, or coat, and a pair of overalls. If you have any acquaintance at Portsmouth or Plymouth, who would send out a parcel to Passages [Pasajes], in Spain, a port town, which is only a mile from this place, I could get it. Directing to Lieut. V_____, 12th Light Dgs., Spain, to the care of Capt. Sir George Collier, or, upon second thoughts, you had better not, as I may get home in the winter, at all events, if I don't, you can get the Genl. to bring them out when he returns.

The Genl. I am happy to say, is in good health, and so is Armstrong, who send their love, also your next friends, Ratler and Taffy, are very well and fat; they would send their respects, poor animals, if they had the power of utterance. I am very anxious to see you all again. I expect to find the girls greatly improved. I am afraid I am a good deal altered. I am not near so fat, I have grown a good deal, and I am a little tinged with brown in the face. I dread staying here in the winter, it is so cold. I shall get my coat lined with sheepskins, and my breeches too, if not warm enough.

I am anxious to hear how Weymouth has agreed with my father, but I never expect to get a letter, as you have left off the custom of writing. Give my love to my dear father and the family, and believe me, your very affectionate son.

John Vandeleur

Although short, this letter contains a summary account of two more dramatic actions, namely the Storm of San Sebastián and

1. Hendaye, on the French side of the Bidassoa estuary.

the Battle of San Marcial. The former took place on the morning of 31 August much as Vandeleur describes, although the story of the explosion seems to have become somewhat exaggerated – in fact, it was a French ammunition store that exploded, apparently by an accident rather than through British fire. Whilst this explosion killed or wounded at least sixty of the defenders, and served as a final straw to break their resolve, the truly decisive moment had already passed – apparently un-noted by Vandeleur – when Sir Thomas Graham ordered his siege guns to reopen fire on the breach, directly over the heads of the attacking troops. This risky stratagem swept the French from the walls and allowed the attackers to gain a foothold, thus rejuvenating a stalled attack. Nevertheless, allied casualties were heavy – amounting to 856 killed and 1,416 wounded – and the survivors of French garrison were able to retreat into the castle, which held out for a further week. The storm coincided with a final French attempt to relieve the fortress, which was defeated in a series of actions fought on the same day along the line of the Bidassoa. Most significantly, the Battle of San Marcial saw the Spanish fight and win a solo combat for the first time in five years, satisfactorily demonstrating the regeneration of that nation's forces under Wellington's direction during the previous twelve months.[1]

Otherwise, most of Vandeleur's news is relatively commonplace – though no less interesting for it – relating primarily to his daily itinerary and preparations for the winter. Vandeleur's proposed unofficial alterations to his uniform are quite in keeping with the attitude of most Peninsular officers, who took their cue from Wellington's stated preference that his officers 'might be rigged out in all the colours of the rainbow if we fancied it'. This indulgence ensured 'that scarcely any two officers were dressed alike! Some with grey braided coats, others with brown; some again liked blue; while many from choice, or perhaps necessity,

1. Oman, *Peninsular War*, Vol. VII, pp. 1–62, 529–30.

stuck to the "old red rag".[1] The results, to be sure, were considered ludicrous by some observers, but generally – as with Vandeleur's modifications – followed practicality rather than fashion.

Ernani, Oct. 3rd 1813[2]

My Dear Mother,

I have received your kind letter dated the 13th Sept., in which I am happy to hear that my father has got a cure from Genl. Morrison.[3] I wish he would cure some of our people in the Peninsula without medicine, and upon the same cheap terms. There is no cure for it but plenty of bark.[4] Thank God I am quite well, and I have not had the slightest attack since the time I mentioned in my former letter.

We are still in the same position, which is considerably strengthened by constructing redoubts upon every hill, and connecting the whole by breastworks. There is a great talk of moving across the river; if so, there will be some wigs on the green,[5] for the country is very strong.

I am very glad to hear that you have met with so much civility at Weymouth. The Willis's were always very polite to the officers of the depôts, but the poor girls were quizzed sadly, they went by the names of Dory Ann, Hatchet Fan, Spapes, etc.; nevertheless they are very nice sort of girls.[6]

---

1. Grattan, William, *Adventures with the Connaught Rangers 1809–1814*, London, Greenhill, 2003, pp. 50–1.
2. In the original text, pp. 125–9.
3. Lt. General Edward Morrison, Governor of Jamaica 1811–13.
4. Chinchona, or Jesuit's Bark – a source of quinine.
5. That is to say, casualties.
6. The nicknames are evidently rather cruel – the first two, and 'Hatchet Fan' in particular, suggesting a rather angular visage on the part of the young ladies in question – but 'Spapes' is a word of which the editor has found no other occurrence, and may represent a mistranscription. Judging by the first two nicknames, however, it may safely be assumed that whatever name was bestowed on the last of the Willis girls was no more complementary than that given to her two sisters.

You mentioned a wish for me to go to England this winter. I had some wish at one time, but upon reflection, I think I had better defer my visit, as it is so difficult for a man to tear himself away from his home and get back to his regt. on time. Besides, my stay would be so very short, that it would not be worth while. I have secured a way of getting my things from England, whenever you will be so kind as to send them. I have got acquainted with a very respectable Spanish merchant, who occupies a great deal of land in this neighbourhood; he speaks English very well: his father was an Irishman, his name Birmingham. He has been so kind as to promise to secure any parcel that comes, and to keep it in his house until I can send for it at Passages. We are quartered at a short distance from it. If you send the things to Gibson, he will see them embarked in the Thames, or thro' his agent at Portsmouth or Falmouth, and by letting me know in what ship the things are embarked, I can give my friend notice, and he can secure them accordingly. I will give you a list of what I want, you will see by it what a way I am in.

I have got my hussar saddle in very good preservation, with the exception of girths, etc. Ratler is so fat I am obliged to borrow a pair from the genl. The things I am in want of are:- a plain saddle with holsters; a plain curb-bridle; a regimental bridle; mounting for my present one; that is, new leather; a new crupper, a new breastplate, two circingles,[1] extra girths, and a regimental valise for a hussar saddle; a regimental sheepskin; a staff do. for Genl. Vandeleur; new pattern regimental cloth shabrack; two regimental collars; two strong common do. for stable; epaulettes, cloth and buttons to make a jacket of the new pattern; lace, cloth, and buttons to make up a jacket of the old pattern; 3 yds. grey cloth, sufficient to make two pairs of overalls, 1½ blue cloth for an evening pair; buff cloth sufficient to make two waistcoats, with buttons and trimmings. These things you had better desire Soloman to send to Gibson, in order to have them packed up with the saddlery, but make Gibson give a receipt for the things, otherwise Soloman will never send them, for he is rascal enough to do a thing of that kind.

---

1. A misspelling of surcingles; an item of horse tack used, amongst other things, for fitting pack saddles.

Capt. Webb of the 12th is going home.[1] The Genl. bought one [of his horses] and I have bought the other at 65 guineas. Enclosed is a bill for £30, which I got for a country horse that did not answer, this will more than cover the 15 more which the horse cost me. At the same time you will tell my father how sensible I am of all his kindness, which I hope he will never have cause to repent placing on me. There is nothing in the above but what is absolutely necessary. I am now 15 months in the country and 3 in England in which time I have never had more jackets than I started with. If my father has not subscribed to the erection of the triumphal pillar to Lord Wellington, tell him he certainly ought. This is the opinion of the Genl. who has subscribed £10. I have drawn the bill for the accommodation of Webb, in two parts. One to Mr. Dowbiggan [Dowbiggen].

The way I would wish the parcels to be directed is – Lieut. Vandeleur, 12th Light Dragoons, to the care of Mr. Birmingham, Merchant, Passages, Spain. Pray be as expeditious as possible, as the uncertainty of our stay so near this port is of consequence. Give my love to my dear father and the family. The Genl. is in excellent health, I never knew him better. I am happy to add, Armstrong is quite recovered.

Your most dutiful and affectionate son.
John Vandeleur

This goes under cover to the Quarter-Master-General

The cure that Vandeleur's father obtained, and which he himself seems to have benefited from in combating his own bout of ague, was at this date the most effective remedy for fevers of all sorts. Quinine, derived from cinchona bark, was employed primarily for cases of malaria, as opposed to other forms of fever which were treated with a variety of measures including bleeding, purging, and some decidedly dubious concoctions of herbs, drugs, and alcohol. These practices were developed in the West Indies, that graveyard of British soldiers, and it was no doubt from his

1. Captain William Webb; see p. 93.

time on Jamaica that General Morrison acquired the familiarity with them that enabled him to aid Vandeleur's father. However, malaria was also endemic in much of Spain and Portugal, and so similar treatments were required for troops under Wellington's command. Under ideal circumstances, between one and one and a half ounces of powdered bark were to be given upon signs of the onset of fever, administered as a tincture dissolved in wine or some other liquid, with smaller quantities in the intervals between attacks.[1]

Medical concerns aside, it is telling – if not particularly surprising – to see that a resumption of letters from home was variously accompanied by a renewed resolve to see things through in the Peninsula, a disappearance of homesickness, and a renewed demand for financial and material support. This last, in particular, helps confirm a number of the details of the uniform of light dragoon officers at this time, including the adoption of both blue and grey overalls: the former served to replace the white britches that were worn for full-dress at home. If the brown overalls mentioned by Vandeleur in his letter of Christmas Day 1812 were ever issued, they had evidently been suppressed by this date. The reference to requiring materials for a 'jacket of the old pattern' is also interesting, confirming that items from the pre-1812 uniform were still being worn long after it had officially been superseded – something that is also evidenced in the transitional attire worn in some portraits of this era.[2] It is also significant that Vandeleur was quite happy to order the raw materials only, suggesting that regimental tailors were well able to undertake the actual construction of these garments.

---

1. Howard, Dr Martin, *Wellington's Doctors: The British Army Medical Services in the Napoleonic Wars*, pp. 191–6.
2. The evolution of light dragoon uniforms is detailed in Fosten, Brian, *Wellington's Light Cavalry*.

Camp near Hendaye, Oct. 17th 1813[1]

My Dear Mother,

You have heard ere this that we are in France, altho' not very far. We passed the river on the morning of the 7th, and completely surprised the enemy. On the evening, previous to dinner, we got the order to march at 11 o'clock that night and assemble in front of the artillery at Onzarzun,[2] where we took our place in the rear of the 1st division (as it was an infantry business). We then commenced our march to Irun. Two miles before we arrived, the 5th division, with Genl. Wilson's Brigade of Portuguese,[3] took the left hand road to Fuente Rabia, where they crossed the river in 3 columns, drove back the right flank of the enemy, and by that movement forced them to abandon the position which their left occupied near the bridge. This was of the greatest consequence, as the ford by which we were to cross was completely commanded by a battery which they had constructed on a hill over the bridge. The moment the 1st division appeared on the Yrun [*sic*] side of the ford, the enemy retired to a position a mile in the rear of the former, from which they were quickly dislodged. This position we occupied where we still are all in camp.

The forage is all consumed. We are the only dragoon regt. up here. We have been doing duty for some time. All the rest of the cavalry are up to their bellies in fine hay and straw, doing nothing, as far back as Pampeluna, but Col. Ponsonby is such a man that he is never quiet unless we are in the middle of everything. All the inhabitants have fled from their houses, which are stripped of every article of furniture, and their doors, windows, etc., all broke by the Spanish peasantry, who assembled before we crossed, armed with old fire-locks, etc., men, women, and children, and made a most desperate sally into France,

1. In the original text, pp. 129–33.
2. Oiartzun, roughly equidistant between San Sebastián and Irun.
3. Brevet Colonel John Wilson, Royal York Rangers (previously Loyal Lusitanian Legion, and before that 97th Foot), seconded to the Portuguese service and commanding the brigade formerly under Pack, composed of the 1º and 16º Infantaria and the 4º Caçadores. Wilson was wounded in the course of this fighting; see Oman, *Wellington's Army*, p. 371.

and plundered and destroyed everything in less than an hour. Every body is in camp at present except a few such as staff people. The Genl. has a house, or rather hovel, near the camp, and a stable which holds all his horses, mine, and Armstrong's. I live in my tent, which is better than being in a dirty house. I lined it with baize, which makes it very warm at night, and prevents the scorching sun piercing thro' the canvas by day. The weather has been very warm, and even now sometime it is very hot in the day time, but the nights are excessively cold.

Lord Wellington, I suppose, will advance as far as St. Jean de Luce, which is about two leagues from here, and there I expect we shall winter. There is great talk of Pampeluna soon falling. Now that we are again on outpost duty, the Genl. has quite a new and regular method of living. He gets up every morning at 4 o'clock, mounts his horse, and rides up to the picquets, which he generally reaches a little before daylight; he visits all the chain of outposts, and gets home about 8 o'clock. We breakfast then, and after breakfast he mounts again and takes a ride to get an appetite for his dinner. He generally canters about 5 or 6 leagues. He dines at 7; he generally has two friends, or officers of the brigade, to dine with him, so that he sits down about 6 people every day. He smokes his pipe after dinner, takes his coffee, and goes to bed about ½ past 8 or 9 o'clock.

Did you receive my last letter from Ernani? I have made up my mind not to go home this winter, as I think there may be something to do; besides, if I get these clothes, etc., which I wrote for, I think I had better stay and take care of the Genl.'s horses and baggage in case he goes. I have no further news to communicate. I hope the things are sent, as the winter is coming on, at which time it would be most disagreeable to go naked. Send me some gloves, if not too late.

Now that you are returned home, I may hear from you a little oftener, as you will have more spare time on your hands. Give my affectionate love to my father. I hope the journey back from Weymouth has not injured him. The man who made my bed and canteens – Thompson & Strachan – has sent an agent to this country for the purpose of collecting his debts. Amongst other people, he sent me a bill for the canteens, etc., which I, of course, refused to pay as I conceived you had already settled with him.

God bless you, my dear mother. Pray write a little oftener.

Your very affectionate son.
John Vandeleur

The fighting to which Vandeleur refers here is the opposed crossing of the Bidassoa, carried out on 7 October 1813. In consequence of the successful passage of the river, Wellington was then able to establish himself on the French bank, and drive Soult from the defensive positions overlooking it. Although it was mostly infantry work, the troopers of the 12th and 16th Light Dragoons were under fire during these operations, and some losses were incurred to artillery fire.[1] After this initial push, however, Wellington again rested his forces for a time, with the consequent return – for the 12th, at least – to the outpost duty described by Vandeleur. Whilst his account tells us little of what regimental duty was like at this time, the insight into the routine of the brigade commander is again interesting. William Hay, still serving as a troop officer with the 12th, had a harder time of things, remarking that officers and men alike 'were nearly starved to death with cold; and our nags were only kept alive by eating chopped whins'. However, Hay also recollected that, with the French being in similar straits so far as the weather and supply situation were concerned, a 'tacit understanding' developed between the opposing picquets and vedettes so that neither side needlessly brought on a fight.[2] This situation could not go on indefinitely though, for, with Napoleon defeated at Leipzig and a potential end to the war in sight, Wellington was again preparing for an advance.

1. Oman, *Peninsular War*, Vol. VII, pp. 110–36; Hay, *Reminiscences*, pp. 124–6.
2. Hay, *Reminiscences*, pp. 126–7.

Chateau de Jeanlais, Near St Jean de Luce,
Dec. 12th 1813[1]

My Dear Mother,

I take this moment of quietness advantageously by writing a few lines, merely to satisfy you, and to say I am unhurt. We have had hard fighting for three successive days without intermission, and, I am afraid, have lost many men on both sides. I have had a horse shot under me, so had Armstrong; the Genl.'s orderly was shot thro' the neck, and how we escaped all being wounded God only knows.

We commenced on the 9th at daylight by advancing rapidly and driving in their advanced posts. We followed it up, and fought every inch of the way to Bayonne, in front of which they took up a position in the rear of some batteries which they had previously constructed, from which it was not possible to move them. Unfortunately the ground, we held was so weak that it was judged expedient for us to retreat during the night to our old position which was effected most cleverly, without losing a man. We patrolled during the night nearly as far as Bayonne, and found them in motion about 4 o'clock on the following morning. They came back to their former post, and actually attacked us on the same ground that we had advanced from the day before. They came down in great force and drove in the picquets of the light divisions, which were on our right; they then came down on the left column, but were stopped by the picquets, who behaved very well. The French brought up guns and used every effort, but could not move until nearly 4 o'clock, when they succeeded in driving in the infantry skirmishers pell-mell on top of the cavalry and artillery. Everybody then rode forward and exerted themselves to get the infantry on.

At this unfortunate moment, while I was endeavouring to rally the infantry, my horse was shot through the lungs. The enemy were coming on fast, and I had to run as hard as my legs would carry me to avoid being taken. I ran to the 16th Drgs. and got a troop horse and returned to the fight. I met Armstrong on foot, whose horse had been

1. In the original text, pp. 134–8; the location is in fact near St-Jean-de-Luz.

shot dead; he was going for a troop-horse also. I joined the Genl., who by this time had succeeded in getting the infantry and the picquets of the 16th Dragoons to charge, which turned the scale, and everything was going well; but the fire was very hot and lively. Unfortunately, the Genl.'s orderly, who was close to us, was knocked down by a ball thro' his neck; he is still alive, but I am afraid he will not survive it. The Genl. was extremely fortunate; the first day his horse got a graze, but it did no harm.

But to return to my despatch. The fighting continued extremely hard until night put an end to it. Both parties remained in *statu quo* until next morn, the 11th. Daylight was cheered by the roaring of French cannon and musketry. They made several desperate attempts, but failed every time. At 2 o'clock fire became very slack; but at 3 they came down with the bayonet, shouting and drumming. The Portuguese gave way, and there was general disorder for some minutes. The Genl., with great presence of mind, took his small picquet to the rear of the fugitives and charged them and beat them most unmercifully until we made them stop, and again advance. Supported by the British they regained their ground and, as before, night put a stop to the proceedings.

I forgot to mention that on the 9th Genl. Hill crossed the river with 3 divisions. The absence of these divisions weakened us so much that they thought they could drive us back, and consequently brought 9 divisions against our little force, which only consisted of 2 divisions and 2 brigades; but at night we were strengthened by 2 divisions more. I hear a great deal of firing to our right; I suppose they are trying Genl. Hill's people.

The horse I lost was a very fine mare, which I bought for 45 guineas. I got her very cheap, as she was very wicked, and the man I got her from could not ride her. I hope Government will allow me something for her. An officer of the 15th lost his horse on the 23rd Oct. in the retreat from Burgos.[1] Government have not yet paid him. My other horse will

1. Either there has been a minor error of transcription, or Vandeleur is confusing things here. The 15th Hussars were not in the Burgos retreat, nor were they in proximity to him at the time of writing. Possibly 15th should read 16th, for the 16th Light Dragoons, which makes sense in both contexts.

not be fit to work for two or three months yet, which was the reason I bought this mare. How fortunate it was not Ratler. You must excuse any incorrectness, as I am much hurried. I have not heard of my boxes yet. Give my love to my dear Father and the family.

> Your ever dear son,
> John Vandeleur

The weather is terribly cold, and all the mountains are covered in snow.

Wellington did not advance again until 10 November, when he launched the series of offensives collectively known as the Battle of the Nivelle. Having taken time to prepare his dispositions, Wellington was able to overwhelm Soult's new defensive line and tumble the French back towards Bayonne with the loss of over 4,000 men. Bayonne, on the River Adour, was the main base for Soult's army, and the river provided a good defensive barrier. Further complicating matters for a further allied advance was the fact that the River Nive ran northwards to join the Adour at Bayonne, leaving Wellington with the unenviable choice of either confining his offensive to the narrow strip of land between the Nive and the sea, or else dividing his army and advancing on both banks of the Nive, with only limited means of communication between the two wings. Again, careful preparation and planning was required to ensure that a further advance could be made with a good chance of success, and it was not until the second week of December that Wellington was ready to begin his new offensive. This led to the twin battles of the Nive and of St-Pierre, fought between 9 and 13 December 1813, vividly described in the above letter and the one that follows it.

Vandeleur's Brigade had remained part of the Left Wing of Wellington's army, coming now under the overall command of Lieutenant General Sir John Hope since Sir Thomas Graham had been required to return to Britain due to the state of his health. As well as the cavalry, Hope's command for this action consisted of the First, Fifth, and Light Divisions of infantry and three independent infantry brigades, two Portuguese and one British. Hope's objective was to draw off Soult's attention by advancing between the Nive and the sea, allowing the army's Right Wing under Sir Rowland Hill to cross the Nive and establish itself on the eastern bank. Operations were set in motion on the morning of 9 December, with Hope pushing his feint attack almost to the defences of Bayonne itself. However, since the ground that had been taken could not be held, Hope ordered a withdrawal; due to some confusion, a portion of his troops retired all the way back to their starting positions near St-Jean-de-Luz, leading to the disjointed response that Vandeleur describes when Soult launched his counterattack on the 10th. By attacking Hope rather than Hill, Soult sought to turn Wellington's plan against him, and initial French success seemed to indicate that this strategy was proving effective. Part of the Fifth Division eventually began to buckle under the French pressure, leading to the dramatic scenes described in the letter, before the arrival of the First Division stabilized the situation and drove the French back.

The following day, Soult tried again but to even less effect; the only significant French success seems to have been the temporary discomfiture of the Portuguese infantry brigade under Colonel de Rego Barreto, part of the Fifth Division, whose fugitives were rallied by Major General Vandeleur as described above. Thus checked, Soult now elected to try and make use of the one advantage remaining to him: namely the fact that control of the bridges in Bayonne itself allowed him to send troops from one bank of the Nive to the other far more quickly than Wellington could. During the night of 12–13 December, Soult passed a sizeable body of troops through the town so as to build up his strength east of the Nive, preparatory to mounting an offensive that is sometimes treated as part of the main action and sometimes dignified by the distinct appellation of the Battle of St-Pierre. In all events, and whatever name one chooses to use, Vandeleur was entirely correct in his closing supposition that the outbreak of firing audible to the right indicated a French attack on Hill.[1]

Chateau de Jeanlais, Near St Jean de Luce,
Dec. 19th 1813[2]

My Dear Mother,

I am sure you have most anxiously awaited this letter, as you have read of all our fighting lately. When I wrote my last letter I informed you of Marshal Soult's going off to try Sir Rowland Hill who commands the right flank of our army. Soult attacked with great fury our allies, the Portuguese, who received them with tremendous coolness, gave them a most tremendous fire, and drove them back with the bayonet. The French next tried my former brigade, the 50th, 71st, and 92nd, who withstood all their attempts, and repeatedly charged them with the bayonet, and succeeded in driving them back with great loss. The 71st and 92nd lost an immense number of men and officers; the former, I am sorry to say, not less than 10 officers, [and] their Colonel, McKenzie.[3] The number of men I do not know, but more than half. I am concerned to say that our worthy friend Southwell was taken prisoner with Major Brotherton, 14th Light Drgs. and 15 men.[4] Southwell has been heard of; he is perfectly well. Some say the major is wounded, but it is not ascertained.

They say the British loss on that day alone was 1000 men, and the French about 4000, but I know that our loss was much more, for I have myself seen upwards of 2000 British wounded. The French loss must have been treble ours, for they were most gloriously beaten. I do not think the French Marshal will try us again. He had nearly the whole of his army opposed to the left column, Sir John Hope, for the first three

1. Oman, *Peninsular War*, pp. 209–61.
2. In the original text, pp. 138–43.
3. Brevet Lt. Colonel Maxwell McKenzie, 1/71st. His Peninsular service with the battalion, from May 1811, did not coincide with Vandeleur's, but they no doubt knew one another from service at home.
4. Major Thomas William Brotherton and Lieutenant Hon. Arthur Francis Southwell, both of the 14th Light Dragoons. See commentary.

days; he found he could not manage us. He then went to Sir R. Hill, where he got most terribly handled.

The same night that this victory was obtained, our regt. got an order to march at 8 o'clock to Cambo,[1] which is on the right, but rather in the rear of the position. The distance was about 16 miles, but the state of the road was so excessively bad, that we could not arrive until 12 next morning, altho' we marched all night, which unfortunately was both dark and stormy. The reason of this sudden march was on account of an unexpected force of a brigade of cavalry, and a brigade of infantry, commanded by the Genl. of Cavalry, Paris,[2] appearing at Hespasem,[3] which is rather in the rear of Genl. Hill's right, therefore to prevent these fellows from doing any mischief the 1st Hussars, 18th do.,[4] and our regt. were ordered to that place, with a small force of Spanish infantry. Our regt. was sent there merely for fear of anything until the English Hussar Brigade, Lord Somerset's, the 10th, 7th, and 15th were sent for.[5] They came up yesterday morning in beautiful condition, and well they might, for since they came into the country, they have been fed with English Hay and never done a day's duty.

Since the 12th have been in this country they have always had the out-post duty of that part of the army which they were attached to, and never were quartered in the rear of the army to regain their condition except last winter, when every man in the army was in quiet quarters at a great distance from the enemy. We can boast of what no regt. in the army can, except the ones that came out the other day, that we never lost a single man by surprise, not a picquet or patrole has ever

---

1. Cambo-les-Bains, on the Nive twelve miles south-southeast of Bayonne.
2. Général de Brigade Marie-Auguste Paris.
3. Hasparren, six miles northeast of Cambo-les-Bains.
4. 18th Hussars and 1st KGL Hussars, together forming the brigade of Major General Victor von Alten.
5. Major General Lord Edward Somerset had replaced Grant as commander of the Hussar Brigade when the cavalry had been reorganized after Vitoria. The 7th Hussars, the last new cavalry regiment to join Wellington's command, had arrived in September replacing the 18th transferred to Alten's Brigade in July. See Oman, *Wellington's Army*, p. 367.

been taken, nor a man deserted or even tried by a Genl. Court Martial.

I am afraid your correspondent, who told you a story about nuns, is rather partial to drawing a long bow.[1] I have just been looking for a letter about money and accounts, but I cannot spare time to find it. In my next I will answer it more fully. I have sent a return of my mare to Lord Wellington. I expect to get £36 for her in the course of time, but a very long time, perhaps two or three years hence or perhaps two or three weeks.

You say in one of your letters 'you must be rich.' If Government would give me the 7 months' pay they owe me, perhaps I might. You also say 'your father has made you so many presents'. I am and ought to be very thankful, but I am sure it never was my father's intention to have them charged against my little income as Mr. Stewart has done.[2] Consider all the wear and tear of baggage, animals, and horses in this country, everything so excessively dear, the enormous sum I am obliged to pay to get a bill cashed, the expense of servants, washing, shoeing horses, etc., etc. Government very liberally takes off the 8½d per horse in this country, but they impose a new sum of 1s per day for rations for a Portuguese servant and myself. Forage is so scarce now that I feed my horses on potatoes. We get corn, but no hay nor straw of any description. How can a man be rich? However, poverty is no crime, and I hate to hear people complain. I have my horses, Ratler and Taffy, fat; I have a horse in farcy, from which I will not be able to recover

1. That is to say, exaggerating. It is unclear what this story refers to, although see pp. 88–9 for commentary on nuns. Stewart, *XII Royal Lancers*, pp. 37, 89, suggests that this may be the origins of the regimental tradition of playing a selection of hymns at watch-setting, one version of this legend stating that this practice was originally ordered as penance for men of the regiment forcibly entering – in some accounts, plundering – a convent. In that such a whimsical punishment hardly fits the nature of the alleged crime, it seems more likely that the hymn-playing tradition in fact stems from a papal audience granted to some officers of the regiment in 1794.
2. The identity of 'Mr. Stewart' is unclear, presumably the family's banker, or an associate thereof, although this does beg the question of why Stewart and not Wakeman, who was dealing with such matters in 1811.

him for some time, perhaps never.[1] I have been very unfortunate in my horses; however, notwithstanding all, there is no reason to complain very much; I owe nobody a guinea, and I am as happy as I ever was. The boxes which you sent, as ill luck would have it, are gone to Bilbao, but I hope not landed there, as the fleet are ordered back to Passages, but the wind and sea is now so high, that I doubt much whether they can put to sea.

Give my love to my dear father and family, never will he enjoy health as long as he is living in that marsh at Barbourne. I wish you could persuade him to move. Everything is quiet; the weather is very bad, and a great part of the troops are in camp. Your ever affectionate son,

John Vandeleur

Pray write a little oftener. Remember the packet sails once a week; you seem to have forgotten that it sails so often. J. V.

Picking up the narrative where the previous letter left off, Vandeleur begins by completing the story of the fighting around Bayonne. Wellington's response to Soult's attack on Hill was complicated by two things. The first of these was the fact that the allied pontoon bridge across the Nive had been swept away, preventing the troops on the western bank from immediately reinforcing those on the east; until the bridge could be repaired, or troops complete the twenty-mile round trip via the ford at Cambo-les-Bains, Hill was on his own. In the event, however, Hill was able to defeat the French with the resources that he had at hand, although not without heavy casualties of which those that Vandeleur relates from his own old infantry brigade were entirely typical. The second problem, and the one that most directly affected Vandeleur, was the appearance of fresh French troops in the allied right-rear. Vandeleur conflates them into a single entity, but in fact there were two distinct forces: a division

1. A highly infectious skin condition, related to glanders. See commentary.

of light cavalry under Général de Division Pierre Soult, brother of the marshal, and an infantry brigade under Général de Brigade Marie-Auguste Paris. Troops of the former were responsible for the fight at Hasparren in which the 14th had two of its officers taken captive, along with a sergeant and a private of the same regiment. Brotherton was indeed wounded, multiple times in fact, and his account of his experiences is reproduced as Appendix II. Paris's troops, meanwhile, engaged the Spanish division of Teniente General Pablo Morillo, which had been covering Hill's far right flank.[1]

Neither of these movements caused any significant disruption to the allied operations, although the upset to the 14th was a cause of some embarrassment. Nevertheless, the defeat of Brotherton's small party was but a minor setback; the shifting of additional cavalry to oppose the French movements was essentially a precautionary measure only, and there was never any significant threat. For Vandeleur these movements did allow a comparison between the veteran 12th and the newly arrived hussars, in which – not surprisingly – he came out ringingly in favour of the former. Vandeleur's boast about the 12th never having lost a man was, however, true only for the duration of his own service with the regiment. Like many units newly deployed to the Peninsula, the 12th underwent something of a steep learning curve upon first arriving in Portugal, having several men taken prisoner whilst on outpost duty during the fighting at Aldea de Ponte in September 1811, and later having a picquet surprised and nearly overrun at Castel Piones during the covering operations for the siege of Burgos a year later. Additionally, a total of six men deserted during the regiment's first few months on active service; nevertheless, there was some justification in Vandeleur's sense of superiority over the hussars, who were still in the midst of a similar learning curve of their own.[2]

---

1. Oman, *Peninsular War*, Vol. VII, pp. 262–81.
2. For which, see Bamford, *Sickness, Suffering, and the Sword*, pp. 284–5.

The vexed issue of finances seems to have caused a minor familial rift at this point, judging by the rather defensive tone of the later part of this letter. The problems inherent in officers keeping themselves equipped on service have already been alluded to, but Vandeleur does seem to have got himself into an unfortunate situation with respect to his horses. Whilst Ratler and Taffy had both evidently proved themselves reliable mounts, his attempts to keep a larger stable may have caused him to overstretch himself, a situation made worse by ill-luck. To lose a horse in battle, as Vandeleur did at the Nive, was an event for which he could expect to receive compensation, albeit at some unspecified time in the future when the claim had been processed. However, this misfortune was then compounded by having a second horse – which, along with the healthy Ratler and Taffy, implies a stable of four having been kept up – come down with farcy. Caused by the bacteria *Burkholderia mallei*, this highly contagious condition and the related complaint of glanders – both still notifiable diseases today – were two of the biggest killers of military horses during this era. Glanders, possibly the worse of the two if only because the symptoms were less obvious until the disease had really taken hold, affected the lungs and nasal passages, whilst farcy affected the skin.[1] Although some veterinary surgeons claimed cures – possibly as a result of misdiagnoses of conditions with similar symptoms – there was no effective treatment and infected animals were generally destroyed to limit contagion. Therefore, Vandeleur's best chance of making good his loss here was if the animal was ordered to be shot to prevent the spread of infection, in which case he might expect – again, in due course once a claim had been processed – to receive official compensation.

---

1. See Department of Environment, Food, and Rural Affairs, 'Glanders and Farcy', at http://www.defra.gov.uk/ahvla-en/disease-control/notifiable/glanders-farcy/.

Dax, 6th March 1814[1]

My Dear Mother,

You will be surprised to hear our recent movements (provided you have not already heard them in the English papers). Lord Wellington has executed one of the cleverest movements that ever was recorded in history. His passage of the Adour will ever be considered by military men who have studied their profession as a most masterly piece of generalship. It was affected without losing a man by land, altho', I am sorry to say, we lost some seamen.

Two days before we crossed, Lord Wellington moved the whole almost of his troops toward the right, making Soult believe he intended crossing the river high up. In the meantime, he moved up all the Spaniards, and put them immediately in front of Bayonne and commanded a feint attack on the entrenched camp. During the operation the 1st division and our brigade, which had marched in the middle of the night toward the mouth of the Adour, escorting a number of boats, which were placed on carriages etc., succeeded in putting the boats into the river while it was dark, and landing about 500 of the Guards, two guns, and a squadron of the 12th Dragoons, before we were discovered. There were a number of large boats, which had come from St. Jean de Luce, for the purpose of making a bridge, that attempted to get in, but I am sorry to say that from the tremendous surf that several of them were upset and a number of our gallant fellows drowned.

During the night the French came down on us in great force. We saw the danger; we had no other retreat than death by drowning, therefore the handful of brave men over the river, amounting to about 500 Guards, infantry, and about 160 drgs. of the 12th, withstood about 4000 men. In the dark we were obliged to fight a desperate game, which fortunately succeeded. We made so good a resistance that the enemy thought that we had a very strong force across the river, and therefore retired, and let us alone for that night. We worked hard all

1. In the original text, pp. 143–8; the town of Dax is situated thirty miles northeast of Bayonne.

night and got about 1000 men across the river. They never molested us after. Fortunately the weather became calm, and the whole of our boats got into the river, and we have now established a most wonderful bridge 500 yards long in a river that is almost as tempestuous as a sea. We were obliged to swim our horses across, carrying the men and saddles in the boats.

The French have retired in every direction. Lord Wellington had an affair with them at Orthes,[1] in which he took 8 pieces of cannon and 700 prisoners. Lord March, his A.D.-Camp, is shot thro' the body.[2] I don't know whether he will live or not. Genl. Ross is wounded.[3] I heard last night from a peasant that Lord Wellington had an affair with them at Grenade in which he took all their artillery and baggage, but I am afraid my friend was too sanguine. I have no doubt but that Lord Wellington beat them well, but I doubt whether the advantages are quite so numerous.[4]

The left column, to which we are attached, are blockading the citadel of Bayonne, which is on this side of the river. The French people have received us with the greatest good nature and hospitality. We have been living for three days at the Maire's house at Dax, where I have enjoyed every luxury possible, sleeping in feather beds, fresh butter for breakfast, fireplaces in the rooms, mangers in the stables, beautiful hay for my horse, in fact I am afraid I shall be spoiled for a soldier if I live much longer in this way.

1. The Battle of Orthez, fought on 27 February 1814, which saw Wellington again defeat Soult in the open field.
2. Captain Charles Lennox, Earl of March, 52nd Light Infantry, extra ADC to Wellington for most of the Peninsular War, but when wounded as Orthez was serving as a volunteer with his own regiment. He was shot in the chest by a musket ball, which was never removed, but nevertheless was able subsequently to take home Wellington's victory despatch after the battle. ADC to the Prince of Orange at Waterloo, and in 1819 succeeded his father as Duke of Richmond.
3. Major General Robert Ross, commanding a brigade in the Fourth Division. Upon his recovery, received a command in the American War; victorious at Bladensburg but then killed in action before Baltimore.
4. Grenade is north of Toulouse, but there was no fighting there. Possibly a garbled account of one of the smaller actions fought around this time.

Our brigade has been most unfortunate in being obliged to remain with the left column, which I suppose will be left here some time. All the heavy dragoons are ordered up from the rear. Our only chance is that some of them will be stopped here instead of us. I have my horses in good condition, therefore I don't wish to remain idle in this place. Marshal Beresford with 3 divisions has got between Soult and Bordeau [Bordeaux], therefore he is obliged to retire on Toulouse.

I am glad to find my father has determined to quit Worcester. I was exceedingly concerned to hear of the death of my poor grandmother. Her illness was very short. It was very unfortunate you did not get intelligence sooner of her illness, as it would have been very gratifying to you to have attended her during her last moments. Mrs. James's son is going home on promotion.[1] He will be able to give you an exact account of my health, appearance, etc., which I am sure will please you. I frequently see Elton, who never fails enquiring in the most friendly manner after you and my father.[2] I have seen West who has improved for the better,[3] also Rivers who has just come out here.[4]

In case of a peace, I mean to apply for a leave of absence to remain a year in France, to study the language more correctly. I shall go into the interior, where I shall have no chance of meeting an Englishman. Pray is there a talk of a peace in England? Excuse me, I must conclude and go to

1. There were several officers with the surname James serving in the Peninsula at this time, but the only one to have been recently promoted was First Lieutenant George James, Royal Artillery, who had obtained that step in rank the previous October. He does not, however, appear to have gone home so if this is the man to whom Vandeleur refers, he is error on that point. It is of course, quite conceivable that Mrs. James – presumably a neighbour in Worcester – had a son by an earlier marriage whose identity cannot therefore be established.

2. First Lieutenant Isaac Marmaduke Elton, Royal Engineers; served in the Peninsula July 1813–April 1814.

3. From the context, this was most likely First Lieutenant George J. West, Royal Engineers. As well as being mentioned in the same breath as two other engineer subalterns, he seems the most likely of all the officers with that surname then in the Peninsula to have crossed Vandeleur's path at this time, having been involved in the Adour bridging operations.

4. First Lieutenant Charles Rivers, Royal Engineers, who had arrived in the Peninsula the previous December.

bed. My love to my father, who I hope has got over the winter well, and to the rest of the family not forgetting George. How is poor William?[1]

> Your most affectionate,
> John Vandeleur

    This letter begins with an excellent account of the establishment of the famous 'bridge of boats' across the Adour estuary between Bayonne and the sea, which enabled Wellington to mount a full blockade of the town and thus deprive Soult of his main operational base. Constructed under the supervision of Lieutenant Colonel Henry Sturgeon of the Royal Staff Corps, with the cooperation of sailors from the squadron under Rear Admiral Charles Penrose, the bridge was an impressive piece of engineering, but it was not established without a fight, and, indeed, the whole operation was at risk of going awry had not Sir John Hope extemporized a crossing with his own resources once it became apparent that the boats being brought round by sea could not enter the river. The one problem with Vandeleur's version of events from a historian's point of view is that he has the first detachment of the 12th Light Dragoons crossing earlier than most other accounts would tend to suggest was the case. In that the wording of the letter is sufficiently ambiguous to render it unclear whether or not Vandeleur was himself with the party who made the first crossing, it seems most likely that he is using 'we' to describe the whole allied force, and that the misplaced chronology stems from a misunderstanding of second-hand information. Certainly, the 12th's own record of services is clear on the point that the first squadron of the regiment did not cross – swimming their horses as Vandeleur describes – until 24 February, two days after the commencement of operations. Of course, it is entirely possible that Vandeleur, with the freedom of movement allowed to an ADC, crossed earlier, did take part in the defence of the bridgehead, and is describing

---

1. It is unclear who 'poor William' was, but judging by the next letter his prospects were not good.

things first-hand – although in that case it is hard to understand how he could have been mistaken about men from the 12th having been present so early and in such numbers.[1]

With Soult's field army no longer able to base itself on Bayonne, the French marshal was obliged to fall back to the east, leaving a division behind to reinforce the Bayonne garrison. Having also had to send substantial numbers of troops to reinforce Napoleon, who was now fighting in northern France, Soult was significantly weakened and this enabled Wellington to leave Hope's Left Wing, reinforced by Spanish troops brought up from the rear, to mask Bayonne whilst he took the rest of the army after Soult. As Vandeleur describes, Soult was defeated again at Orthez, and driven back towards Toulouse; at Bayonne, meanwhile, operations took the form of a blockade rather than a siege, and with limited French forces in the field outside the fortress, there was little for the cavalry to do. To temper the boredom that inevitably followed, however, there came increasing signs that peace was now not far off, a point emphasized by Vandeleur's request for any news from home that might support this development.

Bordeaux, 8th April 1814[2]

My Dear Mother,

I have just received your letter of the 6th March. I am very sorry to find that my poor father has been so unwell. I am certain that he will never be better as long as he continues in that house.

You have long since heard of our entrance into Bordeaux, therefore it is useless to repeat what you know already; but I will explain to you in as few words as possible what kind of place it is. It is built on the river Garonne, perfectly flat, no hills or vales in the city like Lisbon, it is built of stone like Bath. There was formerly a very strong citadel, but since the Revolution [it] has been destroyed by Bonaparte. There is a very fine cathedral, a superb theatre, and several smaller ones. The streets

1. Oman, *Peninsular War*, Vol. VII, pp. 330–40.
2. In the original text, pp. 148–52.

are very wide and most of them have an avenue of trees in the centre, with a good walk for the foot passengers. There is every convenience possible to be procured in London, with the exception of tea, coffee, and sugar. The inhabitants have evinced the greatest friendship and cordiality towards us. The Duke D'Angouleme is here.[1] We had the honour of escorting him into Bordeaux. The white flag[2] is hoist on all the old ships and churches, in fact the people have shook off the yoke, and are now able to breath freely.

The Genl. is at Dax with the 16th. I have left him for a short time to take advantage of hiring a master for the French in Bordeaux, with whom I study every morning. I can speak French with tolerable facility; having learned the idioms in England, it is not difficult as I have so much practice. I am most fortunately lodged in the house of a very clever doctor, who speaks English, Italian, German, and French. He is like a father to me, so kind and good natured. He hears me read for an hour each day, and in return I hear him with the English. One day we speak English, and another French. The Genl. talks of sending for Mrs. Vandeleur and living in Bordeaux. The society is good, and the country beautiful, and cheap, in which case when there is a peace I should like to continue here for some months to make myself perfect master of the French tongue.

You mention in your letter a wish for my procuring a coat lined with fur. I have been able to enquire about it, but I find the fur here is about treble the value that it is in England, on account of the ports being shut against all commerce with Russia, Lapland, and those countries from whence comes the fur. There is no fur to be had in France except what comes from the above places. There is some wolf fur that comes from the Pyrenees, but it is too heavy, and has a very disagreeable smell. Your best plan would be to get a number of young lamb skins, bleach them in the sun and wet them with alum water. It is the warmest and lightest fur possible. That is what we lined our pelisses with in Spain

1. Louis-Antoine de Bourbon, Duc d'Angoulême; eldest son of the Comte d'Artois, and nephew to the Bourbon claimant, Louis XVIII.
2. The white standard of the Bourbons, not flags of surrender.

when we were in the Pyrenees; however, I have bought some beautiful fur to face a pelisse for you and the two ladies, which I shall send the first opportunity.

I suppose long ere this you have had news of our entry into Bordeaux. Your two friends Ratler and Taffy are still in existence, as fat as two pigs, but as rough as possible from the cold and hard work. Poor beasts, they know me as well as I do them. If I ever get them to England, I will never part with them. Poor Taffy, who is about 3 years older than Ratler, begins to shew his work by his legs puffing. He was a cheap horse. I could get 60 guineas from him now from any officer in the regt., he is so well known. I hope my poor father is getting better, but that poor child William, my heart grieves when I think of him. I hope this war will soon be at an end, and you will see me once more ride into the gates upon old Ratler.

God bless you, my dear mother. Give my love to all.

> Your ever dear child,
> John Vandeleur

There is little here to add to this letter, which rather nicely sums up the rounding down of the war on the Biscay coast. With the Bayonne garrison apparently quiescent, the thoughts of many turned towards preparations for the peace. Thus, now that the allies had the advantage, the Duc d'Angoulême turned up to press the Bourbon claim. This placed Wellington in an awkward position, as the British government had not at this point decided on the policy to adopt as to who they would prefer to see on the French throne after the peace. However, when the Mayor of Bordeaux declared for the Bourbons, Wellington was presented with a *fait accompli* and sent a force to occupy the city, giving Angoulême a base for his attempts to further the cause of his house. Lieutenant General Lord Dalhousie was left with the Seventh Division and the 12th Light Dragoons to hold the city and pacify the surrounding area, giving Vandeleur the excuse to leave his staff duties and make the visit described above.

As Vandeleur anticipated, the end was now very close. On 10 April Wellington attacked Soult outside Toulouse, driving him from his defences but only after taking substantial losses. Two days later, with the allies now occupying Toulouse after Soult evacuated the city, news arrived of the abdication of Napoleon and the end of the war. Toulouse, then, had been an unnecessary battle, fought after the conclusion of the peace. Even more unnecessary was the sortie by the Bayonne garrison on 14 April, an action that cost 1,700 casualties, but which Vandeleur thankfully missed due to his trip to Bordeaux. In all events, though, even if it had ended on a sour note, the Peninsular War was over and Vandeleur able to return home as he had hoped and wished for.[1]

1. Oman, *Peninsular War*, Vol. VII, pp. 341–405, 433–512.

Chapter 5

The Hundred Days

~

With the Peninsular War at a close, Major General Vandeleur was appointed to oversee the overland march of the British cavalry and horse artillery from Bordeaux to the Channel ports, from where they were shipped to England. John Vandeleur accompanied him in this task as an unofficial extra ADC, and then returned to regimental duty with the 12th Light Dragoons. That part of the regiment that had returned from the Peninsula was initially posted to Hounslow, and then reunited with the depot at Dorchester. William Hay, who had been detached from the 12th during the final months of the Peninsular War to serve on the staff of Lord Dalhousie at Bordeaux, found life back at home extremely dull when he re-joined the regiment over the winter of 1814–15. It may have been as a result of similar feelings of boredom, or to follow up on his earlier stated desire to improve his French, that John Vandeleur soon applied for leave, which was granted to run from 7 October 1814 to 9 March 1815, in order to travel to Flanders.[1] Here, Major General Vandeleur was serving as commander of the Second Division of the small British force that had been sent to the Low Countries at the end of 1813, and which had taken part in the attacks on Antwerp and Bergen-op-Zoom early the following year. Now under the command of Lieutenant General the Prince of Orange, these troops were intended to show support for the United Netherlands, and help add to Britain's voice in the affairs of the region in

1. 12th Light Dragoons Monthly Returns, The National Archives, WO17/272, 288.

the negotiations then under way at Vienna to settle the political structure of post-war Europe.

John Vandeleur returned to the 12th upon expiry of his leave, just in time to be caught up in a series of policing operations as the regiment was deployed to quell riots provoked by the promulgation of the new Corn Laws. Just as these operations were coming to a close, word was received of the escape of Napoleon from Elba. This news caused the immediate redeployment of the 12th to the continent as part of the British contribution to the armies of the hastily formed Seventh Coalition. After being reviewed at Canterbury by Vandeleur's old commanding officer from the 71st, now Major General Sir Denis Pack and himself on his way to the continent to take up an infantry command, the 12th sailed from Dover to Ostend, where they disembarked on 3 April. Upon landing, they were assigned to a cavalry brigade that also comprised the 11th and 16th Light Dragoons. Initially numbered the Second, and then re-numbered the Fourth, this brigade was commanded by Major General Vandeleur, who, like Pack, had recently received a knighthood for his earlier services. Along with six other British brigades, and one of Hanoverian hussars, Major General Vandeleur's Fourth Cavalry Brigade formed part of the Cavalry Corps under the command of Lieutenant General the Earl of Uxbridge.

Rather lower down the organizational scale, Lieutenant John Vandeleur found himself again serving as a troop officer, this time in the troop of Captain Edwin W. T. Sandys. Since Sandys was one of the three senior captains in the regiment, he served in practice as commander of one of its three squadrons, leaving Vandeleur to lead the troop in action. Notwithstanding this extra responsibility, Vandeleur continued to hanker for a return to life as an ADC. He made the error, however, of conveying that desire to his family, which promptly landed both himself and the general in something of a pickle, as this first letter home explains.

Gamerage Nr Gramont, 17th May 1815[1]

My Dear Mother,

I received your letter, which delighted me very much to hear that my father was so well as to use his gig again. I was really astonished to see Robert gazetted in the 18th Hussars.[2] If you had waited a fortnight longer Tom would have got into the 51st.[3] I saw Storer about a fortnight back.[4] He is in our old quarters at Renaix.[5] He desired to be most affectionately remembered to you and my father.

I am very sorry to find by your letter that my father has written to Lord Wellington, asking to appoint me extra A.D.-Camp, because it will appear that Genl. Vandeleur, in consequence of being refused in Spain, does not choose to be under an obligation to the Duke, and that he will not condescend to ask a favour. Besides it is a thing directly contrary to the rules of the service, and to all military etiquette. By the letter the Genl. is placed in a very difficult situation. He is very angry about it. He says that Lord Wellington would never appoint a man A.D.C. to a general officer without that general first applying himself. I am convinced that my father took this step thinking it would be very advantageous to me, but it has done me infinitely more harm than good, for the consequence is that Lord W. will put the letter in his pocket and think no more about it; also that Genl. Vandeleur will never be able to ask to get me appointed. I am sorry that you wrote the letter without consulting the Genl. The only remedy now left is that he writes another

1. In the original text, pp. 153–8. Gamerage does not appear on modern maps, but Grammont (in Flemish, Geraardsbergen), is situated twenty-five miles west of Brussels and was at the centre of the area where Wellington's cavalry was cantoned.

2. Robert Vandeleur's first commission, as an ensign in the 85th Light Infantry, was gazetted 22 March 1815, but on 27 April he was appointed instead to a vacant cornetcy in the 18th Hussars.

3. Thomas Vandeleur succeeded to the ensigncy that had been vacated by his brother Robert. However, the 85th were at home, having just returned from North America, whereas the 51st Light Infantry were in Flanders.

4. Captain Richard Storer, 51st Light Infantry.

5. Renaix (Ronse in Flemish), thirteen miles west of Grammont.

letter, of which I give you the outline as the Genl. dictated for me. I was going to Brussels purposely to be presented to Lord Wellington by the Genl., which of course did not take place in consequence of the letter as it would appear a pre-meditated scheme.

Their [*sic*] is another thing that the genl. desires me to beg, that you will also desist in getting an exchange for Robert into the 5th for the present.[1] They are not on active service nor are they expected. You would injure Robert greatly by taking him from his regt. that is on service, to put him in one at home. It is the report of the day that we are to have no fighting. The French are very quiet; I cannot conceive how it will end.

Will you thank my father in my name for his kind present. I only regret that he thinks I spend my money lavishly. I dined with Richardson of the Life Guards yesterday at Nenoue.[2] He is very well and desires to be remembered to you. Lady V. is still at Ostend; she is very well, and her little family. The Genl. is in good health and so is William;[3] they desire their love. I got acquainted with young Harelock [*sic*].[4] I will get some person to write a letter to Nash in his name.[5] I remain, dear Mother, your very affectionate son,

J. Vandeleur

You must commence by complementing him on the honors he so justly gained last war, and the hopes that this will terminate equally glorious, and that my father would have paid his respects when the Duke was in England, had he not been prevented by illness.

---

1. The 5th Dragoon Guards; see commentary.
2. Cornet and Sub-Lieutenant William Stewart Richardson, 1st Life Guards. Location in fact Ninove, situated between Grammont and Brussels.
3. William Armstrong, who was again serving as ADC to Major General Vandeleur.
4. Lieutenant W. Havelock, 43rd Light Infantry, ADC to Lt. General Karl von Alten.
5. Presumably the same Nash earlier referred to as a friend of Vandeleur's.

(Copy)

My Dear Duke, I take the liberty of again writing to you to beg leave to withdraw the request I made in a former letter, which was done without the knowledge of my son, Lieut. Vandeleur, 12th Light Dragoons, who prefers serving with his reg. in the hope of being promoted. My son has had the honor to serve under your Grace, 5 campaigns in Spain and Portugal. He was dangerously wounded at the Battle of Fuentes D'Onoro, and is now nearly six years a subaltern, without any chance of preferment, unless your Grace (with who I have the honor to be connected thro' the Longford family) would be so kind as to recommend him for a troop or company, either with or without purchase, which favor shall be remembered with gratitude by your most obedient humble sert. etc. etc.

Let the letter be as short as possible . . .
I will write to De Bath in the 85th.[1] I dined in company with Sir Wm. Ponsonby,[2] at the Genl.'s the other day. He asked after my father. This, I believe, is my birthday. Send me the letter and I will deliver it myself.

Vandeleur's letter catches something of the confusion into which the British Army was thrown by the return of Napoleon. Regiments that had been in the process of winding down after the long war that had just ended, and which in some cases had been well on the way to resuming a peacetime establishment of officers and men, were now forced hurriedly to reorganize themselves for war. This did, at least, allow an opportunity for young men who had missed out on the last war to rush for a chance to distinguish themselves in the new conflict, as was the case for Vandeleur's

1. William Plunkett de Bathe, previously encountered in the Peninsula as a captain in the 94th Foot, had been one of the 'elegant extracts' transferred to the 85th Light Infantry in 1813 when the regiment's entire complement of officers was replaced en masse. Presumably the point of writing was to ask de Bathe to look out for Thomas Vandeleur.
2. The cousin of the 12th's commanding officer, now commanding the Second Cavalry Brigade, better known as the Union Brigade.

two younger brothers. There was a clear family preference – based, one assumes, on the services of the previous generation – for service in the cavalry rather than the infantry, as evidenced by John Vandeleur's own transfer from the 71st to the 12th Light Dragoons, and now seen also in Robert's move from the 85th to the 18th Hussars before he had even had a chance to join the former regiment. It is for this reason, quite apart from it also having been their father's old regiment, that it has been assumed that the reference to a mooted transfer of Thomas Vandeleur to 'the 5th' relates to the 5th Dragoon Guards. Further, Vandeleur's caution that the regiment was not expected on service could hardly relate to the 5th Foot, whose 1st Battalion was on its way to join Wellington's army, although it did not arrive until after Waterloo. As things turned out, however, Vandeleur's concerns that his parents' interference might prevent his brothers seeing action was overtaken by events. Robert, although transferring to the 18th Hussars, did not join them in Flanders, whilst the 85th Light Infantry remained at home and so Thomas was as far from the action as an ensign there than he would have been as a cornet of the 5th Dragoon Guards.

Vandeleur, of course, had cause of his own to rue parental meddling in the progress of his career, for the ill-advised attempt to intervene on his behalf with the Duke of Wellington had thoroughly backfired. That said, the whole affair, and particularly the sample letter that Vandeleur provides for his father to copy to Wellington, gives a useful insight into the world of military patronage, and the continued importance of 'interest' and family connections.

In the space of a month such concerns would suddenly become insignificant as Napoleon's Armée du Nord crossed the Netherlands frontier and the fighting of the Hundred Days began in earnest.

Camp in front of Nivelles, June 20th 1815[1]

My Dear Mother,

I write merely to inform you that we are all three safe, after one of the hottest actions that ever was fought. We have been fighting for 3 successive days, but the last was without doubt the warmest day the British troops ever saw. The cavalry have suffered very severely. The genl. was slightly grazed on the wrist by a spent ball, which fortunately has not even bruised him. My poor little mare was shot thro' the heart; she fell on my thigh, but has not hurt me. I was so pressed at the time that I was obliged to abandon my saddle, bridle, collar, valise, and cloak. The last is a great loss, as I had my dressing things and a change of everything. The loss of my cloak also is a very serious misfortune, as the nights are often very cold.

The result of the day is that we have completely beaten the French who attacked us, commanded by Bonaparte in person, taken upwards of 100 pieces of cannon, and a great number of prisoners. The loss of the British must be at least 10,000 men, the French considerably more. The 12th have lost 130 men out of 380, the 16th, 62, and the 11th, 54. Our brigade made some desperate charges. Col. Ponsonby is most desperately wounded, piked thro' the body and his arm broken by a sabre cut. We were obliged to leave him on the ground until after the battle, which finished about 11 o'clock. Immediately it was over I asked leave to go look for his body among the dead; every body said I would never find it, but I was determined to find him, and I did, but he was nearly dead. I took a canteen of water with me, which revived him a little. I got him onto a horse and got him in at 6 o'clock. I was all night looking for his body.

I am very much fatigued being continually on horse back, day and night, for these last three days. I am sure that we have not slept more than 7 or 8 hours, the whole three days. I am afraid Capt. Sandys is

---

1. In the original text, pp. 158–60.

killed,[1] Bertie[2] and Lockhart[3] are dead, Dawbiggen wounded. Our regt, behaved most nobly. We are now only two weak squadrons. Bonaparte has retired (leaving everything behind him) across the Sambre, where he is likely to remain. I have no time at present to give you a detailed account, and I am so fatigued that I can hardly see my paper. The battle was fought near Waterloo. We have advanced to Nivelles this morning, probably we shall go on a few leagues tomorrow, where I think we shall halt, when I shall write again.

> I remain, my dear mother, your affectionate son,
> John Vandeleur

As was the case after Vitoria, there are two letters covering the fighting at Waterloo. This first gives only a brief account of what had happened and the fate of the officers of the 12th. The bulk of the casualties suffered by the 12th were incurred early in the day, when they and the 16th Light Dragoons charged in order to help extricate the survivors of the British heavy cavalry who, after an initially successful charge that threw back Napoleon's first major infantry assault, had failed to rally and found themselves at risk of being destroyed by French counterattacks. The left-most squadron of the 12th was itself taken in the flank by French cavalry, and forced to retire, but the other two squadrons, along with one from the 16th, continued their attack into the heart of the French position. Vandeleur, in the centre squadron under Captain Sandys, took part in this section of the attack. The charge as a whole bought some time for the heavies to rally, but meant that the two light dragoon regiments then themselves suffered heavily in retiring. Matters were not helped by the fact that

---

1. Sandys was in fact only wounded, but dangerously so.
2. Lindsey James Bertie: cornet, 12th Light Dragoons, October 1811, lieutenant May 1812. Served in the Peninsula April 1812–April 1814; placed on half pay when the regimental establishment was reduced during the peace, returned to full pay March 1815.
3. John Elliott Lockhart: cornet, 12th Light Dragoons, April 1814.

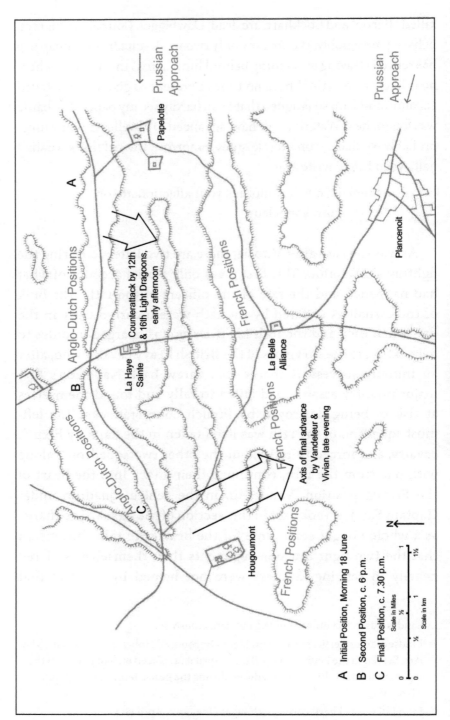

Map 3: Vandeleur at Waterloo.

Lieutenant Colonel Ponsonby was wounded whilst in the act of going to halt the advance of the right and centre squadrons. With Major Bridger also temporarily unhorsed, the regiment was left without leadership at a vital moment, which may have contributed to its losses. Ponsonby was left behind on the battlefield, and his ordeal has become one of the famous stories of Waterloo. His own account of his sufferings, which only ended when Vandeleur came and found him as described in the letter, are given in Appendix IV.[1]

Camp in Front of Cateau,
23rd June 1815. A Halt Day[2]

My Dear Mother.

I wrote to you rather in a hurry from Thinnes the day after the battle, I must give you a more detailed account of how it happened. We were marched away suddenly from our quarters on the 16th inst. At daylight the cavalry assembled at Enghien, the Infantry marched in the night, we passed them at Braine le Comte. We began to hear a heavy cannonade, which was an attack Bonaparte had made upon the Prussians at Floris [Fleurus] on our left.[3] He attacked our advanced posts at Genappes,[4] at the same time on our right with his cuirassiers, and succeeded in driving them in. Our brigade and the Hussars brigade came up at a trot, just in time to see the end of that business. We showed a front, that stopped anything further that night. Our infantry had orders to retire next morning, which they did without any

---

1. As well as eyewitness accounts from the 12th, coverage of the Waterloo campaign is summarised from Barbero, Alessandro, *The Battle: A History of the Battle of Waterloo*; Fletcher, Ian, *Galloping at Everything: The British Cavalry in the Peninsular War and at Waterloo 1808–15. A Reappraisal*, pp. 221–78; Fortescue, Hon. J. W., *A History of the British Army*, Vol. X, pp. 256–438; Hofschröer, Peter, *1815: The Waterloo Campaign*. I am also grateful to Paul L. Dawson for sharing his as-yet-unpublished research into the cavalry action at Waterloo.

2. In the original text, pp. 160–5; location in fact Le Cateau-Cambrésis.

3. In fact Fleurus; Vandeleur is here referring to the Battle of Ligny.

4. Vandeleur is here describing the fighting at Quatre Bras, which battlefield is in fact located three miles south of Genappe.

loss. The cavalry were drawn out in two lines, where they remained until about 2 o'clock, waiting the approach of the French cavalry, who suddenly came out of a wood and formed line. We immediately retired quietly. They followed us and skirmished the whole way until we arrived at our position at Waterloo. The 15th charged several times that day, and experienced some loss.

The next morning, the 18th inst., everything was quiet, until towards 12 o'clock we discovered the whole of the French cavalry moving away to our left; this was a feint to draw us away from our position, however we stood fast. They then commenced a vigorous attack upon our right, which they often drove back, but we always regained our ground. He then made an attack about 5 o'clock on our centre with nearly the whole of his cavalry and his Imperial Guard. He headed this attack in person, but our infantry, which was formed in squares with cavalry between them, gave them the most dreadful fire you can possibly imagine. The cavalry on both sides charged and recharged continually. The Life Guards behaved well. There are only about 40 men left in the 2nd regt.

At last about ½ past 7 or 8 o'clock our infantry began to shake and lost a little ground. Lord Wellington at this moment rode up and cheered them on; they then rallied and not only regained their ground but marched straight on. This decided the fate of the day; the French began to move away, our cavalry took advantage of this movement, and charged them, which caused great confusion. We followed them on, charging and killing them like sheep for about 6 miles until it got dark. The result of this day's operation is 25,000 killed, 26,000 prisoners, upwards of 200 pieces of artillery, and almost all their baggage fell into the hands of the Prussians. Our loss is reported at about 11 or 12,000 killed and wounded. The last letter I wrote was written the day after the battle, so that I had not an opportunity of hearing that the deroute was so complete.

Colonel Ponsonby and Capt. Sandys are still alive, but very bad indeed. Dawbiggan is doing well. Poor Bertie and Lockhart have been found and buried. I mean to purchase Bertie's horse and appointments. We have been marching hard every day since, at the rate of 30 miles a day. We take numbers of prisoners every day. The weather has been extremely bad, continued showers, accompanied by much thunder and lightning. Capt. Windsor is killed.[1] Tell Mrs. Vapal that Capt. Elton is safe.[2] The Greys have buried 8 officers. Westly is killed,[3] Windham is wounded,[4] Richardson of the Life Guards is wounded, but by [no] means badly,[5] L'Estrange is killed.[6] There was a report of the Genl.'s death, but I can answer for him. Cambray [Cambrai] is taken, Mauberge [Maubeuge] is taken. Nobody knows the actual state of affairs but Lord Wellington.

The Genl. commands the whole of the British cavalry. He mentioned my name in his despatch to Lord Wellington. He is going to ask him to appoint me extra A.D.C. I cannot conceive why my father will not write that letter. I expect soon to be able to write from Paris. Everybody says we will have no more fighting. God bless you my dear mother, believe me ever yours,

J. Vandeleur

My love to all. I forgot to mention that the Genl. lost a cart with his wine and all his maps, which was very valuable. Some people created an alarm among the baggage that the enemy were coming. The fellows set off and did not stop until they got to Antwerp. One-third of the army have lost their baggage. Waggons upset, horses fell over each other, guns over them again. Mine is safe.

1. Captain Edward Charles Windsor, 1st Royal Dragoons. His mother, having spent her available fortune on her son's commission, was awarded a pension of £50 per annum. See also pp. 45–6.
2. Captain William Elton, 1st Dragoon Guards; the identity of Mrs. Vapal, and her connection with the captain, are not clear.
3. Cornet Edward Westby, 2nd Dragoons.
4. Lieutenant Charles Wyndham, 2nd Dragoons.
5. Cornet and Sub-Lieutenant Richardson; see p. 143.
6. Brevet Major Edmund L'Estrange, 71st Highland Light Infantry, mortally wounded by a roundshot whilst serving as ADC to Major General Sir Denis Pack who was in command of the Ninth Infantry Brigade, Fifth Division.

Vandeleur's account of events on the 16th and 17th is sound enough so far as it goes, although since the 12th did not arrive on the field of Quatre Bras until dusk was falling and the battle at an end, his understanding of events on that field is necessarily second-hand. When news of the Prussian defeat at Ligny reached Wellington the following morning, causing orders to be given for the retreat to the position on the ridge of Mont St. Jean, the cavalry under Uxbridge were given the task of forming a rear-guard to give the rest of the army time to disengage and move north. The Fourth Cavalry Brigade of Major General Vandeleur, along with the Sixth Cavalry Brigade of Major General Sir Richard Hussey Vivian, was tasked with covering the eastern flank of the retreat, and thus missed the major fighting of the day around Genappe. Vivian's three Hussar regiments – 10th, 18th, and 1st KGL – were engaged at several points during the day, but Vandeleur's light dragoons were only briefly under fire. Strangely, considering that they are the only hussar regiment mentioned by Vandeleur, the 15th Hussars were not heavily engaged either, since the fighting at Genappe fell to the 7th Hussars and the Life Guards. Possibly a second-hand account has been included here in garbled form.[1]

There is no space here to give a full account of Waterloo. The circumstances of the 12th's part in the morning fighting have already been discussed in the commentary to the previous letter, so it remains only to complete the story of the regiment's activities for the remainder of the day, and to elaborate on a couple of significant points arising from Vandeleur's account of the fighting as a whole. The initial mention of a French movement to the allied left, and the assumption that this was a deliberate feint, is interesting: in fact, initially only the 7eme Hussards, under the celebrated memoirist Colonel de Marbot, were detached in this direction, in order to watch for the arrival either of the Prussians, or of French reinforcements under Marshal Grouchy. Only later were additional light cavalry moved in this direction, followed by infantry once

1. Fletcher, *Galloping at Everything*, pp. 229–36.

the Prussians hove into view. There then came the attack of the French I Corps against the allied centre-left, which was met by the infantry of the Fifth Division and the counterattack of the two heavy cavalry brigades, leading in turn to the intervention by the 12th and 16th Light Dragoons described in the previous letter.

After the regiment had regrouped after its charge, a remounted Major Bridger took command of the survivors, and, along with the rest of the brigade, the 12th were moved first to the allied centre and then, late in the day, to the right of Wellington's main line, above Hougoumont. These movements enabled Vandeleur to get a good idea of the development of the rest of the battle, although he errs – at least in part – in attributing the attacks made during the late afternoon to the Imperial Guard. Parts of the Guard Cavalry did charge the allied squares, but the main brunt of these attacks was borne by the regiments of cuirassiers making up the bulk of the French III and IV Cavalry Corps. Quite possible, however, Vandeleur shared the opinion held by many British officers that these troops were also part of Napoleon's Guard. Later, when the Guard really did attack in earnest, two columns of Middle Guard infantry moving against the allied First and Third Divisions, Vandeleur adds another voice to those who state that the French did have some initial success, and that Wellington's line wavered for a time before the French were finally driven back. This would seem in particular to relate to the infantry of the Third Division, which had already taken very heavy casualties earlier in the day, and which required reinforcements to help restore its line. Once the Imperial Guard had been repulsed, however, the surviving British cavalry – much of which, as Vandeleur says, had been in action throughout the day – were able to advance again.

The brigades of Vivian and Vandeleur, having been brought round from the left flank during the course of the day, were fresher than most, and continued to advance until darkness prevented any further movements – since this was high summer, this means that the pursuit cannot have halted much short of midnight, although the state of the ground means that Vandeleur's estimate of six miles is rather an exaggeration. Major General Vandeleur had, by this point, succeeded to the command of the entire allied cavalry following the wounding of the Earl of Uxbridge, and would hold this appointment until Stapleton Cotton – now ennobled as Lord Combermere – arrived in mid-July. As a result of the general's acting appointment, he was at last able to obtain for John Vandeleur the appointment of extra ADC, which was announced by a General Order of 24 June 1815.[1]

Roissey, 4 Leagues from Paris, 1st July 1815[2]

My Dear Mother,

We have been marching continually since I wrote last, without any opposition whatsoever. I have not had time to write to you before. We have marched at a rate of 6 or 7 leagues a day. Yesterday we marched 10 leagues and came up with them at Mont Mastre and St. Denis,[3] where, of course, we leave them until the infantry come up; they will be up today, and probably attempt those 2 places to-night. We took about 150 prisoners yesterday morning, and killed a few fellows. Probably we shall get into Paris to-morrow or the day after. A deputation waited on the Duke of Wellington yesterday morning, but he would not listen to their proposals. There is a report that Bonaparte is confined in a house at Malmaison, and Fouche has offered to give him up to the Duke of Wellington. The people of Paris are in a great fright, they don't know what to do.

The Genl. has got me appointed extra A.D.C., but I get no extra pay unless I am put in genl. orders at Horse Guards. I have written 3 times about a letter to the Duke of Wellington, which I request my father will

1. Adjutant General to Sir J. O. Vandeleur, 26 June 1815, in Wellington, 2nd Duke of (ed.), *Supplementary Despatches, Correspondence, and Memoranda, of Field Marshal Arthur, Duke of Wellington*, London, John Murray, 1858–1862, Vol. VIII, p. 171.
2. In the original text, pp. 165–7; location in fact Roissy-en-France, fifteen miles northeast of the centre of Paris, and today the site of the Charles de Gaulle Airport.
3. The Paris suburbs of Montmartre and Saint-Denis.

send, that I may present it myself. I shall not ask for it again. If the letter was written when I asked for it, the chance is I should have got a troop by the last action.[1]

I suppose you have a list of the killed and wounded by this time. Poor Sandys is dead of his wounds. Bertie was killed on the spot. Col. Ponsonby is out of danger. The two officers of my troop were killed out of 3, and only myself, a sergt., and 14 men left. I do not know how the deuce I escaped. I rode Taffy, who is very fresh at the moment. He certainly is the hardest and best horse for fatigue that I ever saw. I rode him two days and one night continually, with the exception of three or four hours on the evening of the 18th, when I crossed my mare. Ratler was at Antwerp with my baggage.

The Genl. is very well and in high spirits. Lady V. is still at Ostend. They all send their love. Pray send this letter or you will be too late. I hope my father continues to use his bath chair and gig. I suppose the weather is hot in England; these last four days have been extremely warm and dry. It is thought the British army will be kept some time in France after the affairs are settled, in which case do not sell my gig. Richardson is quite well and has rejoined his regt. George Nugent is well.[2] I hope the next letter will be dated Paris.

> I remain, my dear mother, your affectionate son,
> J. Vandeleur

The post is just going off.

As Vandeleur notes, Captain Sandys had died of his wounds, having been taken to hospital in Brussels. William Hay was with him, and remarked on his calmness and unselfishness in his final hours.[3] It may be inferred that the third officer of Sandys's troop, after the Captain and Vandeleur himself, was the unfortunate Lieutenant Bertie. Bertie's name is missing from the allocation of troop officers given out on embarking for the continent, which

1. That is to say, a promotion to captain.
2. Cornet George Nugent, 16th Light Dragoons.
3. Hay, *Reminiscences*, pp. 202–9.

shows Vandeleur as Sandys's only subaltern, but he was one of three additional lieutenants, all recalled from half-pay, who joined between then and Waterloo. Since the other two new arrivals both survived unscathed, it follows that Bertie was the third officer in the troop. Sandys's command was the centre squadron of the 12th, which places him and his troop in the midst of the hardest fighting during the regiment's charge. Under these circumstances, the high casualty rates of both officers and men are scarcely to be wondered at.

The fact that Vandeleur confirms that he was riding the faithful Taffy during the charge is interesting, since it implies that his mare was shot from beneath him – as described in his letter of the 20th – not during the charge but in the later fighting when the 12th had redeployed to the centre-right of Wellington's line. For Vandeleur to have been, as he says in his earlier letter, 'so pressed at the time' that he had to abandon his kit along with his dead mount would suggest that the 12th were more heavily engaged than other accounts would suggest; alternatively, of course, it may be that the regiment was on the move when Vandeleur was unhorsed, and that he did not have time to linger.

There was little action during the advance on Paris, for the Prussians had taken the lead in the pursuit, and continued to do so once Wellington's forces had come up and positioned themselves north of Paris as Vandeleur describes. The day after the date of Vandeleur's letter, the Prussians began to move around to the south of Paris so as to cut the city off, although in doing so their cavalry received a bloody nose from the still-combative French. Negotiations, however, were already under way to bring an end to hostilities, which, with Napoleon having already abdicated for a second and final time, were now without a cause. Although mopping up of some of the French fortress garrisons would go on for some time, to all intents and purposes the fighting came to an end with the allied occupation of Paris on 7 July.[1]

1. Hofschröer, *1815*, Vol. II, pp. 238–78.

Chapter 6

Two Courts Martial and a Coronation

~

After hostilities came to a close, John Vandeleur initially continued as extra ADC to Sir John Ormsby Vandeleur, who reverted to a brigade command once Lord Combermere arrived to replace Uxbridge permanently as commander of Wellington's cavalry. In November 1815, the army that had fought under Wellington's command at Waterloo was formally broken up, and a far smaller Army of Occupation formed in its stead. Major General Vandeleur did not receive a command in this new army, and returned to Britain. However, the 12th Light Dragoons did form part of it, and so John Vandeleur remained in France as a regimental officer. The 12th remained on the continent until November 1818 during which time they were re-equipped as lancers and eventually formally redesignated in March 1817 as the 12th (Prince of Wales's Royal) Lancers. As such, they were one of five light dragoon regiments so converted, a process which required the dispatch of a party of men to the Cavalry Riding Establishment at Pimlico over the winter of 1816–17 to receive lance instruction, following which they could then return to their regiments and pass on their knowledge. John Vandeleur commanded the training party sent by the 12th. Once back in England, the 12th Royal Lancers were stationed at Chichester, before relocating to Hounslow and Hampton Court in July 1819.

There are, unfortunately, no letters from the immediate post-Waterloo era included in the 1894 compilation, although it is inconceivable that none were written during Vandeleur's time in France. Possibly their contents were deemed insufficiently interesting for publication when the original text was assembled, but the same can quite clearly not be said for the correspondence that makes up the bulk of the post-war letters, concerning the near-disgrace of John Vandeleur's younger brother Robert. Robert, it will be remembered, had been first commissioned in March 1815, quickly transferring from the 85th Light Infantry to the 18th Hussars. He then swiftly rose to a lieutenancy in the 18th, gazetted in October 1815, but this proved to be a bad piece of timing since it made him one of the most junior officers in that rank when the regimental establishment was reduced the following spring, forcing him onto half pay. Robert remained thus unemployed until February 1818, when he obtained a full pay lieutenancy in the 38th Foot by means of an exchange with a Thomas Greening Twigg. Since a half pay commission, even in the cavalry, was worth less than a full pay infantry commission, Robert was obliged to pay Twigg the difference between the two commissions.

In June 1818, shortly after Robert's appointment, the 38th sailed for the Cape of Good Hope, where the conflict between European settlers and the indigenous Xhosa tribe had flared up into the Fifth Cape Frontier War. In April 1819, elements of the 38th took part in the decisive defeat of the Xhosa at Grahamstown, but it seems that Robert was not involved in that action, his company having remained at Cape Town. It may be that the boredom of garrison life, heightened by having been left out of the action, contributed to the unsavoury train of events that Robert was obliged to relate to his elder brother, and John in turn to their father.

Kensington, 5th August 1819[1]

My Dear Father,

You will be surprised at so early an answer to your letter, but I am going to write not about my own affairs but Robert's. I have just heard

1. In the original text, pp. 168–73.

from him, dated Cape Town, 1st May, by which he gives me account of a disagreeable adventure he was led into, but has acquitted himself with satisfaction to everybody. You have heard of the unfortunate duel that took place in the regt. in which Capt. Hussy lost his life.[1] To be brief, Robert was his second, and has written to me the following account:-

'When I entered the 38th, I was placed in Capt. Hussy's Compy. He took a fancy to me, and of course I felt grateful for it: unfortunately he was a very quarrelsome man (altho' a perfect gentleman and a man above the generality of society one meets) when he had taken a little wine, and much given to abuse. Several instances are known in the regt. when I have made up his quarrels, and made him sensible of his error in the morning; but, poor man, the last terminated by his death under these circumstances. He abused Lieutnt. Osborne of the regt.[2] at the mess-table, and made use of very gross and ungentlemanlike language: the consequence was, the latter threw a glass of wine in his face. It was the general opinion of the regt. that there was but one way of settling it; I was called upon; it was impossible to refuse. I did all in the power of man to prevent their meeting – the result was, the first shot struck Hussy on the fifth rib, which resisting, gave the ball a direction through the stomach, which produced his instantaneous death. My conduct upon the occasion has met with the entire approbation of the regt. I could not have acted otherwise, and I feel duly of having discharged my duty as a Christian, and a man, in endeavouring to prevent it. The consequence of this unhappy business was, the civil power – which is composed of Dutchmen, and laws not at like our own – endeavoured to lay hold of us, which, Lord Charles Somerset hearing of it,[3] took it

1. Captain George Hussey, a veteran with extensive service in the Peninsula, as well as on Walcheren, who had held his present rank since September 1812.
2. Darragh Osborn; first commissioned as an ensign in the 38th Foot in June 1807, promoted lieutenant May 1809, served through almost all of the Peninsular War with either the 1st or 2nd Battalions of his regiment, being absent from the theatre only between January 1809 and April 1810.
3. General Lord Charles Somerset, Governor of Cape Colony from 1814 to 1826. A son of the 5th Duke of Beaufort, his brothers included Lord Edward Somerset who had commanded the Hussar Brigade in the Peninsula, and Lord Fitzroy

into his own hands, and as his power is supreme he ordered a General Court Martial to assemble, before which Ensign Moore (the Marquis of Drogheda's own nephew),[1] and I were arraigned "For aiding and attending as seconds to the parties concerned in a duel, on or about the morning of 24th March 1819, in which Capt. George Hussy, of the 38th Regt., was killed, such conduct being prejudicial to good order and military discipline, and contrary to the Articles of War." We were both acquitted for want of evidence. Lord Charles immediately sent for us, and gave us a most paternal lecture, did not in any way blame our conduct; but made us promise never to act as seconds again, which I assure you is my firm intention to abide by'.

Thus ends Robert's account of it. He sent me a copy of the proceedings, by which it appears that the only evidence against him was his being seen by the sentry pass thro' the gate early in the morning in plain clothes. I am afraid my poor Mother will be very much shocked when she hears of the business. I am certain you will agree with me that he was in no way to blame, and that in refusing to accompany Hussy, he would have completely forfeited his own honor – altho' I admit the principle of duelling is founded upon an erroneous point; but still it is a necessary evil, without which there would be no check on over-bearing society. Poor Bob says he is more afraid of your disapprobation than any thing in this world, and I am perfectly convinced he speaks his real sentiments. I therefore hope and trust you will withhold any angry feeling against him, and allow me in my next letter to assure him of your sympathy for what has happened. He writes in very good spirits. He says that the governor takes a great deal of notice of him, that the Grenadier compy. to which he is attached remains at Cape Town, and has not proceeded against the Caffres.[2]

Somerset, the future Baron Raglan. Lord Charles, however, was primarily a politician and courtier rather than a fighting soldier.

1. Ensign Frederick Moore, son of the Hon. Ponsonby Moore whose brother was, as Robert Vandeleur reports, General Charles Moore, 1st Marquess of Drogheda.

2. Kaffirs: although now considered pejorative, this was then a neutral term applied to black southern Africans in general, although here being used specifically to indicate the Xhosa.

Lieutnt. Osborne is to leave the regt. forthwith. Robert begs particularly that he may not be exchanged as his prospects are so good. Lieutnts. Cook and Green will never return to the regt.[1] I am pretty certain that Hopper, who is at Canterbury, will retire on account of his health.[2] Robert then becomes first for purchase as Mackay is on his way to England, to get Capt. Gathie's compy.[3]

He speaks in high terms of the people at the Cape, and seems to like it very much. He by his own account must be a favourite amongst the people. There are very few of the officers who go into society. He complains of the Cape being very expensive, and from their situation they are obliged to entertain people passing on to India. He requests that my mother will send him some things, such as a blue frock coat, a dress blue coat, and five pairs of boots; in return for which he will send her at the proper season, a box of the most beautiful bulbous roots, which grow in great perfection at the Cape. He also wishes to have some of the recent publications, and if there is a possibility of getting your newspapers when you have done with them, they will be a great treat. I shall have the opportunity of sending by the hand of Mr. Dibdin a box: he is going on to India and promises to take any thing to my brother that I wish. I dine at his father's next Saturday.

Bob tells me it costs him three shillings a day to keep his horse, and he humbly begs an increase of income. As you were not aware of this before you made me such a generous offer, I shall defer your putting it into execution until I hear your answer to my brother's request, which I hope will be a favourable one.

1. Adolphus Cooke, lieutenant since July 1812, who was, however, still with the regiment in 1821. Samuel Green, a lieutenant in the 38th since September 1812 having been first commissioned into the regiment as an ensign in October 1810, did indeed leave as expected, exchanging into a half pay appointment in the 22nd – and pocketing the difference in commissions – in September 1819.

2. Edward Hopper, a lieutenant since March 1811, was still with the regiment in 1824, so Vandeleur was wrong on this count.

3. Apparently a reference to George Mackay, who, was however, still a lieutenant two years later. 'Gathie' would seem to be a mistake for Captain (Brevet Major) John L. Gallie.

He wishes to have White's *Farriery*,[1] and a new saddle and bridle. All these things had better be got in London and packed together by Lawrie my saddler, who is in the habit of sending saddles to India.[2] He begs particularly to mention to my mother the want of these articles. He was always her pet, so I hope she will influence you on his behalf. He says 'the winter is commencing (1st May) it is very raw and cold'. I hope he is provided with flannel.

My love to my mother and sisters, to whom Bob requests that I will speak in the most affectionate manner, and begs to know what height Fanny is, and the breadth of Bessy's foot.

Your very affectionate son,
John Vandeleur

The situation in which Robert Vandeleur found himself, and the response both of his own brother and of his fellow officers at the Cape, is indicative of the importance of honour and 'face' amongst British officers of the Napoleonic era. In theory, duelling was illegal and an officer who fought a duel – assuming he survived it – was liable for prosecution along with his second. Yet by far the majority of officers chose to put their personal honour as gentlemen before their commitment to the letter of military law; indeed, an officer who refused a challenge, or failed to issue one when deliberately provoked, could forfeit all respect from his fellows.[3] John Vandeleur's opinion, that duelling was a necessary evil, may safely be taken as typical of the time, and the conduct of the court martial of the two seconds, detailed in the following letter, clearly

1. *The Improved Art of Farriery,* by James White.
2. Peter Lawrie was an established saddler with premises on Oxford Street. His business success in supplying the army in India brought him considerable wealth, and in later life this saw him knighted and serve as Lord Mayor of London.
3. For such a case, and a wider discussion of attitudes to duelling at this time, see Bamford, Andrew, '"Dastardly and atrocious": Lieutenant Blake, Captain Clune, and the recall of the 55th Foot from the Netherlands, 1814', *Journal of the Society for Army Historical Research,* Vol. 92, No. 371 (Autumn 2014), pp. 34–46.

demonstrates that they had the full sympathy and support of their fellow officers. That said, a duel – particularly a fatal one – was a scandal nonetheless, and it is not to be wondered that Lieutenant Osborne was obliged to leave the 38th in consequence of the death of Captain Hussey. A death and a departure caused a shake-up of the regiment's officers, and the closing part of the letter details one of the main preoccupations of the peacetime officer, namely the chance of promotion.

Without the combat vacancies created in wartime, promotion during peacetime could often be very slow, and an officer's standing on the regiment's list of seniority was all important. If Robert were to have transferred to another regiment, he would have become its most junior lieutenant irrespective of his time in rank within the 38th, and so it behove him to hang on where he was and hope for a captaincy by seniority. In the event, however, the hopes of the two brothers that this would come to pass were mistaken; the majority of the officers named did not leave the 38th, and Robert eventually obtained a transfer, still as a lieutenant, back to his old regiment the 18th Hussars. He eventually obtained a captaincy by purchase in October 1821, moving to the 84th Foot as a result. Five years after that he obtained his majority but went onto half pay, and when he retired in 1851 it was as a brevet lieutenant colonel.

Kensington, 14th November 1819[1]

My Dear Father,

According to your desire, I send you a copy of the proceedings of the Court Martial. I have for some time been waiting for a frank, but have not succeeded in obtaining one.

Sir, I beg to enclose a copy of the charge preferred against you by His Excellency the Commander of the Forces, upon which you are to be tried by the general Court Martial, now sitting at the Castle – together

---

1. In the original text, pp. 174–81.

with a list of the witnesses to be examined on the *part of the prosecution*. I have the honour, etc.

(Signed) Wm. Underwood, A. Dep. J. A.[1]

To Lieut. Robt. Vandeleur, 38th Regiment.

Charge. – Lieut. Robt. Vandeleur, of His Majesty's 38th Regt. put in arrest by the orders of His Excellency, the Commander of the Forces, on the following charge:- for aiding and abetting and attending as a second to the parties concerned in a duel, on or about the morning of 24th March 1819, in which Capt. George Hussey of the 38th Regt. was killed. Such conduct being prejudicial to good order and military discipline and contrary to the Articles of War.

(Signed) M. G. Blake, Depty. Adjn.-General.[2]

Head Quarters, 28th March, Wm. Underwood, A. Depy. J. Advocate.

Proceedings of a General Court Martial Held on Thursday, April 24th, for the trial of Lieutn. Vandeleur and Ensign Moore 38th Regt. arraigned by order of His Ex. Ld. Henry Chas. Somerset, Governor and Commd.-in-Chief.

1st Evidence. – Lieutn. Col. Miles being duly sworn,[3] deposeth as follows:- *1st Question.* – On what day and from whom did you receive the information of the death of the late Captain Hussey?
Answer. – By an anonymous letter on the morning of the 24th inst.[4]
2nd Question. – State to the Court the particular information you received.
Answer. – After parade on the morning of the 24th, I went to barracks, and near the mess-room I was met by Lieut. Bain who gave me the

1. Captain William Underwood, 21st Light Dragoons, Assistant Deputy Judge Advocate.
2. Major Mathew G. Blake, Deputy Adjutant-General on the staff at the Cape.
3. Lt. Colonel Edward Miles. Newly promoted to substantive rank, Miles had held his lieutenant colonelcy by brevet since January 1812, and had served extensively in the Peninsula where he was wounded at Salamanca and San Sebastián.
4. He presumably meant ult., since he was speaking of the previous month.

anonymous letter,[1] which was placed on his table during parade-time, saying, if he would direct a party and the quarter-master to take a waggon to a certain place under Table Mountain, he would there find the body of the late Captain Hussey. I directed Lieutn. Bain immediately to get a waggon, which he did, and desired the quarter-master to accompany him with a party to the place mentioned in the note, where they found the body. I also went myself with the Adjut., Major Evans, and Doctor Cathcart, Regt. Surgeon.[2] On my arrival here I directed the body to be moved to the barracks, and directed the surgeon to open it, which he did and extracted the ball which he believed caused his death. He shewed me the ball, which appeared to be a musket ball shaved down.

3rd Question. – Did any circumstance reach your knowledge which led you to believe who were the persons concerned in the duel in which Capt. Hussey was killed?

Answer. – It was reported to me in the mess room on the 22nd ultimo. They were present when the quarrel arose with Capt. Hussey and Lieutenant Osborne.

[Remark by me, J. V. – Does he mean the circumstance was reported *in the mess room on the 22nd* to him? – in that case Col. M. could have prevented the duel – or does he mean it was *afterwards* reported? They were present when the quarrel arose? This Judge-Advocate is a stupid fellow.]

4th Question. – Was it in consequence of this report that you placed them under arrest?

Answer. – Yes.

2nd Evidence. – Quarter-master Southall being duly sworn,[3] deposeth.

1st Question. – Did you on the morning of the 24th March receive instructions from Lieut. Col. Miles to go in search of the body of the Capt. Hussey?

1. Lt. Patrick Bain.
2. Lt. and Adjutant James Mathews; Major Thomas Evans; Surgeon Martin Cathcart.
3. Quartermaster Thomas Southall.

Answer. – I did.

2nd Question. – Did you find the body?

Answer. – Yes.

3rd Question. – Relate to the Court the circumstance.

Answer. – I was directed by the order of the Commandg. Officer to accompany Lieut. Bain in search of the body, which we found under Table Mountain covered with a blue coat. I saw it put into the waggon and accompanied it to the barrack. It was put into a room, the key of which I gave to Dr. Cathcart.

Question from the Court. – Were the prisoners or either of them aiding and abetting in the duel of the 24th March last, in which Capt. Hussey was killed?

Answer. – Not to my knowledge.

3rd Evidence. – Surgeon Cathcart, 38th Regt., being duly sworn, deposeth as follows: -

1st Question. – Did you examine the body of the late Capt. Hussey on the morning of the 24th March after it was brought into barracks?

Answer. – I did.

2nd Question. – In your opinion what was the cause of his death?

Answer. – A wound by a ball much less than a musket ball. It entered the collar-bone on the right side, passed thro' the lungs on the left side of the chest, broke the 4th or 5th rib on the left side, and lodged in the left shoulder blade.

3rd Question. – Were the prisoners or either of them aiding or abetting in a duel which took place on the 24th March last, in which Capt. Hussey was killed?

Answer. – Not to my knowledge.

4th Evidence. – Private George Potter being duly sworn, deposeth.

1st Question. – Were you on sentry at the barrack gate on the morning of the 24th March?

Answer. – Yes.

2nd Question. – At what hour?

Answer. – From four to six.

3rd Question. – During the time you were on sentry did you see Lieut. Vandeleur or Ensign Moore or either of them go out of the barrack gate?

Answer. – I saw Lieut. Vandeleur, but cannot say as to Ensign Moore.

4th Question. – Was Lieut. Vandeleur accompanied by any other person?

Answer. – He was, but I cannot say who it was who was with him.

5th Question. – Can you recollect what hour the persons described went out of the barrack gate?

Answer. – I opened the gate about ten minutes – it might be about ten minutes past 5; it was about 5 when the gun was fired and the gates were opened about ten minutes after.

6th Question. – How were the persons you may have seen dressed?

Answer. – They were in coloured clothes.[1]

5th Evidence. – Henry England, Private, 38th regt., being duly sworn, deposeth.

1st Question. – Were you on sentry at the barrack gate on 24th March? At what hour?

Answer. – I was from six to eight.

2nd Question. – Whom did you relieve?

Answer. – George Potter.

3rd Question. – During the time you were on sentry did you see Lieut. Vandeleur or Ensign Moore or either of them come into the barracks?

Answer. – I saw Lieut. Vandeleur come in.

4th Question. – Was he accompanied by any other person?

Answer. – There were two other gentlemen with him. One was Lieut. Osborne. I don't know who the other was.

5th Question. – How were the persons described dressed?

Answer. – In coloured clothes.

Defence. – The prosecution being closed, the prisoners being called upon for their defence they rose and stated: 'Being conscious no part of the evidence produced against us can prove the crime with which

1. That is to say, in civilian clothes rather than in uniform.

we are charged, we consider it unnecessary to further infringe the time of the honourable Court, to whose decision we cheerfully submit'.

Here follows a list of the evidences which hath already been detailed in the proceedings.[1]

The result has caused universal joy throughout the regiment. My plans must therefore be completely altered. You seem to have misunderstood my letter. My meaning was that as you made me the offer before Robert's request, there might be some difficulty in prejudice to Robert; but this not being the case, I hope you do not mean to retreat from your proffered kindness – and you will greatly add to my comfort by allowing it from the 1st of Jany., as by those means I shall be enabled to set up a Tilbury horse.[2] My mare was sold for 20 guineas; she is decidedly broken winded; I could not warrant her. I got a wetting the other night on my way to a party and was obliged to turn back. By allowing me this which is a trifle from your coffers, I can get a Tilbury for £37, which will leave £13 to be added to the 20 will purchase a very decent horse. This time of year, they are now dog-cheap.

I am very much afraid that the poor general has met with a disappointment in some money speculations. He does not even keep a saddle-horse, and is living in the most economical manner possible. He was always dabbling in French funds and I fear he has burnt his fingers. If it is not too late, send my cloak with Robert's things, and pray send him some comfort for the mind as well as the body. I mean some books. I have ordered the saddle and bridle. Pray tell my good mother not to be angry with me for not writing. I wish to defer it until I can describe to her my new equipage.

---

1. This list was not copied; evidences in this context means witnesses.
2. Named for the firm who manufactured them, a Tilbury was a light weight, two-wheeled, open carriage which became fashionable around this time; a Tilbury horse, therefore, was the animal needed to pull it.

My love to all. I am sorry to say Colonel M'Donald told me there were upwards of 2000 candidacies for cornetcy's and ensigncy's.[1]

Your affectionate son,
John Vandeleur

On the face of it, this is a record of a most peculiar court martial, with the discrepancy that John Vandeleur himself noted – the 'J. V.' aside in square brackets – just one of many occasions where evidence was not elaborated on and statements not followed up. Yet of course that was rather the point. Some things, of course had to be admitted: Captain Hussey was undoubtedly dead, and the bald facts of his death could not be avoided, nor the detail of the means by which his death had come about, at least insofar as the medical aspects were concerned. Otherwise, all commission witnesses – or 'evidences', as they were styled – seem to have been engulfed by a fog of collective amnesia. The only hard facts, that Vandeleur left barracks on the morning in question and that he and Ensign Moore later returned, were established by the testimony of the two sentries, who were not bound up in this gentlemanly conspiracy of silence but who, equally, were not pressed for any further details that might incriminate someone. In effect, what was being done was to ensure that whilst all due process was followed, the testimony given would be such as to ensure that the accused could, without stain on their honour, state that 'no part of the evidence *produced against us* can prove the crime with which we are charged' [emphasis added]. Every man in the room likely knew full well that Robert Vandeleur and Frederick Moore had been the seconds in the fatal duel, and most could likely have, had they so wished, given testimony to prove it. But the sympathies of the court were with the accused – refusing to support a fellow officer as a second when called upon would, after all, have in itself meant a loss of personal honour – and so the fiction was

---

1. Colonel Sir John MacDonald, Deputy Adjutant-General at Horse Guards; it is not clear on whose behalf Vandeleur had been enquiring about commissions.

maintained that no-one could quite remember the details of the sad affair, allowing the neatly framed response by the accused that in turn allowed the court to give a not guilty verdict. Such circumventions of due process, it might be noted, were perfectly common, and for duellists too, never mind their seconds.[1]

It will be recalled that Sir John Ormsby Vandeleur's finances had never been particularly robust – hence his expressed preference to live abroad after the conclusion of the Peninsular War – and this latest upset over dabbling in unwise investments had evidently not helped. Seniority eventually carried Sir John to the rank of full general in 1838, but he saw no further active service before his death in 1849. His young relative, meanwhile, was evidently becoming something of a man-about-town, placing him under financial pressures of his own if he was to maintain the expensive lifetime of a cavalry officer in peacetime London. A very early photograph, taken when the sitter was in middle age, shows Vandeleur with a particularly impressive set of whiskers, typical of those sported by late-Regency cavalrymen, and the intent to purchase a fashionable Tilbury carriage – the open top sports car of its day – also spoke of a wish to follow the trends of the age.

As has already been noted with regards to the career of Robert Vandeleur, peacetime promotion was extremely slow. John Vandeleur did not obtain his captaincy until 1822, and that by purchase rather than seniority, although he did compensate by purchasing his majority only three years after that. It may reasonably be inferred that the impetus for this sudden advancement was the death of his father in 1822, upon which he came into his inheritance. Both these promotions kept Vandeleur with the 12th Lancers, but in order to get his next step he was obliged to take an

---

1. For an example, and wider discussion, see Divall, Carole, *Inside the Regiment: The Officers and Men of the 30th Regiment During the Revolutionary and Napoleonic Wars*, pp. 173–6. Divall also produces evidence of a far greater instance of offences relating to drinking and/or duelling in overseas garrisons than in Europe, which entirely fits the circumstance of the Hussey–Osborne duel; it was, after all, a glass of wine that the lieutenant threw at Hussey.

infantry commission and to go on half pay. From December 1827, therefore, Vandeleur was a half-pay unattached lieutenant colonel of infantry – unattached signifying that he was a supplementary officer holding rank in the Army as a whole and not in a particular regiment – and he remained thus for over a decade. Only in June 1838 did he return to full pay, exchanging into the 10th Hussars as a regimental lieutenant colonel.

In part, this return to full pay may have come about because of his responsibility as a family man, for he made good use of his time on half pay to woo and wed his widowed cousin, Alice Stewart. Alice's paternal grandfather, Crofton Vandeleur, was the elder brother of John Vandeleur's grandfather. Her first husband, the Rev. Charles Moore Stewart, had died in 1831 only a year after their marriage. Loss of Irish census records renders it difficult to date the marriage of John and Alice, or to confirm the details of their family beyond the fact that their only son – named, perhaps inevitably, John Ormsby Vandeleur – was baptized in January 1840. There seem also to have been at least four daughters, possibly five, the last born in 1846 when the 10th Hussars were stationed at York.

Whilst Vandeleur took his young family with him to that posting, he had left them at home when the regiment was stationed in London for the coronation of Queen Victoria, the aftermath of which is described in the following letter.

Hounslow, July 1838[1]

My Dearest Alice,

I received your affectionate letter of the 4th, and I am truly sorry to find that you were disappointed seeing me; but cheer up, it is a long street that has no turn, and I hope the time is approaching that I shall obtain leave. The fact is I find my Major is not quite so efficient an officer as I first supposed,[2] and all hands seemed to think that if he had

1. In the original text, pp. 181–4.
2. Major John Clement Wallington.

had command of the regt, during the last month, that he would have got it into some sort of scrape, but I am now going to apply for leave of absence, but whether I shall get it directly or not I cannot say.

I must now give you a further account of our proceedings after the Coronation. As I described, we returned very much fatigued to Hounslow.

The next Wednesday we marched 22 miles in the wet to Woolwich, where we were quartered in pot-houses. The next day, Thursday, the review took place. Marshal Soult,[1] the Prince Nemours,[2] Prince George,[3] thousands of foreign officers, all the ambassadors, etc., etc., were present, I never saw such a splendid sight. The 10th Hussars kept the ground, which was a very fatiguing duty, 12 hours, on horseback during all the heat, for we had nobody to keep the ground at the review. But we had to keep the mob from running into the space where the *dejeuné* was given, and where all the artillery soldiers sat down in the open air to dinner, rather tantalizing for my poor hungry Hussars, however we were obliged to grin and bear it. The next day we were ordered 22 miles back to Hounslow. Here we counted on a little rest, but no. On my arrival a letter was put into my hand directing me to march the next day to Wandsworth and to other villages near London, no great distance, but we were separated and badly put up.

The following day, yesterday, we formed a part of this great review in the park, which was very splendid, the day was so fine and clear. The Queen was received with a salute. She passed down the line in her carriage, and then we passed her, first at a walk, and then at a trot. When your husband rode past at the head of the Hussars, Her Majesty made him a bow. Well after a great deal of charging, firing, etc., etc., the 10th marched down Park Lane past Lord Londonderry's House,[4] by his own directions, where Marshal Soult was stationed in the balcony to

1. Soult was in London as Ambassador-Extraordinary on behalf of King Louis-Philippe.
2. Prince Louis, Duc de Nemours, second son of King Louis-Philippe.
3. HRH Prince George of Cambridge, cousin to the new queen.
4. General Charles Vane (formerly Stewart), 3rd Marquess of Londonderry. Brother of the late Lord Castlereagh, Stewart had served under Wellington

see us. We gave him a military salute as we passed and then returned to a most splendid *dejeuné*. I presented all the officers to Lord and Lady Londonderry, and they promised all sorts of things to do for us (which of course they will forget). We came home here last night, and I am now preparing a detachment to send to Kensington tomorrow morning.

I am going to dine with the Marquis of Anglesea tomorrow,[1] and I am going over this evening to Hampton Court, to see about a house. I forgot to say that Lord Bloomfield, with whom I dined at Woolwich, is one of the most delightful men I have ever met, he and I are great friends and he is very anxious to see you.[2] You will be well recd.

Here. I must now, my dear Alice, bid adieu. You will hear again in 3 days. Don't go about without Michael or Willm. Some one will run away with you. I wish to God, you and the picks were here.[3] I am so tired at night that I sleep, but I often dream of you.

> Adieu and love, Yrs., most affectly.,
> J. V.

This is evidently the second of two letters describing the involvement of the 10th Hussars in the coronation, the first of which must be assumed to be lost. The Coronation itself took place on 28 June 1838, with an enormous procession through London that was viewed by unprecedentedly large crowds which required a strong military presence to line the route. For his part in the celebrations, Vandeleur received a Coronation Medal in gold. Many foreign dignitaries attended, as might be expected, and it was on this occasion that Wellington, catching sight of Marshal

---

in the Peninsula as a cavalry brigadier and later as Adjutant-General. He was Colonel of the 10th Hussars.

1. Formerly the Earl of Uxbridge, who had been elevated to a marquisate after Waterloo.
2. Lieutenant General Lord Bloomfield; now retired, previously private secretary to George IV.
3. That is to say, their children, 'picks' being an abbreviation of pickaninny which at the time was neither a derogatory term nor applied universally to those of African origin.

Soult who was attending events as representative of King Louis-Philippe, is alleged to have caught his old adversary by the arm with an exclamation of 'I have you at last.' Apocryphal or not, the story marks something of the character of the event, looking to the future rather than to the past. Indeed, it would be pleasing to end on this note, with the nation beginning a new age and our hero having found domestic happiness, but there was to be a final sour note before the eventual end of John Vandeleur's military career.

As is evident from the above letter, Vandeleur evidently had some doubts about his new command. The 10th Hussars had always been a fashionable regiment; its style had been set by King George IV during his tenure as its Colonel when he was still Prince of Wales, and Beau Brummel had once been numbered amongst its officers. It will be recalled from Vandeleur's letters from the Peninsula and Waterloo campaigns that the men of the Army's light dragoon regiments had little regard for their showier brethren in the hussars, but as the nineteenth century drew on, increasing numbers of light cavalry regiments – those, at least, that had not undergone conversion to lancers – adopted the more ornate dress of the hussars, and changed their titles accordingly. Whether or not John Vandeleur came to take up command of the 10th with his old prejudices intact is unclear, but both this letter and later events made it clear that he was disinclined to allow any pretensions to fashion to get in the way of the military effectiveness of his new command.

Exactly what his new second-in-command, Major John Clement Wallington, had or had not done in order to justify the low opinion of him that Vandeleur expressed in the above letter is not certain. Wallington was an officer of long standing in the regiment, with which he had fought at Waterloo as a lieutenant, and may have seen Vandeleur as an interloper and a block on any aspirations to command that he himself might have entertained. Certainly, if the regimental history of the 10th is anything to go by, there was some concern within the regiment that their new commander had been so long on half pay.[1]

What is certain is that Vandeleur had every intention of maintaining his regiment in a condition of full effectiveness, one important aspect of which being that all officers should be properly mounted, having both a charger and a second horse. Thus, when Lieutenant William Hyder applied, in 1842 when the regiment was stationed in Ireland, for a leave of absence, Vandeleur refused it to him on the grounds that the only horse he owned was unfit for purpose and that until Hyder had rendered himself effective by obtaining a proper mount, he would not be permitted to take leave. Hyder then, it was alleged, bought one charger from a Mr. Silver Charles Oliver – formerly an officer of the 10th – and attempted to obtain from the same source the loan of a second horse to pass off as his second, thus demonstrating that he was effectively mounted and permitting him to go on leave. This was, indeed, a rather frivolous case, albeit one that cast doubt on Hyder's honour and status as a gentleman, but the manner in which it was brought was rather more complex, for it was only three years after the fact that the case came to trial. What had happened in the interim is that Vandeleur, who had evidently realized that in Hyder he had something of a bad apple, had sought to discipline the subaltern and, so Hyder alleged, to create a breach between him and his fellow officers, and force him from the regiment. Hyder complained of this perceived persecution to his father, who in turn wrote to the Duke of Wellington – since 1842 again serving as Commander-in-Chief of the Army – complaining of Vandeleur's conduct. Wellington in turn demanded an inquiry, which turned up the circumstances detailed above and led to Vandeleur being ordered to prefer charges. He explained the situation to the court martial, which took place at Leeds in September 1845, under the presidency of Major General Sir William Warre, in the following terms:

---

1. See Liddell, Col. R. S., *The Memoirs of the Tenth Royal Hussars (Prince of Wales's Own) Historical and Social*, pp. 218, 239.

Mr. President, and Gentlemen of this Honourable Court, I shall not trespass on your time by going into any unnecessary detail of what my feelings must be as a Commanding Officer of one of Her Majesty's Regiments, but proceed at once to the charge. When the Regiment was quartered at Ballincollig, in October 1842, Lieutenant Hyder made a personal request to me to recommend him for two months' leave of absence to go to England. I replied to the effect that as he had no regimental horses to do duty on I did not consider him an effective Officer and that I could not entertain his application till he produced two proper and efficient horses for that purpose. On this he Lieutenant Hyder, went to Mr. Oliver, of Inchera, in the County of Cork, a gentleman of high character and considerable property, and who had, some years ago, himself served in the 10th Hussars, and made an arrangement with that gentleman for the purchase of a bay horse, and at the same time endeavoured to persuade Mr. Oliver to lend him another chesnut horse, to pass off on me as a second charger, at the same time stating, that unless he produced two horses to me as chargers, he could not obtain leave of absence – in fact, using in substance the expression I made use of on giving my refusal a day or two before. He, Lieutenant Hyder, further proposed, that if the horse was sent he should be taken the greatest care of, that he should be led out to exercise daily with the Troop horses, that no one should get on his back, and, finally, that he should be sent back on his, Lieutenant Hyder's, return from his leave of absence. It is needless for me to add, that a proposal of such a nature, made to a man of honour and a Gentleman, was most disdainfully rejected. As this matter took place in 1842, it will be my duty to prove that it never came to my knowledge till May, 1845, and that its having then accidentally escaped detection is no justification of the gross deceit attempted to be practised. It became imperative upon me to apply to Mr. Oliver, and he gave me a detailed account of what I have described; consequently, on the arrival of the Regiment at York, I was directed by Field-Marshal the Duke of Wellington to place Lieutenant Hyder under arrest, and to deliver the charge now before the Court to that Officer, the said charge being framed by his Grace's order, and not by me. I now attend here as the Prosecutor; and, as I am without Counsel or other adviser, trusting to the impartiality of a Court of British Officers, I shall endeavour strictly to adhere to the rules of evidence, and not to introduce anything which does not bear upon the matter at issue.[1]

Hyder had obtained civilian legal counsel to assist him in his trial, and the case quickly descended into a lengthy courtroom battle, fought for the most part on a series of legal technicalities and marked by attempts to blacken the character of the prosecution witnesses. Vandeleur, for his part, did not always help himself with a series of lively and forthright responses, in which the wit evident in his letters as a young man remains apparent. A fine taste of this is given by the following exchange from early in the trial, when Hyder was allowed to cross-examine his accuser:

Q. Is it your invariable custom to refuse leave of absence unless or until an Officer has two chargers?
A. It is my custom not to give an Officer leave of absence, or any other indulgence, who shows ...
The Deputy-Judge Advocate. – The question is. Is it your invariable custom?
Lieutenant Colonel Vandeleur. – I say it is. I had no cases of the sort before.
The Deputy-Judge Advocate finally read the answer thus: It is my invariable custom to refuse every kind of indulgence to Officers, who show a disinclination to mount themselves.
The Prisoner submitted that the question must be answered. Yes or no; and that it had not yet been answered.
The Deputy-Judge Advocate repeated the question, and the Court directed the witness to speak to the point.

1. Quoted in Hyder, William, *Proceedings of the General Court Martial, Held by the Order of Field Marshal the Duke of Wellington, the Commander in Chief, for the Trial of Lieutenant William Augustine Hyder 10th Royal Hussars, on the Prosecution of Lieut. Colonel Vandeleur, 10th Royal Hussars*, pp. 2–3.

(Here a conversation took place between the Court and the prisoner, and the following question was substituted):-

Q. Do you invariably require an Officer to have two chargers before you give him leave of absence?

A. No; not when I see that that Officer shows a proper inclination to mount himself. Frequently an Officer asks for leave to go and buy a horse as a charger.

Q. Have you not frequently granted leave of absence for a considerable period to Officers who had only one charger?

A. Yes; being under the impression that those Officers would not remain without a second charger.

Q. Have you never given leave of absence to an Officer who had no charger?

A. Not that I recollect. I hope I have a right to command my Regiment as I think proper, without being subject to this sort of cross-examination.

Lieutenant-Colonel Vandeleur was asked if he wished the latter part of his answer to be taken down; and he replied in the negative.

Q. When I first applied for leave did you not know that I had a black gelding with which I joined the Regiment?

A. (With much animation.) I knew that you had a *black cart-horse* when you joined the Regiment but I believe it was a mare.

The Deputy-Judge-Advocate repeated the question and Lieutenant-Colonel Vandeleur replied. – Yes; I was aware that you had a black horse that was totally unfit for the Ranks.

The President. – A man may have a dozen horses. The point is was it a charger? I think it was an imputation uncalled for to style a horse of that description a *cart-horse*; and you had better abstain Colonel Vandeleur from language so calculated to irritate the Prisoner.[1]

Eventually, having managed to cast sufficient aspersion on the character of the vital witness Oliver, and on Vandeleur himself, Hyder was able to obtain a not guilty verdict, which is reproduced, along with the findings of the court and the Queen's comments

1. Hyder, *Proceedings of the General Court Martial*, pp. 5–6.

on the case, as Appendix V. Notwithstanding that he had been ordered to bring about the prosecution, Vandeleur came in for some criticism in the findings of the court, which could have done little for his standing with his regiment or his attempts to instil order into it. Nevertheless, it was apparent from testimony that Hyder's own character was hardly without fault, and within a year he had left the 10th and retired from the Army.

By the time of the Hyder court martial, the 10th were stationed at York where, in early 1846, they received orders to prepare for service in India. The regiment was evidently well-thought of by the city, and the following newspaper cuttings were included with the original publication of the letters, having evidently been kept by Vandeleur.

Extracts from the *York Herald*[1]

The 10th Hussars

This distinguished regiment having left York Barracks, we cannot allow the opportunity to pass without expressing our high opinion of the conduct of both officers and men during their sojourn amongst us. Colonel Vandeleur and his brother officers were ever ready to promote the pleasure of the citizens by the presence of their Band on all public occasions, and their munificent hospitality at the entertainments which they gave at the *De Grey Rooms* will long be remembered. This regiment is about to proceed on foreign service, and the fact that every officer goes out to India with it, is highly creditable, and must redound to the honour of the corps. From ourselves and our fellow citizens, we heartily wish them farewell.

Departure from York of the 10th Hussars

In the hurry of our last publication, we omitted to mention the departure from York, on the previous Thursday, of the 10th Hussars. The high character of this truly gallant regiment, and their brave conduct during the arduous service of the late Continental War, requires not an eulogium from us. It is, however, our duty as public journalists to

1. Reproduced at the end of the original text of Vandeleur's *Letters*, pp. 184–6.

notice their kind and gentlemanly deportment, whilst stationed at our Barracks, and the universal feelings of respect entertained for them, by the citizens at large, and markedly shown by the general expressions of regret at their recent departure. This was sure to be the case, for they were ever ready to assist in promoting the public amusements of the city, and their band was not only allowed to play in the *Museum Gardens* at stated periods, for the gratification of the citizens, but was readily permitted to enliven every public scene when requested. In short, the liberality of the officers in subscribing £10 towards the erection of an orchestra in the *De Grey Rooms* was but one amongst a number of spirited instances of their generosity. We, however, cannot spare room further to enumerate. It is sufficient to state that their high sense of duty was strongly exhibited by the fact, that when called upon to proceed to active and dangerous services in distant lands, there was no demur, no wish to cast 'a longing lingering look behind,' so as to shun the threatened danger. All were ready, and when the trumpet sounded, they proceeded with high spirits and dauntless step, on their march of destiny, and of honourable combat. The citizens saw and admired the gallant spirit of the regiment, and an immense mass of people assembled at the railway station on the morning of departure and relieved their friendly feeling to the regiment by loud and repeated cheers, repeated as the train moved on, and till the sound of its motion died away in the faint murmuring of the distant breeze.

The 10th Hussars sailed to India from Gravesend in May 1846, and an embarkation return for their passage was included in the original 1894 compilation of the Vandeleur letters; since in the original it was slotted into the midst of the Napoleonic material, it has been extracted and reproduced here as Appendix VI. Having got the regiment out to India in good order, but no doubt also troubled by the unpleasantness of the Hyder court martial, John Vandeleur now elected to retire. With effect from 7 August of that year, he exchanged into the home-based 4th Light Dragoons, preparatory to retiring from the Army completely by sale of his commission on 29 December. Vandeleur's final regimental rank was that of lieutenant colonel, but he had held a brevet as full colonel since 1841.

Little is known of his later life, but his retirement was spent with his family – still a young one at his time of leaving the Army – at Ballinacourty, County Limerick. It was there, on 1 April 1864, that he died at the age of seventy-one.

Appendices

Appendices

Appendix I

Report on the 12th Light Dragoons After the Retreat from Burgos

～

Major General George Anson's half-yearly confidential Report of the Six Troops of the 12th Light Drags. in his Brigade of Cavalry, ending 24th December 1812.[1]

Commanding Officer
Lt. Colonel the Honble. F. C. Ponsonby has commanded since the last period. This officer has been repeatedly and most deservedly noticed by the Commander of the Forces for his Ability, Judgement, and gallant conduct in the Field; he has paid every attention to the Discipline of the Regiment which however is not well versed in the Manoeuvers, having been originally badly instructed.

Field Officers & Officers of Troops
Major the Earl of Waldegrave promoted to the 54th Foot and no other Field Officer has yet joined. An active Major would be a great acquisition to the Regiment. The captains are competent to the command they hold in his Majesty's Service. The Subalterns are willing and anxious to learn their Duty, and appear active and Intelligent. The greatest Unanimity prevails in this Corps.

Adjutant, Regimental Quartermaster, Paymaster
The Adjutant Lieut. Gitterick is a zealous active officer, but has not all the necessary qualifications for an adjutant. The books are kept in good

---

1. The National Archives, Series WO27: Office of the Commander-in-Chief and War Office: Adjutant General and Army Council: Inspection Returns WO27/111 1812 Second Half-Year to 30th Foot.

order. The Regimental Quarter Master has been employed at Lisbon forwarding the Clothing. The Paymaster is present with the Regiment.

Troop Quarter Masters, Troop Serjeant Majors
The Troop Quarter Masters and Troop Serjeant Majors appear competent to the situations which they fill, and are honest in their transactions.

Non Commissioned Officers
The Non Commissioned Officers are apparently active and intelligent and support their authority which I suspect is sometimes misapplied.

Trumpeters
The Trumpeters are but indifferent.

Privates
The Privates are a good body of Men, of a proper standard and healthy in their appearance. They are well set up on Foot, and attentive when on duty, rather loose in their conduct at other times, and require a tight hand over them. No Man is kept on the strength of the Six Troops who is not clothed.

Interior Œconomy
The Interior arrangements and Œconomy appear to be well attended to.

Books
The principal books which can be conveniently carried upon service are very well kept. The men sign their Accounts in the presence of an Officer who witnesses their Signature. There is no Troop debt. The Troops have been paid up to September 1812 and the Men have seen their Accounts made up to the 24th December 1812.

Regimental Necessaries
The Regimental Necessaries are charged at a fair and reasonable price.

Complaints
None.

Horses of Cavalry Regiments
The Horses are of a full size, active but not of a strong make. It requires great care and good feeding to keep them in condition. When in order there are many fine looking Horses. Indifferently trained. The Remount which has lately joined is a better description of Horse for Service.

Field Exercise and Movements
I cannot say much in favor of the Movements and Exercise of this Regiment the Men have a great deal of dash amongst them but ride ill. It is difficult in this country to find even ground & move a Squadron; were it practicable the condition of the horses at this season of the year would not admit of it, consequently the field exercise cannot be attended to with that regularity which is required.

Courts Martial
No irregularities to my knowledge has occurred in the Proceeding of Courts Martial.

Regimental Hospital
The Hospitals and attendance upon the Sick are conducted according to the Regulations of the Army and the Medical Duties are well performed. The Sick is rather numerous but the Mortality is not great.

Veterinary Department
Mr. Castley the Veterinary Surgeon is intelligent and competent to the Duties of his situation. The Horses are shod according to Regulation. The Farriers are instructed in their business and appear tolerably good. No appearance of Glanders or any other disease of consequence.

Arms
The Arms are kept in a Serviceable State.

Clothing Accoutrements and Appointments
The Clothing has been delivered in due time and in good condition. The appointments of this regiment have not been attended to sufficiently in former days; some of the saddles were so bad as to materially injure

the Horses backs. The supplies of saddles have not been sent to the Regiment according to the Return of the Annual Inspection 1811. They have lately received one hundred saddles which they should have had before they came to this country. Lt. Colonel Ponsonby has written home frequently for the information of his Colonel reporting the real state of things. As far as the effectives they are now complete, but more attention should be paid to the annual inspection return transmitted home and signed by the Commanding Officer and the Two Senior Captains, that the deficiencies therein specified might be immediately supplied.

Appendix II

Major Brotherton's Account of his Capture[1]

—

Sir Hussey Vivian, who was the General commanding our brigade, being a great friend of mine, and anxious to afford me an opportunity of distinguishing myself, arranged that I should lead the charge (a sort of forlorn hope) with a certain number of picked men, to drive the enemy out of the village of Hasparren, which they occupied in force. Accordingly, early in the morning of the 13th, I descended towards the village with my party, immediately supported by a half squadron, and found the enemy, the 13th Chasseurs, and Chamboran (2nd) Hussars, posted behind a narrow bridge, at the entrance of the village. I immediately ordered the trumpeter to sound the 'charge,' so that those behind us who were to support should advance at the same time, and putting myself at the head of my men, rode at the enemy; but as the bridge was a very narrow one, only myself, Lieutenant Southwell (a distinguished officer, whom I had chosen to accompany me), and my orderly, could pass over at a time, which we accordingly did. The enemy received us with a volley from their pistols and carbines, when we were close upon them. Southwell's horse fell dead, and he fell under him. However, myself and orderly closed with the enemy. The orderly had his bridle-hand nearly chopped off, and was run through the body, and I was then left alone amidst the enemy. I was belaboured with cuts and thrusts from all sides, defending myself as long as I could against such odds. However, after receiving eleven thrusts, three of which only

---

1. Quoted in Hamilton, Colonel Henry Blackburne, *Historical Record of the 14th (King's) Hussars*, pp. 130–1.

wounded me (as I wore a buffalo leather cuirass which I had made at Madrid, after having been run through the body at Salamanca), I was wounded through the neck, in the right hip, or to speak more plainly, in the bottom, on the right side, and another stab in the thigh, which would have proved the worst of all, had it not been for a bunch of letters which I had that morning received from England, and which I had put into one of the pockets which were then worn with pantaloons. The sword penetrated the letters, and went a quarter of an inch into the thigh, close to what is called, I believe, the femoral artery, which, had it touched, probably it would have proved fatal; but the blow which rendered it impossible to make further resistance was a sabre-cut, aimed at my head, which fell on the peak of my helmet with such force that it bent it on my nose, which it flattened and nearly broke, and completely stunned me. As I said, this blow disabled me from further resistance, and, indeed, no signs of any assistance appearing, rendered it useless to resist any longer. Surrounded as I was by fellows cutting and thrusting at me in all directions, and so occupied was I in parrying, that I had not time for assaulting in my turn. It was my intention to surrender, but a little circumstance caused me to be much more roughly treated than I otherwise should probably have been. I had, previously to advancing to the 'charge,' twisted my silk sword-knot round and round my wrist, by way of securing my sword the more effectually; and when stunned by the cut on my helmet, which I have just before mentioned, and summoned on all sides by vociferations to surrender (*rendez vous*), my sword was seized, but as it was so tightly fastened to my wrist, this was taken for an intention not to surrender it ; and a fellow cocked his pistol, and put it to my head to blow out my brains, when I had just sufficiently recovered to articulate *Je me rends!*

Appendix III

Orders and Instructions for Outpost Duty, 1815

—

Regimental Orders of Colonel Ponsonby, Renaix, 12 April 1815[1]
The Commanding Officer desires that the following Instructions may be read on three Parades by the Officers commanding Troops when every Officer, Non Commissioned Officer and Private is present.

As the Regiment is likely to be put on the Out Post Duty it is Colonel Ponsonby's wish that the following Regulations shall be considered as the Standing Orders of the Regiment on this subject.

Officers and Non Commissioned Officers in command of Picquets or Patroles are to be particularly careful in sending in Reports of the Enemy's Movements, nothing can be so disgraceful as a Dragoon galloping in with a false report of the Enemy's advance, the Patrole or Picquet must himself ascertain the truth and then have it conveyed as rapidly as he thinks the circumstances require to the Commanding Officer in the Rear. All Reports must be made in writing except when the Enemy is advancing so rapidly that no time is to be spared.

Officers or Non Commissioned Officers on Patrole must never halt to feed in a Town and wherever they do halt which should be in an open place a Vidette must be placed.

A Flag of Truce is known by a person coming forward his Hand kerchief or pulling off his hat, or more frequently by a Trumpet or Drum. The Vidette is not to permit him to pass but is to make a signal by circling his Horse. The Officer of the Picquet is to receive the Letters

1. 9th/12th Royal Lancers Regimental Museum, Derby: 912L:2088/5 '12th Lancers Order Book 1815–1872', pp. 2–3.

from the Flag of Truce and give a Receipt for them, Non Commissioned Officers are to do the same but no person is to be allowed to pass the Vidette without further Instructions from the Officer Commanding the Outposts.

If any movement of the Enemy takes place in front of the Vidette, except the relief of the Enemy's Vidette he is to circle, the Picquet is to turn out and the Commander to ascertain the movement before he reports.

If near the Enemy the Picquet must be on the Road and upon all occasions a dismounted Man who can see the Vidette must be placed to warn the Picquet if the Vidette makes a signal.

Half the Picquet must always be bridled.

Any Officer or Non Commissioned Officer who suffers the Picqeut or Patrole to be surprised is inevitably disgraced.

Every Man knows how fatal drunkenness must be either on Patrole or Picquet – there is every temptation but the Men must resist; they must recollect that they subject themselves to be tried by a General Court Martial and to be shot if Guilty of Drunkenness when on duty before the Enemy, but he hopes they will consider how much the honor of the Regiment depends upon them particularly in this.

If any prisoners are taken they are to be treated kindly, any man found plundering will be seriously punished. All horses taken are the property of the Regiment, and if sold the money is divided amongst the whole[.] no man is to go to the Rear without an Order from an Officer, no man must plead ignorance or the example of an other Regiment, when the orders of His own Regiment are so positive.

It is hoped that the Non Commissioned Officers and Men will endeavour to get sufficiently acquainted with the French Language to ask questions and to understand the Answers – to describe places carefully, and in every respect to be alert and intelligent, as many of them were in the last Campaigns.

Brigade Standing Orders 3 May 1815[1]

After Every March all Dragoons are to be made acquainted with the Name of the Head Quarters of the Brigade and of Head Quarters of the Regiment, Squadron, and Troop to which they belong, before the Troops are dismissed, they are to be shown the Houses in which the Officers Commanding their Squadrons and Troops live.

On arrival in new Quarters, Officers will immediately take the best means of informing themselves of the Roads communicating with the different Quarters of the Brigade, and intelligent men will be made acquainted as much as circumstances will permit, with those leading to them, but particularly with those that lead to the Head Quarters of the Regiment and Brigade in Order to be sent with any Report if necessary.

M. Childers, Major of Brigade[2]

Brigade Orders, Meerbeke, 5 May 1815[3]

The accompanying form of Reconnoitring Report [overleaf] is to be adopted in the 2nd Brigade of Cavalry.

It is desirable that these Reports should be accompanied by sketches when practicable. Officers Commanding Troops will make a General Report to the Major General, comprising the information obtained by each Officer sent to reconnoitre a Copy of which will be kept by the Adjutant.

The above will only be required on entering a new Cantonment.

M. Childers, Major of Brigade

1. Ibid., pp. 3–4.
2. Major Michael Childers, 11th Light Dragoons.
3. 9th/12th Royal Lancers Regimental Museum, Derby: 912L:2088/5 '12th Lancers Order Book 1815–1872', p. 4.

<u>Form</u>
Reconnoitring Report _____ Regiment _____

Names of Villages	Distances	No. of Troops Capable of Containing	Roads	Roads Practicable for Artillery	Nature of the Country	Forage	Remarks
From To							
			Paved or Clay	If practicable for Guns the initials P.R. will be sufficient	Woody, Hilly, Open, or Enclosed	Nature of the quality as near as can be ascertained	

NB The Column Specifying the Number of Troops a Village is capable of containing refers to the first Column.

Appendix IV

Lieutenant Colonel Ponsonby's Account of the Waterloo Campaign[1]

~

In the Month of March we received an order to march to Ramsgate and to embark for the Netherlands in consequence of Bonaparte's arrival in Paris.

We Landed at Ostend and proceeded to the Frontier near Tournay without halting. General Vandeleur commanded the Brigade and the Duke reviewed us at Oudenarde on the Ground where the Duke of Marlborough gained the battle in 1708.

Early in May we marched to the neighbourhood of Enghien, and early in June the Duke and Blucher reviewed the whole of the British Cavalry in a plain near Gramont. We had 5,200 on the Field with 6 Troops of Artillery.

On June 15th I was going to the Duchess of Richmond's Ball at Brussels. An Officer however came up to my quarters and told me that a sharp skirmish had taken place on our front and that the enemy were advancing; I determined not to go and about 3 in the M[ornin]g we received an order to assemble at Enghien.

We were on the ground at 6 o'clock in the morning the rest of the Cavalry having further to come, did not arrive till nine or ten. We moved towards Nivelles halting in the middle of the day to feed.

We now heard the constant roar of Artillery very distinctly and as we passed Nivelles at a Trot we met a great many wounded. Dawson ADC to Lord Anglesey came to us, he told us of the death of the Duke of Brunswick. We arrived on the Ground of Quatre Bras, but the action

1. Quoted in Ponsonby, *Ponsonby Family*, pp. 119–22.

was over, and there was only a skirmish going on, with a cannon shot or a shell now and then.

The Ground was covered with French Cuirassiers and a good many of our men and also Brunswickers. Night came on we bivouacked on the ground. Early in the morning the Duke having ascertained the retreat and the defeat of Blucher, gave order for all the Infantry to retire to Waterloo. The Cavalry with two Battalions of the 95th remained as a rear guard to mask the retreat of our Infantry. The whole of the Cavalry were drawn up on some rising ground and remained there till after two. It was a most interesting time for the Duke who had every reason to expect the whole of Bonaparte's army would immediately fall upon him, before he could collect his army on the position of Waterloo.

I was with him, the Duke, just in front of this line of Cavalry when we were all observing the preparations and movement of the immense mass of Troops before us. He was occupied in reading the news-papers, looking through his glass when anything was observed, and then making observations and laughing at the fashionable news from London.

The French Cavalry were now mounted, it was past two and the whole of their army were seen getting under arms. We commenced our retreat in three columns. I was with the left column. We had nothing however but a skirmish. The centre column had a sharp affair, but we all arrived at Waterloo without suffering any material loss. The rain fell in torrents, it was so heavy that my large thick cloak was almost wet thro' in a few minutes. The whole country became almost a swamp.

We bivouacked just in rear of the position, the rain continued all night. I dined with General Pack in the Village, and slept on the road.

In the Morning (the 18th) my Servant who had not gone off to the rear like almost all the Servants of the Army had a good breakfast for me, and a change of things. It is a very curious thing that few of us expected a battle. Why, I cannot tell, but so it was. About 10 however the Artillery began and soon after we saw large bodies of the Enemy in motion. The first attack was very formidable, it was repulsed and my cousin General Ponsonby charged and had great success.

We were on the left and seeing a large mass of Infantry in retreat and in confusion, my Regt. charged. It entered the mass and at the same time a Body of French Lancers charged us on our flank. Nothing could equal the confusion of this melee, as we had succeeded in destroying, and putting to flight, the Infantry. I was anxious to withdraw my Regt. but almost at the same moment I was wounded in both arms, my Horse sprung forward and carried me to the rising ground on the right of the French Position, where I was knocked off my Horse by a blow to the head.

I was stunned with the blow and when I recovered finding I was only wounded in my arms and seeing some of my Regt. at the foot of the Hill I attempted to get up, but a Lancer who saw me immediately plunged his Lance into my back and said 'Coquin tu n'es pas mort.' My mouth filled with blood and my breathing became very difficult as the lance had penetrated my Lungs but I did not lose my senses. The French Tirailleurs who had joined that Battalion when the charge took place took up their ground again at the crest of the rising Ground where I was; the first man who came along plundered me. An officer then came up and gave me some brandy; I begged him to have me removed but this he could not do. He put a knapsack under my head and said I should be taken care of after the battle. He told me that the Duke of Wellington was killed and that several of our Battalions in the night had surrendered. There was a constant fire kept up by those about me, a young Tirailleur who fired over me talked the whole time always observing that he had killed a man every shot he fired. Towards the Evening the fire became much sharper, he told me our Troops were moving on to attack and with his last shot he said 'Adieu Mon Ami, nous allons nous retirer.' A squadron of Prussian Cavalry passed over me. I was a good deal hurt by the Horses – in general Horses will avoid treading upon men but the Field was so covered, that they had no space for their feet.

Night now came on, I knew that the Battle was won. I had felt little anxiety about myself during the day as I considered my case desperate, but now the night air relieved my breathing, and I had hope of seeing someone I knew. I was plundered again by the Prussians. Soon after an English Soldier examined me. I persuaded him to stay with me. I suffered but little pain from my wounds, but I had a most dreadful thirst and there were no means of getting a drop of water, I thought the night would never end. At last Morning came, the Soldier saw a Dragoon, he was fortunately of the 11th in the same Brigade with me. He came and they tried to get me on his Horse, but not being able to do so, he rode to Head Quarters, and a waggon was sent for me. Young Vandeleur of my Regt. came with it, he brought a Canteen of Water. It is impossible to describe the gratification I felt in drinking it. I was of course very much exhausted having lost a great deal of blood from five wounds. I had been on the ground for near 18 hours. I was taken to the Inn in Waterloo, it had been the Duke's Quarters. Hume dressed my wounds. I remained about a week in this Village and was then carried into Brussels. I returned to England in the Month of August.

Appendix V

The Finding of the Court, and Approval and Confirmation Thereof by the Queen[1]

~

Horse Guards, 18th October , 1845

Sir,

Field-Marshal the Commander-in-Chief having had the honour to lay before the Queen the proceedings of a General Court Martial holden at Leeds, on the 1st of September, 1845, and continued by adjournments to the 18th of the same month, for the Trial of Lieutenant William Augustine Hyder of the 10th Royal Hussars, who was arraigned upon the undermentioned charge, viz:-

For conduct unbecoming the character of an Officer and a Gentleman; for that he, the said Lieutenant William Augustine Hyder, being quartered with his Regiment at Ballincollig, did, on or about the 17th day of October, in the year 1842, at Inchera, near Cork, and with intent to deceive his Commanding Officer, Colonel Vandeleur, endeavour to prevail on Sylvester Oliver, Esq.,[2] to lend him a horse to retain for two months at Ballincollig aforesaid as his second charger; he, the said Lieutenant Hyder, proposing at the same time to the said Sylvester Oliver, Esq., that no one should, during such two months, get upon the said horse.

Upon which charge, the Court came to the following decision:-

1. Quoted in Hyder, *Proceedings of the General Court Martial*, pp. 155–7.
2. As the defence pointed out, Oliver's actual Christian names were Silver Charles; although this error technically destroyed the case for the prosecution, it was not followed up.

The Court having maturely weighed and considered the evidence in support of the Prosecution, together with what the Prisoner has urged in his defence (and laying out of their consideration the letter addressed by Major-General Henry Wyndham to Colonel Vandeleur)[1] is of opinion that the Prisoner, Lieutenant William Augustine Hyder of the 10th Royal Hussars, is NOT GUILTY of the charge preferred against him, and does therefore ACQUIT HIM OF THE SAME.

The Court, having acquitted the Prisoner, Lieutenant William Augustine Hyder of the 10th Royal Hussars, of the charge preferred against him, cannot refrain from animadverting in the strongest terms of disapprobation on the violent, coarse, and uncalled-for language, which he, the Prisoner, has had recourse to in his defence, in allusion to the character of S. C. Oliver, Esq.

I have his Grace's commands to acquaint you that Her Majesty was pleased to approve and confirm the finding of the Court.

Her Majesty was pleased to observe that it appears that after the assembly, and during a short adjournment of the Court, a civilian, the principal witness for the Prosecutor, did, in the presence and with the acquiescence of Colonel Vandeleur, the Prosecutor, destroy certain documents, which, at the instance of the Prisoner, such witness had been duly required to bring with him for production before the Court – one of such documents being a letter having reference to the subject-matter of the charge against Lieutenant Hyder, addressed, on the 9th of May, 1845, by Colonel Vandeleur, to the said witness; and Her Majesty was pleased further to express her displeasure that Colonel Vandeleur, hastily acting, as he declares, under an impression that these documents were not in a fit state to be produced in Court, and that the fair copies in his possession would be much better, should have acquiesced in a proceeding the impropriety of which must on reflection be obvious to him: notwithstanding that Lieutenant Hyder having been acquitted, has not suffered prejudice; and notwithstanding that Colonel Vandeleur had in Court, and was ready to produce, a paper which

1. This letter was a character reference for the witness Oliver.

he alleged to be a true copy of such letter, and as to the authenticity and truth of which copy Colonel Vandeleur who wrote the letter, the clerk who copied it, and the witness who received it, might have been examined, if Lieutenant Hyder had thought fit to do so.

Her Majesty, moreover, was pleased to remark that much irrelevant matter appears to have been gone into, and more particularly that the character of a witness for the prosecution was irregularly and unjustly sought to be impeached, by examining witnesses to particular facts, supposed to have taken place many years ago, and unconnected with the matter before the Court, whereas, according to the established law and practice, evidence to the general character of the witness for veracity was alone admissible; and furthermore, that witnesses were also irregularly examined, to contradict the evidence of that witness, on matters totally irrelevant to the issue.

> I have the honour to be,
> Sir,
> Your most obedient, humble servant,
> (Signed) Fitzroy Somerset

H.M. 10th Royal Regiment of Huzzars: Return of the Number Embarked at Gravesend

~

In What Ship Date	Field Officers	Captains	Subalterns	Staff	Sergeants	Trumpeters	Farriers	Corporals	Privates	Total, Sergeants rank and file	Women	Children	Total
Brahmin 30 Apr. 1846	–	2	3	–	9	2	2	8	106	127	16	12	28
Larkens 5 May 1846	2	–	6	2	14	5	2	10	169	199	26	26	52
Hindostan 5 May 1846	–	1	2	2	10	2	2	8	157	179	23	21	44
Persia 7 May 1846	–	1	4	–	9	1	2	9	108	129	20	19	39
Total	2	4	15	4	42	10	8	35	540	634 163 797	85	78	163

Of the above – 8 Men
2 Women } are deponet.
4 Children

John Vandeleur, Lt. Colonel[1]

1. In the original text, p. 156.

Select Bibliography and
Further Reading

~

Anon., *Journal of a Soldier of the 71st, or Glasgow Regiment, Highland Light Infantry, from 1806 to 1815*. Edinburgh, Balfour & Clarke, 1822

Anon., *Vicissitudes in the Life of a Scottish Soldier*. London, J. Moyes, 1827

Bamford, Andrew, *Sickness, Suffering, and the Sword: The British Regiment on Campaign 1808–1815*. Norman, University of Oklahoma Press, 2013

____, *Gallantry and Discipline: The 12th Light Dragoons at War with Wellington*. Barnsley, Frontline, 2014

Barbero, Alessandro, *The Battle: A History of the Battle of Waterloo*. London, Atlantic, 2005

Burnham, Robert (ed.), 'Lionel S. Challis' "Peninsula Roll Call"', at http://www.napoleon-series.org/research/biographies/GreatBritain/Challis/c_ChallisIntro.html

Crumplin, Michael, *Men of Steel: Surgery in the Napoleonic Wars*. Shrewsbury, Quiller, 2007

Dalton, Charles, *The Waterloo Roll Call*. London: Eyre and Spottiswoode, 1904

Divall, Carole, *Inside the Regiment: The Officers and Men of the 30th Regiment During the Revolutionary and Napoleonic Wars*. Barnsley, Pen & Sword, 2011

____, *Wellington's Worst Scrape: The Burgos Campaign 1812*. Barnsley, Pen & Sword, 2012

Fletcher, Ian, *Galloping at Everything: The British Cavalry in the Peninsular War and at Waterloo 1808–15. A Reappraisal*. Staplehurst, Spellmount, 1999

Fortescue, Hon. J. W., *A History of the British Army*. 20 vols; London: Macmillan, 1899–1930

Fosten, Brian, *Wellington's Light Cavalry*. Oxford, Osprey, 1982

Glover, Michael, *Wellington's Army in the Peninsula*. Newton Abbott, David & Charles, 1977

Hamilton, Colonel Henry Blackburne, *Historical Record of the 14th (King's) Hussars*. London, Longmans, Green & Co., 1901

Hay, Captain William, *Reminiscences 1808–1815 Under Wellington*. London, Simpkin, Marshal, Hamilton, Kent, & Co., 1901

Haythornthwaite, Philip J., *The Armies of Wellington*. London, Cassell, 1994

_____, *The Waterloo Armies*. Barnsley, Pen & Sword, 2007

Hildyard, Lieutenant Henry J. T., *Historical Record of the 71st Regiment Highland Light Infantry*. London, Harrison and Sons, 1876

Hofschröer, Peter, *1815: The Waterloo Campaign*. 2 vols; London, Greenhill, 1998, 1999

Howard, Dr Martin, *Wellington's Doctors: The British Army Medical Services in the Napoleonic Wars*. Staplehurst, Spellmount, 2002

Hyder, William, *Proceedings of the General Court Martial, Held by the Order of Field Marshal the Duke of Wellington, the Commander in Chief, for the Trial of Lieutenant William Augustine Hyder 10th Royal Hussars, on the Prosecution of Lieut. Colonel Vandeleur, 10th Royal Hussars*. London, Charles & Edwin Layton, 1845

Liddell, Colonel R. S., *The Memoirs of the Tenth Royal Hussars (Prince of Wales's Own) Historical and Social*. London, Longman's, Green & Co. 1891

Muir, Rory, *et al.*, *Inside Wellington's Peninsular Army*. Barnsley, Pen & Sword, 2006

Oman, Sir Charles, *A History of the Peninsular War*. 7 vols; Oxford, Oxford University Press, 1902–30

_____, *Wellington's Army 1809–1814*. London, Edward Arnold, 1913

Ponsonby, Major General Sir John, *The Ponsonby Family*. London, Medici Society, 1929

Reid, Stuart, *Wellington's Highland Warriors*. Barnsley, Frontline, 2010

Robertson, Ian C., *Wellington Invades France: The Final Phase of the Peninsular War*. London, Greenhill, 2003

Stewart, Capt. P. F., *The History of the XII Royal Lancers (Prince of Wales's)*. London: Oxford University Press, 1950

Tomkinson, Lieutenant Colonel William, *Diary of a Cavalry Officer in the Peninsular and Waterloo Campaigns 1808–1815*. London, Swan Sonnenschein & Co., 1894

Vandeleur, John Ormsby, *Duties of Officers Commanding Detachments in the Field*. London, T. Egerton, 1801

Index

~